Forensic Science

Geoffrey Davies, *Editor*

A symposium co-sponsored
by the Division of
Analytical Chemistry and
the Division of Chemical
Education, Inc. at the
168th Meeting of the
American Chemical Society,
Atlantic City, N.J.,
September 8–9, 1974

ACS SYMPOSIUM SERIES **13**

AMERICAN CHEMICAL SOCIETY

WASHINGTON, D. C.   1975

Library of Congress CIP Data

Forensic science.
  (ACS symposium series; 13)

  Bibliography: p. Includes index.

  1. Chemistry, Forensic—Congresses. 2. Criminal In-
vestigation—Congresses.
  I. Davies, Geoffrey, 1942-   II. American Chemical
Society. Division of Analytical Chemistry. III. American
Chemical Society. Division of Chemical Education IV.
Series: American Chemical Society. ACS symposium
series; 13.

HV8073.F58   614'.19   75-9986
ISBN 0-8412-0280-X   ACSMC8 13 1-204

ACS Symposium Series

Robert F. Gould, *Series Editor*

FOREWORD

The ACS SYMPOSIUM SERIES was founded in 1974 to provide a medium for publishing symposia quickly in book form. The format of the SERIES parallels that of its predecessor, ADVANCES IN CHEMISTRY SERIES, except that in order to save time the papers are not typeset but are reproduced as they are submitted by the authors in camera-ready form. As a further means of saving time, the papers are not edited or reviewed except by the symposium chairman, who becomes editor of the book. Papers published in the ACS SYMPOSIUM SERIES are original contributions not published elsewhere in whole or major part and include reports of research as well as reviews since symposia may embrace both types of presentation.

CONTENTS

Preface vii

1. Forensic Science Education—A Perspective 1
   Ralph F. Turner

2. Some Critical Personnel Policies in Forensic Science 8
   William Fox

3. Educators in Forensic Science—The Men in the Middle 10
   W. W. McGee

4. An Introductory Forensic Science Course in a Law
   Enforcement Program 22
   Richard Saferstein and Robert Epstein

5. Graduate Education and Research in Forensic Chemistry at
   Northeastern University 28
   Barry L. Karger, James M. Parker, Bill C. Giessen, and
   Geoffrey Davies

6. LEAA's Forensic Science Research Program 43
   Joseph L. Peterson

7. Application of Materials Science Methods to Forensic Problems—
   Principles, Serial Number Recovery, and Paper Identification 58
   Bill C. Giessen, Donald E. Polk, and James A. W. Barnard

8. Examples of SEM Analysis in Forensic Evidence Applications ... 75
   John Sabo, Gary Judd, and Stark Ferriss

9. Recent Developments in Bullet Search Systems 83
   Al Johnson

10. Progress in Firearm Residue Detection 88
    Edgars Rudzitis and Morris A. Wahlgren

11. A Comparison of Neutron Activation Analysis and Atomic
    Absorption Spectroscopy on Gunshot Residue 97
    W. D. Kinard and D. R. Lundy

12. Recovery and Identification of Residues of Flammable Liquids from
    Suspected Arson Debris 108
    Cecil E. Yates, Jr.

13. Forensic Applications of Differential Scanning Calorimetry 114
    Jesse H. Hall and Bruce Cassel

14. Ink Analysis—A Weapon Against Crime by Detection of Fraud .. 134
    Richard L. Brunelle and A. A. Cantu

15. Forensic Bloodstains and Physiological Fluid Analysis 142
    W. C. Stuver, Robert C. Shaler, Peter M. Marone, and
    Ralph Plankenhorn

16. Effect of Environmental Factors on Starch Gel Electrophoretic
    Patterns of Human Erythrocyte Acid Phosphatase 151
    Cornelius G. McWright, James J. Kearney, and James L. Mudd

17. Forensic Toxicology: The Current State of the Art and Relationship
    to Analytical Chemistry 162
    Bryan S. Finkle

18. A Comparison of Heroin Samples 170
    S. P. Sobol and A. R. Sperling

19. New Applications of Photoluminescence Techniques for
    Forensic Science 183
    Peter F. Jones

Index 199

PREFACE

This volume is based on papers presented at the symposium entitled "Educational and Scientific Progress in Forensic Science." The primary sponsor was the Analytical Chemistry Division, with co-sponsorship from the Chemical Education Division and the American Academy of Forensic Sciences. The symposium program consisted of invited contributions from all sectors of the forensic science community. These presentations attracted large audiences and prompted lively discussion, reflecting the growing interest of the educational, scientific, and professional communities in forensic science.

Forensic science is a broad field which encompasses all aspects of the application of scientific principles to the establishment of criminal guilt or innocence, including such specialties as pathology, psychiatry, and jurisprudence. Criminalistics, a subdivision of forensic science, involves the collection and laboratory examination of physical evidence from the scene of a crime or a suspicious occurrence (e.g., an unexplained death) and court testimony on its significance in a particular case. Items submitted to the criminalistics laboratory might include a blood sample from a suspected drunken driver, a weapon obtained from a crime scene or suspect, bloodstained clothing, or a suspected forgery. The increasing recognition of the investigative value of such evidence and its widening acceptance by the courts has created educational, manpower, technical, and legal opportunities and problems in the criminalistics profession. Several of these areas were identified and discussed at the symposium. It is worthwhile to outline some of the current major issues facing the nation's criminalistics laboratories in the context of the topics covered in this volume.

Education

There are three major subdivisions of the process of physical evidence evaluation—collection, laboratory evaluation, and court presentation of results and their significance. How should personnel be trained for each of these functions? It need hardly be pointed out that the crime investigator should be well aware of which types of evidence are useful for investigative purposes, what evidence the local, regional, or federal laboratory is capable of processing, and how the chosen evidence is to be collected and transmitted to the laboratory so that the results of the laboratory examination will not be jeopardized.

There are wide variations in the nature and magnitude of the case-load and in the manpower and technical capabilities of the nation's criminalistics laboratories (Peterson). Ideally, the crime scene itself should be surveyed by a trained criminalist who is also responsible for the proper collection and transmission of physical evidence. Unfortunately, this practice is only found in the most advanced criminalistics operations, and even here it is almost entirely restricted to major crimes (bombings, homicide, suicide, hit-and-run auto deaths, etc.). While this approach will never be practical for the investigation of all criminal acts, it would permit realistic collection of evidence and its proper transmission to the laboratory for scientific evaluation. The criminalist must be aware of what he is looking for and of the accuracy, precision, and investigative significance of his measurements.

How is the criminalist to be trained? Turner is amusingly accurate when he points out the attributes of the complete forensic scientist, "He must have, in superior measure, the separate and collective expertise which all of you possess, knowledge of criminal law and procedure commensurate with that of Melvin Belli and F. Lee Bailey, the thoroughness and integrity of Hans Gross, the cleverness of Vidoq, the audacity of Sir Bernard Spillsbury, the experience of Milton Helpern, and the consummate intuitive skill of Sherlock Holmes." The attainment of such broad attributes can only come from years of active practice in a well staffed and efficient criminalistics laboratory with adequate support for the study of new techniques and methodology and the significance and legal value of improved measurements. In some jurisdictions the local criminalistics laboratory is staffed by police officers who have essentially acquired their skills "on-the-job" (Fox). Although field experience is essential to the practice of forensic science, such personnel may be ill-equipped to broaden their laboratory's capabilities in the examination of a sufficiently wide range of evidence. In addition, perceptive cross-examination in court may call their testimony into question on technical grounds, nullifying their efforts in the laboratory and causing personal and laboratory morale to deteriorate (Turner).

The integrity of the evidence must be preserved in criminal investigations, and it seems preferable to examine as much physical evidence as possible in local and regional laboratories so that the complexity of the overall criminalistics process can be minimized. Each laboratory should be well managed and adequately staffed by competent, scientifically trained criminalists who are given the opportunity and encouragement continually to upgrade their education and expertise.

Entry into the profession at the technical level demands a sound training in physical sciences, particularly in chemistry, with a good knowledge of physics, mathematics, and biology. Universities can provide such training, and those which integrate classroom preparation with practical experience in the field are particularly well suited for this task. Many students are attending courses which lack practical criminalistics experience and which are taught by instructors with little or no actual forensic experience (Turner). Most disturbing is the observation that a large proportion of the students in such courses also have inadequate basic mathematical and scientific skills (Saferstein and Epstein).

The creation of a completely new course in forensic science or criminalistics is expensive (McGee). However, given the fact that most universities are capable of providing the basic scientific and legal courses, the only elements to be added are the special coverage of forensic science topics and a field internship. To be useful, the forensic science courses must be taught by professional criminalists who are also competent and enthusiastic teachers; this raises the very practical question as to where such teachers are to be found. In order to be acceptable to the profession, such courses must include practical field experience, and the Law Enforcement Assistance Administration is able to support some internships (Peterson). What appears to be happening is that the manpower demands created by the rapid rise in crime are so great that the law enforcement agencies are being forced to employ new personnel with inadequate training in the hope of training them "on-the-job." Aside from the drain on laboratory manpower for training in basic scientific skills, this is leading to a "sacrific of quality for quantity" (Turner, McGee) and does not bode well for the profession. Greater advantage should be taken of the tremendous resources of the universities in providing the required basic educational background for entry into the profession. Forensic science is a challenging field and should attract the best of our students, not those who feel they cannot compete in the "traditional" scientific disciplines.

Graduate education and research are closely related in the training of specialists for the criminalistics profession. Again, extended practical experience as part of the curriculum will be part of any program of real value, as has been demonstrated at a number of schools. Persons trained in such programs should be able to build upon their experience during employment. However, the workload often increases to such an extent that they have no time for research or for keeping up with new or improved methodology. This is unfortunate, since persons with expert scientific training are best suited to develop and expand laboratory capabilities in response to a demonstrated need.

At a practical level, then, it seems necessary to foster a selected number of professionally oriented courses at both the undergraduate and graduate level to ensure that subsequent employment will lead to personal and professional development opportunities. The utility of physical evidence cannot be advanced without providing adequate training, manpower, and funding to allow attainment of these goals.

Research

The research institutions of the nation can play a substantial role in improving the methodology of forensic science, yet there is a substantial gap between the development of new technology and its application in the field. As noted above, this problem largely exists because of inadequate manpower and training and as a result of heavy workloads in the nation's criminalistics laboratories. Some of the current problems in toxicology are discussed by Finkle. Of particular concern are the extreme sensitivity and specificity required to deal with nanogram quantities of drugs and picogram quantities of drug metabolites in tissue extracts, as well as the general lack of realistic programs in forensic toxicology. Karger *et al.* discuss the interrelationship between graduate training and research. For example, the research and educational development work in Boston is being funded by the Law Enforcement Assistance Administration under an agreement which created a consortium of schools throughout the nation. The consortium goal is to develop effective training and research programs in law enforcement.

Research in forensic science must be aimed at early solutions to urgent current problems. To be useful, laboratory techniques must be rapid and reliable, and, to be legally admissible, they must also give reproducible data which are scientifically acceptable. In an increasing number of cases, testimony must be supported by statistical data which substantiates the conclusions of the witness. There is a need not only for increased use of powerful examination techniques, but also for the provision of detailed statistical population data to support the interpretation of data from several important classes of evidence, including bloodstains and gunshot residues. The papers by Raduzitis and Wahlgren; Stuver, Shaler, Marone, and Plankenhorn; Kinard and Lundy; and McWright, Kearney, and Mudd all illustrate the application of statistical studies to physical evidence evaluation.

Through the Law Enforcement Assistance Administration, the Federal Government is funding significant research in forensic science (Peterson). Proposals for funding are reviewed by experienced forensic scientists to ensure that those which address themselves to urgent, current problems are given priority. It is significant that the Federal Bureau of Investigation is further developing its scientific research activities.

The technical papers of the symposium cover most of the major current research areas in forensic science. The applications of materials science methods to forensic problems is discussed by Giessen *et al.* Very powerful analytical tools are now available to examine surface morphology and to identify minute particulate evidence, and new methods have been developed for inerasable tagging, for example, of guns. Tagging is currently a subject of great interest in the forensic science field (*see*, for example, the paper by Brunelle and Cantu). The application of the scanning electron microscope to a variety of difficult forensic problems is surveyed by Judd, Sabo, and Ferris, but it is evident that fired bullet identification presently consists of a difficult and time-consuming examination which is in urgent need of development (Johnson), as is the operational detail and statistical evaluation of arson debris (Yates). It cannot be overemphasized that the most viable techniques are those which can be applied at the local level, and the comparison of flameless atomic absorption spectroscopy with more expensive and inaccessible neutron activation analysis in the examination of firearms discharge residues (Kinard and Lundy) is most significant in this regard. There is an interesting contrast of statistical methodology between this paper and that by Rudzitis and Wahlgren which merits further consideration. The demonstration of a reliable means of examining firearm discharge residue at the local level is an example of the right direction for forensic science research.

Hall and Cassel describe a complete, commercially available experimental system for detailed studies of the thermal history and other characteristics of fibers, a common form of evidence material. The Bureau of Alcohol, Tobacco, and Firearms has developed a large library of inks of known manufacture dates and reports excellent cooperation from industry in its tagging project (Brunelle and Cantu). Again, the application of a well established technique (in this case thin-layer chromatography, which is sensitive enough to allow concurrent handwriting and other supportive analysis) proves its value not only operationally but also from the viewpoint of legal admissibility (Brunelle and Cantu).

Physiological fluid analysis by electrophoretic techniques is a very potent identification tool when supported by genetic population data (Stuver, Shaler, Marone, and Plankenhorn). McWright *et al.* report a careful study of the importance of environmental factors in determining the reliability of the genetic typing of bloodstains, another common clue material.

The current high level of narcotic abuse calls for rapid and reliable means of identifying and quantitating drugs in tissues and physiological fluids (Finkle) as well as tracking down illicit supply sources (Sobol and Sperling). The problem of drug abuse is reaching frightening proportions, and it is gratifying to see the applicability of familiar methodologies to these investigations.

The final paper in this volume (Jones) is concerned with the application of a less familiar technique, photoluminescence, to a wide range of investigations, including sensitive firearm residue detection, the discrimination between different glass, polymer, and hair samples, and the identification of seminal stains. The promise here is of relatively inexpensive equipment with wide applicability in the criminalistics laboratory.

Communication

Close collaboration between practitioners has always been an essential key to solving multidisciplinary problems. Educators must provide graduates with a fundamental understanding of scientific principles and sound practical experience in the field. They must be responsive to the real needs of the forensic science profession through strong contact with practicing criminalists. Operating a meaningful and successful forensic science program is by no means easy, but this effort is needed by the nation's laboratories. Useful methodology can only be developed by this same type of collaboration, and research institutions should have a means of field-testing their ideas and listening to the requirements of local, regional, and federal laboratory personnel. The acceptability of evidence must be further improved through a growth of the capability and quality of each laboratory. Personnel in the field should not be so burdened with work and so badly funded that they cannot take advantage of the educational and research efforts of others. The problems are urgent, but there are means available to solve them.

It is hoped that this volume will lead to further advances in forensic science through an increased communication of ideas and skills. The growth of physical evidence utilization has created great educational, employment, and research opportunities which are likely to continue for many years.

It is a pleasure to thank the contributors and to acknowledge the support of the staff of the Institute of Chemical Analysis, Applications, and Forensic Science at Northeastern University in arranging the program. I am particularly grateful to Suzanne Leidel for her expert typing of several of the manuscripts. Robert F. Gould of the American Chemical Society was also most helpful in bringing this volume to fruition.

Northeastern University   GEOFFREY DAVIES
Boston, Massachusetts
March 6, 1975

Forensic Science Education—A Perspective

RALPH F. TURNER

School of Criminal Justice, Michigan State University, East Lansing, Mich. 48823

In attempting to place forensic science education in some kind of perspective, it has been my good fortune to put the finishing touches on this paper while conducting my bi-annual course in Comparative Criminal Justice in London, England, this summer of 1974. At least I have had the advantage of being several thousand miles from my office and I hope that some measure of intellectual perspective has accompanied this matter of physical separation. Dealing with "a perspective" of whatever the topic may be suggests 1) an enormous vanity, presumably supported by considerable experience and 2) a demand that the author be completely open and fair with his readers by revealing his biases and prejudices. With the latter point I am quite comfortable, having done this before several thousand students for 27 years. My training as a chemist suggests some adherence to objective interpretation of events. Modest personal experience in psychology and psychotherapy has given me some insight into human nature, my own included. Testimony in court as an expert witness, beginning in 1938 and carrying through the spring of 1974 (with several subpoenas awaiting me when I return to East Lansing) has given me a certain feeling and respect for the administration of criminal justice, despite its numerous shortcomings, with which we are all familiar. With regard to personal vanity or ego satisfaction in attempting to bring an issue into perspective, I view this paper as just another small effort to refine our thinking and attitudes about forensic science education. This is probably the third or fourth paper I have prepared on this particular topic, and I hope I will have the opportunity to write several more in future years. So much by way of introduction.

Let us begin by posing the question "What seems to be, in my humble view, the current necessary ingredients of American forensic science education?" I say American, for this is presumably the principal area of interest for this symposium; but in so doing one cannot ignore the enormous contributions of our predecessors in Europe and, to some extent, the Far East. Looking

toward Europe also helps us with a definition, or more precisely,
a clarification of terms. Important historical references
illustrate the fact that forensic science had its origins in
problems of forensic medicine. One must note, however, that
Europeans tend to hold a broader and more intellectually sophisticated concept of forensic science than is currently evident in
America. Thus we see the names of Lombroso, Bertillon, Locard,
Freud, Gross, Landsteiner, Jellinek and others frequently
referred to in historical accounts of the development of forensic
science. It is not my aim to present a detailed account of the
historical development of forensic science, but I must bring to
your attention an important recent paper by Frederick Thomas,
entitled "Milestones in Forensic Science" (1). . Paraphrasing
this excellent article, we learn about medical examination and
the description of firearm wounds in the 16th century, scientific
interest in the problem of sudden death in the 17th century,
distinguishing between live and stillborn infants in 1681, the
detection of arsenic in human organs in 1811, the Law of Quatelet
(1869) which was the foundation for Bertillon's later work in
personal identification, the development of schools of forensic
science in Paris (1795), Vienna (1804) and Berlin (1850),
Lombroso's work (1826-1909), the use of mathematical probabilities in a Belgian case in 1929, and the more recent British
contributions of Smith, Glaister, Spilsbury and Nicholls. To
these milestones set forth by Thomas, we can add the American
achievements which are highlighted in part by the Stielow firearms case in New York state, the recognition of personal identification through fingerprints at the St. Louis, Missouri World
Fair in 1904, Weiner's discovery of the "rh" blood factor, the
establishment of the Scientific Crime Detection Laboratory at
Northwestern University Law School in Chicago around 1929, the
opening of the FBI laboratory in 1932, the development of the
polygraph during the same period, the long and eminent history
of the Office of the Chief Medical Examiner in New York City,
the creation of the Department of Legal Medicine at Harvard
University, the informal, and later formal, teaching of criminalistics at the universities of Wisconsin, California and Michigan
State, the first meeting of the American Academy of Forensic
Sciences in St. Louis, Missouri in 1948 and the emergence of the
National Institute for Law Enforcement and Criminal Justice, the
research branch of the Law Enforcement Assistance Administration,
created by the Congress after adoption of the Safe Streets Act
in 1966.
       Having briefly touched upon some historical facets of
forensic science, I think it is clear that the first necessary
ingredient of our educational program is one which will make
students aware of the past. Undergraduate and graduate criminalistics programs have mushroomed from four in the 1940's to
several dozen at the present time. As I understand the philosophy

of these programs, they seem to be geared to producing technicians for a job market that is still very attractive. Some students appear to be fascinated by the potential glamour or mystery of the work, and some instructors detect a source of funds to enhance grantsmanship or irrelevant research. So far, I see little evidence of courses that introduce the student to the broad spectrum of forensic science; courses that trace the development of this scientific sub-speciality from its European and British origins, and courses that illustrate how scientific observation and conclusion have been incorporated in the Anglo-Saxon style of administration of justice are hardly to be found. After all, this is our American heritage, and it behooves the student to understand this as well as he can and to understand also that there are other systems of justice utilized in many parts of the world, for example, in Napoleonic Code countries.

Thus, I have tried to present a case for the student being made aware of the origins of forensic science, understanding that this discipline is not an American invention of the latter 20th century, appreciating the fact that there has been a steady evolution and accumulation of knowledge of an understanding of how science is ultimately only one of the tools used in the administration of justice.

Moving to a second perspective of forensic science education, one naturally considers technical content. Given my practical experience and teaching career in criminalistics, I will have nothing to say about forensic pathology, toxicology, psychiatry or other specialities essentially related to medical training. Formal training in American forensic science (criminalistics in its broadest sense) did not come into being much before the advent of World War II. Paul Kirk at the University of California and J.H. Mathews at the University of Wisconsin were probably the two important educators who first took an interest in moving beyond the apprentice-tutorial type of training which existed in a number of medical schools that were producing forensic specialists at that time. In his private laboratory technician school, R.B.H. Gradwohl, of St. Louis, Missouri, was also training students who acquired expertise in forensic immunology. One must also acknowledge the important contributions of Colonel Calvin Goddard and his colleagues Keeler, Muehlberger, Wilson, and Inbau at the Northwestern University Crime Detection Laboratory in Chicago. This was essentially a working laboratory, independent of any government agencies, yet for the most part serving prosecutorial offices. The group did conduct short courses for prosecutors, and, later, under the auspices of the law school, also for defense counsels. Training in the laboratory, however, was of the apprentice type, assuming that the student had suitable academic preparation.

Returning to Kirk and Mathews, it is interesting to note that both of these gentlemen were chemists who had distinguished themselves in their respective fields of biochemistry and physical chemistry. Considering the fact that proteges of these mentors have had considerable influence in shaping educational practices regarding forensic science training, it is no small wonder to me that we still see the basic curriculum for forensic scientists paralleling that of chemistry, physics or biology majors. I do, however, see some new interdisciplinary programs evolving which are most encouraging, as long as they include elements which I shall refer to later. Probably one useful end-product of this symposium will be a stimulus to rework the existing patterns of forensic science training into new and different formats geared toward producing the more complete forensic scientist.

In a recent article A.C. Maehly (2), Director of the National Laboratory of Forensic Science in Solna, Sweden, reflects on the current state of forensic science. With regard to education he states, "The trend in education has in some ways been less favorable to us. Quality is sacrificed to quantity, and a solid general background to increased specialization. Specialists are needed, of course; otherwise tasks such as document examination, drug analysis, serology and so on could not be carried out satisfactorily. But in our broad field of endeavor, a solid education is of great importance, especially for coordinators and leaders of working groups and institutes." Further on he observes, "A small number of universities should run high-quality schools of forensic science.....For assistants, a specialized training in either physics, chemistry or biology is needed.,...University graduates should have the opportunity of working on their thesis at a laboratory of forensic science." Maehly, from his European viewpoint, has pointed up a potentially serious problem which I see also emerging in America; namely the sacrifice of quality for quantity. I need only to refer to the rapid proliferation of forensic science programs in this country and suggest that we carefully review the quality of these programs. Specifically, quality has been sacrificed when we consider how quickly some of these programs have been organized, how minimal the qualifications of instructors are in some instances, and how seemingly obsessed some programs are with the acquisition of costly and elaborate instrumentation with very little forensic science expertise to build upon.

Returning to the matter of curriculum, this obviously is not the time nor the place to dwell upon specific courses or their detailed content. Other speakers will deal more completely with that topic. Rather, let us consider the ultimate goal of a forensic science training and education program. Simply stated, the goal, as I see it, is to educate and train students to interpret evidence and events correctly, so that such interpretations will prove or disprove the truth or validity of the state-

ment under litigation. This implies the need for both broad and
solid general education called for by Maehly, along with highly
specialized skills in selected areas. Also implicit in this
statement is the need for the student to comprehend that there
is absolutely no limit to the kind or nature of evidence that
he may be called upon to examine and interpret. The student
must also be well aware of the historical nature of technological
progress so that his imagination and ingenuity will not be dis-
suaded by some seemingly difficult problem. Consider the fact
that Hans Gross, at the time he wrote "Criminal Investigation,"
could not report on latent fingerprints, yet he probably viewed
hundreds of them during the course of his investigations. Yet,
a few years later, Henry and his followers paved the way for
utilization of this now commonplace technique. Two decades ago
criminal investigators could do little with the clue of an odor.
Today the science of olfactronics is immensely useful in criminal
investigation. The purpose of these examples is to emphasize
the point that evidence is always present. It remains for the
imaginative, the curious and the well-trained forensic scientist
to interpret the evidence. I can best summarize this point by
stating two hypotheses which I have presented to my students
for years: 1) It is impossible to commit a crime without
leaving a clue and, 2) If all evidence is collected and interpreted correctly it will prove or disprove the truth of the
allegation.

Thus, it becomes apparent that the student must first be
well grounded at the undergraduate and graduate level in an
appropriate physical or natural science. This must include
both the theory and practice of any scientific technique.
Given the increasing sophistication of cross-examination, (and
we should all welcome this), it is important that the expert
witness be acutely aware of the limitations of any technique at
a particular phase of its development and use. Here again we
have lessons to learn from the past. Forensic science educators
must be familiar with past errors and miscarriages of justice
which occured when we pushed too far too fast in such areas as
chemical tests for intoxication, interpretation of polygraph
tests, powder residue analyses, indiscriminate use of neutron
activation analysis and voice print identification, to cite
just a few examples. I also call your attention to a small
emerging group of trial lawyers who are becoming expert at cross-
examining computer-based technology. Consider these implications
when we view the widespread use of automated analyses employing
complicated computerized searches of masses of data. Consider
the plight of the technician who, on rigorous cross-examination,
cannot give convincing and accurate answers to searching questions. Here agian we are reminded of the dangers of sacrificing
quality for quantity.

Now, assuming that we have developed a course of study that deals with the problems which I have alluded to in general terms, what other topics must be considered? One of the most important is the problem of proof. Proof may be a relatively simple matter in each of your various disciplines. However, in the criminal justice arena, I fear that it is more complicated. Without pretending to give answers, I suggest that the student must be confronted with the following questions: What constitutes proof in the eyes of the philosopher, the logician, the attorney, the judge, the scientist and, finally, the jury? How does one define proof? How does one articulate his findings or "proof"? How does one translate and transmit these findings and conclusions to investigators, attorneys and jurymen? Answers to some of these questions can be found in appropriate courses on almost any decent liberal arts and science campus.

Turning to another subject matter area, my experience with forensic science students graduated over a period of 25 years indicates that many move forward into responsible management positions. The usual scientific curriculum does not prepare students for such duties. Probably such training should be carried over to postgraduate years, but it should not be neglected. Obviously it must deal with such matters as personnel selection, finance and budgeting, supervision and management, manpower development, research and development, and policy and decision making. So much for general comments on curriculum.

Finally, what is a third important ingredient in the forensic science training format? I see it as a need to guide the student in understanding the role of science in the total scheme of the administration of justice.   For years we have heard many eminent forensic scientists make strong appeals for the scientist to remain aloof from the crime scene, from the investigator, from the legal counsel, from the accused, and from the philosophy of the law itself. The scientist is told that his objective interpretation of the evidence will be a sufficient end in itself. While there can be no quarrel with scientific accuracy and objectivity, the practitioner who follows this philosophy will inevitably be heading toward difficulties and the possibility of thwarting justice. Here again, the forensic scientist should be conversant with historic miscarriages of justice. Examples are the trials of Socrates and Galileo, the Dreyfus Affaire involving Bertillon, the disputed paternity trial of Charles Chaplin and the problems surrounding the two Coppolino trials. If you thought my earlier reference to the importance of a psychological understanding of human behavior and one's own motivations strange, let me explain briefly. Even though the forensic scientist fancies himself an objective personality, he, too, is subject to the same emotional pressures which buffet investigators and members of a cummunity when they are dealing with particularly difficult or emotionally-laden offenses. Consciously or subconsciously, he may be influenced by these pressures and adopt unscientific behavior. The better equipped he is to understand his own biases and prejudices, the better forensic scientist he will be. I need only to refer to two examples to illustrate my point, namely the incredible forensic handling of the assassination of President John F. Kennedy and the widely divergent scientific opinions thrust upon us today by forensic scientists speaking out on the current drug abuse problem. On this latter point, we do not seem to be any more sophisticated than we were at the time of the enactment of the 18th amendment.

Stated differently, the third ingredient calls for an understanding of the evolution of Anglo-Saxon law and its subsequent adaptation and modification in America. Throughout this evolution runs a continuous thread of concern for just, fair and humane treatment of those fellow men who become subjects of litigation. To be sure, history tells us that we have departed from this admirable course on many occasions. This then, is all the more pressing reason for including seminars dealing with the more abstract relationships between law and science.

In summary, I have attempted to put forensic science education into a perspective as I see it at the moment. I have not dealt with the minutae of curriculum, but rather have tried to present a few broad strokes. I realize that all educators must deal eventually with the small details of course content, sequence, and so on, but I feel it is equally important to keep long range and general goals in mind. Thus I would hope that some of you will be encouraged to study carefully the not-so-recent history of forensic science, select milestones which you feel have been responsible for important forward steps, and then devise programs of your own that will prepare students to meet the challenge and rigorous demands of fair, just and humane administration of justice.

Having said all of this, will you bear with me while I give you (with tongue slightly in cheek) my profile of the ideal forensic scientist which I know all of you hope and expect to produce. He must have, in superior measure, the separate and collective expertise which all of you possess, knowledge of criminal law and procedure commensurate with that of Melvin Belli and F. Lee Bailey, the thoroughness and integrity of Hans Gross, the cleverness of Vidoq, the audacity of Sir Bernard Spillsbury, the experience of Milton Helpern and the consummate intuitive skill of Sherlock Holmes.

Literature Cited

1. Thomas, Frederick, JOURNAL OF FORENSIC SCIENCES, 19, (2), 241(1974).
2. Maehly, A.C., JOURNAL OF FORENSIC SCIENCES, 19, (2), 255 (1974).

2

Some Critical Personnel Policies in Forensic Science

WILLIAM FOX

Oakland Research Associates, Staten Island, N. Y. 10310

The scientific qualifications of the personnel assigned to police units involved in the discovery and evaluation of physical evidence are important in determining the extent of the application of the tools of the physical sciences to the problems of the criminal justice system. With regard to the staffing of these units it has been recognized that "...there is no substitute for the educational background of science, and no amount of enthusiasm on the part of a prospective employee should be accepted in lieu of a sound scientific background..." (1).

It is therefore important to note some pertinent facts related to the assignment of police personnel to scientific units of the semi-military police agencies in this country. A questionaire to which 100 police units responded revealed that "Of the total number of 459 civilian personnel employed in crime laboratories, almost all possess Bachelor of Science or equivalent degrees. Of the 623 full-time police personnel, only a fraction hold Bachelor of Science degrees.... The areas of document examination, firearms comparison.... have the lowest number of degree holders." (2).

The survey also revealed that "An examination of the educational backgrounds of personnel in many crime laboratories indicates a need for considerable upgrading. The number of experts qualified by 'on-the-job' training is excessive....," (2).

The actual situation regarding full-time police service personnel assigned to the scientific units is obscured by the fact that courses in studies dealing with police administration, patrol activities and related matters are titled "Police Science" (3). The John Jay College, that branch of the New York City University System that offers degrees in Police Science and

---

*
Captain, New York Police Department. This paper utilizes only information available from the public record. No information gained as a result of assignments in the New York City Police Department is included herein.

Forensic Science, "received the largest group of underprepared students in any of the four-year colleges" and "had the worst senior-college retention rate after seven semesters" (3). These programs of study can be used to hide a lack of qualification for assignment to scientific units of police agencies, up to and including intermediate and command level supervisory positions.

What seems to have been perpetuated is an "on-the-job" training sequence where unqualified police service personnel receive their training and advancement from equally unqualified peers. As noted by Dr. Paul Kirk "Too many forensic scientists are being trained in a crime laboratory by instructors with a nonscientific background...criminalistics is not yet mature enough to have emerged from the apprenticeship system" (4).

It has been noted that "No new methods of fired bullet identification have been adopted since utilization of the comparison microscope over forty years ago" (5). Does the information revealed in the L.E.A.A. survey (2) that the area of firearms comparison was among those with the lowest number of degree holders suggest contributing factors for the lack of scientific advancement in that field?

Continuing the policies of assigning police officer personnel, without physical science qualifications, to the scientific units of police agencies cannot improve the quality of any of the services required of the police. The fact that such policies have been followed by police agencies in this country has inhibited the utilization of the skills and expertise of physical scientists of many specialities and the application of scientific knowledge and instrumentation to the criminal justice system.

Literature Cited

1. Turner, R.F., "Forensic Science and Laboratory Techniques," Thomas, Springfield, Ill. 1945 and F.B.I. Law Enforcement Bulletin, (1945), 14, 13
2. Joseph, A., "A Survey of Crime Laboratories", 1967 funded by LEAA Grant 013.
3. Lavin, D.E., "Student Retention and Graduation at City University of New York: September 1970 Enrollees Through Seven Semesters", 1974.
4. Chem. and Eng. News, (1967), August 14, p.49.
5. Johnson, A., paper in this volume.

3

Educators in Forensic Science—The Men in the Middle

W. W. McGEE

Florida Technological University, Forensic Science Teaching Laboratory,
Sanford, Fla. 32771

The need to staff forensic laboratories with qualified personnel has created a demand for education facilities to prepare
forensic scientists. Educators in colleges and universities in
many parts of the country are responding to this demand. Very
quickly these brave souls discover that being an educator in forensic science places them directly in the middle of a controversy
in which the educational needs of the forensic science profession
must be placed in a frame work prescribed by college or university administration. At this point, the educator becomes the man in
the middle. To survive this controversy, the educator must recognize each problem area and somehow reach a solution acceptable to
the parties involved.

In this paper, an attempt will be made to illustrate the relationship that exists between education and the forensic sciences, to present some of the problems that can be encountered in
establishing a forensic science degree program, and to discuss how
these problems were confronted in establishing a B.S. degree program in Forensic Science at Florida Technological University (FTU)
in Orlando, Florida.

The purpose of this paper is to identify problem areas so that
they can be recognized and openly discussed. The solutions proposed represent one point of view and should not be taken as the
final answer to each problem.

Background

The large influx of federal money into law enforcement, designed to upgade law enforcement and related professions has produced its share of benefits as well as disadvantages. The forensic
science profession has received its share of this double-edged
"benefit". Crime laboratories which (with few exceptions) had
been subsisting on handouts from local or state revenues suddenly
found themselves with the means of upgrading their facilities to
meet the deluge of narcotic and drug abuse related casework. It

has been said that "drug abuse" called attention to the need for
expanded crime laboratory services to serve the criminal justice
system. It has been L.E.A.A. that has provided the means to this
end.

While science writers today extoll the virtues of computer
controlled laboratory instrumentation, knowledgeable lab scientists
recognize the extent to which automated equipment can "free" the
scientist from his laboratory investigations. A similar appraisal
occurred in the crime laboratory. Crime laboratory directors soon
recognized that no amount of modern equipment could reduce the ev-
er-growing case load if there were not enough laboratory scientists to use the equipment. Adequately prepared laboratory scientists were needed to use the equipment to produce results which
could be interpreted in a meaningful manner relative to the cases
at hand. In other words, we have not as yet found the way to get
the "computer" to testify under oath on the stand!

Personnel-adequately prepared personnel-is the solution to
the problem. But where to find them? Because there is a definite
shortage of recognized expertise in this field, enticing established personnel away from positions in recognized labs is not
only expensive but likely to cause hard feelings. Education.
There are few recognized colleges and universities which graduate
adequately prepared personnel specifically for the forensic science profession. "On-the-job" training. With no other source to
turn to, O.T.J. represented the most direct solution to the problem. It still is one very acceptable means of preparing personnel.

But what about education? Education-educators-college and
university administrators have been severely unresponsive to the
needs of the forensic science profession. In the past, forensic
scientists have turned to college professors for help only to find
that there was no "real life" application for the discovery which
offered so much promise on paper. In those instances where the
process could be adapted to a specific forensic application, the
work would have to be done within the confines of the university.
provided the proper working agreement between the two agencies
could be reached. That is, provided the money was available, provided all patent rights would become property of the university,
provided all publications describing the data would show university personnel as the senior authors, provided, provided, provided !
Combine this overt atmosphere with the experience that most
crime lab analysts have had---that is, watching a college profes-
sor make a fool of himself as an "expert" for the defense, and it
is no wonder that forensic scientists have looked suspiciously at
education.

The forensic science profession is not entirely without fault.
Perhaps, due to the state of flux in which the profession finds
itself, forensic scientists have not been sufficiently articulate
about the personnel needs of the profession. Just what the forensic scientist does within the confines of the CRIME LABORATORY
walls has long been a well guarded mystery; or at least it seems

that way. The personnel requirements, the background and wealth
of experience that constitute the preparation of potential forensic scientists is, at present, poorly understood and not well defined even by forensic scientists. Perhaps it is a question of
evolution. It may simply be a question of not having enough time
and enough "history" to begin to consider personnel requirements.
Whatever the reasons, these factors are clear:
1. There are few successful forensic science/criminalistics
   educational programs at colleges and universities in the
   United States.
2. The number of graduates from these programs is small.
3. There is a mutual feeling of misunderstanding between the
   two groups involved.
4. There is a critical shortage of adequately prepared forensic scientists.
5. There will be a shortage of qualified professionals for
   five to ten years.

The Problems

Being in the middle of the controversy has provided a degree
of perspective concerning the areas of misunderstanding. On the
surface, it would seem that the problem areas, the areas of critical questioning by educators and forensic scientists, seems limitless. While the number of questions which can be asked is undoubtedly limitless, there appears to be a relatively small number
of basic differences which need to be recognized. To illustrate
this point, consider some of the statements made by forensic scientists concerning the profession and its relationship to education.
1. A degree in Chemistry is the only educational prerequi-
   site that is needed to prepare for work in the forensic
   sciences. Why bother establishing a new degree program?
2. We hire chemistry majors because they do the best job for
   us.
3. Forensic science is such a broad heterogeneous field of
   endeavor requiring such a great diversity of skills that
   no one single degree program can ever hope to accomplish
   this task.
4. To be recognized as an expert witness, competent of tes-
   tifying to even one small area of expertise in forensic
   science, requires a great deal of special knowledge.
   There is little demand today for personnel with the general experience that would result from a B.S. degree
   program.
5. Forensic science is a profession. Unlike other pure scientific disciplines (chemistry or physics) it has a func-
   tional code of ethics which must be adhered to. The justice system acts as a continuous check on the conduct of
   the forensic science professional. The only way to learn

this code is to experience it in action in the crime laboratory. A degree program at a college or university
cannot hope to duplicate this experience.

6. In our lab we have toxicologists, drug chemists, firearms examiners, questionned documents examiners, serologists, and trace evidence examiners. Just how in the
world are you going to pack all of this into one degree
program? What are you going to prepare them for?

7. We do not want degree programs that claim that they are
producing expert witnesses. The only way you can become
an expert is to go through a period of "on-the-job" training to gain enough confidence in your work and enough experience in performing a specific analysis to qualify before the court. No degree program can do this!!

8. The biggest problem with many scientific degree programs
is that they have not kept abreast of developements in
that scientific field. Once a degree program is established, with all courses identified, how are you going to
keep the program current?

9. A single degree program graduating 25 students per year
could easily surpass the demand for personnel within a
given local. Fifty degree programs of this size would
rapidly exceed the personnel needs of the entire nation.
We want quality, not quantity!

10. Research. My advice to you is have the students take as
many hours of research as possible. That's the only place
where they learn to think.

At the heart of all of these statements is one question.
What constitutes a degree program in Forensic Science and what can
be accomplished within the structure of such a program?

Today, college and university administrators tend to look at
new education programs not in terms of professional service but in
terms of the constraints into which the new program must fit.
Here are a few of the more important constraints.

1. There is a limit to the number of courses and "hours"
which can be required of a student in a degree program.
Students can "volunteer" to take additional course work
but in a physical sense there is usually a limit to the
time which a student has available for extra courses.
The trend in education today is to make available to students options which will reduce the total elapsed time
(but usually not the number of courses) required for a
specific degree. State universities in Florida usually
limit their science programs to 180 quarter hours.

2. Specialization within a B.S. degree program which requires input from many scientific disciplines is limited.
Some measure of specialization can be achieved by providing elective hours within the program which students can
use to reflect individual interests.

3. The cost of an educational program in forensic science

will be one of the greatest among scientific disciplines taught at a college or university. In terms of laboratory equipment, instruments, microscopes, special chemicals and solvents, fulltime staff, adjunct staff, and particularly in terms of the relatively small number of students that will be involved in the program, it will be expensive.

4. Staff. First of all, who is going to teach the courses, even basic introductory courses, within the Forensic Science degree program? Secondly, how do you attract them away from their present jobs, with the present level of college or university salaries? Finally, how can one department justify the number of individuals (staff size) that theoretically are required to present a credible forensic science degree program?

5. How can classes be structured within a forensic science degree program to meet the needs of the working professional and the full time student?

These are the basic problems to which the educator, the man in the middle, must find working solutions if he is going to have a successful forensic science degree program.

Apparent Solution To Some Of The Problems

On July 19, 1974 the Board of Regents of the State of Florida approved the B.S. degree program in Forensic Science at FTU for initiation in September, 1974. Development of the degree program and support facility took nearly two years to complete. A significant portion of that time was spent talking to forensic scientists in an attempt to articulate the problems just described. Once articulated, specific steps were taken to resolve some of these difficult problems. The specific features of this degree program as they relate to these problems are described in the following paragraphs.

The logo or symbol for the program is shown in Figure 1. The symbol is more than an eye-catching design. It embodies the purpose and intent of the degree program. The Forensic Science program at FTU is a degree program emphasizing "the scientific aspects of physical evidence valuation". In the symbol, education is shown as the connecting bar between physical evidence and the scientific techniques which the forensic scientist uses in his valuation process. The justice system forms the pivot point in this conceptualized balance-like process. The role that education plays is clearly defined. Emphasis on physical evidence valuation will provide the goal toward which course work in law, science, and forensic science can be aimed. In this way, some of the confusion resulting from the diversity of courses needed for the degree program can be eliminated.

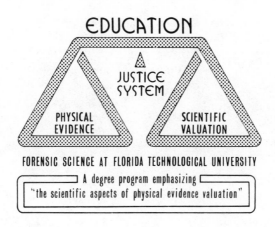

EDUCATION

JUSTICE SYSTEM

PHYSICAL EVIDENCE

SCIENTIFIC VALUATION

FORENSIC SCIENCE AT FLORIDA TECHNOLOGICAL UNIVERSITY

A degree program emphasizing "the scientific aspects of physical evidence valuation"

Figure 1. FTU forensic science program symbol

A typical student curriculum is shown in Table I. As stuctured, the curriculum offers a number of advantages to students. The following features highlight the curriculum.

1. The degree has been established as a professional degree to be housed in the College of Natural Sciences and administered by the Department of Chemistry.

2. Acknowledging critical recommendations from concerned forensic scientists, the degree program will contain in excess of 110 credit hours of science courses, to include a minimum of 44 hours of chemistry and 28 hours of special forensic science courses.

3. A two-quarter internship in a recognized crime laboratory is required of each student. The typical student will begin the internship in the summer following the junior year.

4. The student completes, prior to the internship, a rigorous schedule of required basic course work in science, law, and professional courses in forensic science.

5. Restricted electives provide the student with a measure of flexibility to reflect a special interest (e.g., serological individualization of body fluids) or a special area of forensic science (e.g., toxicology).

How are these features realized within the degree program? Professionalism in a degree program can be achieved in a number of ways. Forensic science courses can be structured to emphasize the code of ethics which guide the actions of the forensic science professional. Laboratory experiments can be directed toward the preparation of evidence for court testimony. Forensic science and law courses can involve moot court testimony. When possible, staff members will be expert witnesses with court experience. Al-

Table I
Typical Forensic Science Curriculum

	Fall	Winter	Spring
First Year			
Biological Science	Biology	Botany	Microbiol.
Chemistry	General	General	General
		Gen. Lab	Analyt.
Communication	English	Speech	
Mathematics	Precalc.	Calculus	Computer Sci.
Social Science			Social Sci.
Second Year			
Chemistry	Organic	Organic	Organic
	Analyt.	Analyt.	Organic Lab
University Studies		History	Humanities
Restricted Electives	Microbiol.	Immunology	Serology
Physics	Physics	Physics	Electronics
Third Year			
Law & Legal Procedure		Law	Legal Proced.
Forensic Science	For. Anal.*	Crmnl. I*	Crmnl. II*
Restricted Electives	Phys. Chem.	Phys. Chem.	Adv. Analyt.
Social Science	Social Sci.		
Statistics	Stat.		
Summer Following Third Year	Cooperative Education Internship		
Fourth Year			
Internship	Internship		
University Program		Univ. Prog.	Univ. Prog.
English		Report Writing	
Restricted Electives		For. Sci.	For. Sci.
Social Science		Social Sci.	

Total Quarter Hours 180

Restricted electives are approved courses in science, forensic science, legal procedure, or criminal justice.

*Abbreviations:
Crmnl. = Criminalistics
For. Anal. = Forensic Analysis Techniques

most by definition, a professional degree program must maintain
direct and open contact with the profession. Active participation
in the profession by staff members is an essential ingredient in
the operation of the degree program. If nothing else, it will
keep members of the profession and the staff on a first name basis.
    What about chemistry courses in the curriculum? The question
of whatconstitutes adequate educational preparation for the forensic science profession is a very controversial one. Almost
without hesitation, when asked what background do you look for
when you hire new personnel, the answer is a degree in chemistry.
Yet, when pressed, this same individual will usually admit that
there are a few things which were not covered in a Chemistry Degree that are valuable to forensic scientists. There is no doubt
that a strong background preparation in Chemistry is essential.
But does the forensic serologist need the same extensive chemistry
background that a drug chemist requires? Should the toxicologist
take the same schedule of courses which the potential fire-arms
examiner takes? Is advanced organic chemistry more important to
the serologist than immunology or serology? Are courses in differential and integral calculus essential to the day-to-day tasks
of the questioned documents examiner? To require all forensic science majors to take the same extensive background in chemistry
(to become chemistry majors) would be equivalent to disputing the
need for subspecialties (fire-arms, toxicology, etc.) within the
forensic science profession.
    The curriculum shown in Table One represents a selection of
courses which is designed for 70% of the students. For these
students, with little or no preconceived knowledge of professional
subspecialties, chemistry courses will be recommended as electives
to provide a strong background. It is conceivable that after several years of operation, separate curricula will evolve for students in drugs analysis, forensic serology, toxicology, or trace
evidence examination. Until this happens, the restricted elective
courses within the program should provide the student with a means
of individualizing or tailoring his course work. (Restricted
elective courses are approved courses in science, forensic science,
or law).
    What is the program position with respect to the expert wit-
ness? Nowhere in the curriculum does the student get the impression that upon graduation he will automatically become, with the
receipt of his diploma, an expert witness. Recognition as an expert witness is the function of the court and it is still the duty
of the forensic laboratory to provide the bulk of the practical
experience necessary to qualify for this title. A forensic science degree program can be designed to provide the foundation upon
which actual laboratory experience will build. But it is through
actual work experience that the forensic lab requires confidence
in the graduate's ability to perform in the adversary system.
    What is the function of the internship within the degree pro-
gram? It can serve many functions; for one, it is an effective

device for providing students of a degree program with a measure
of work experience. Realistically, the required internship will
serve as a screening device. If the degree program is to fill the
personnel needs of the forensic science profession within the State
then the program must produce 5-10 graduates per year. The internship should provide a mechanism for keeping student enrollment
in line with profession needs by exposing them, their abilities,
and attitudes to the forensic laboratory personnel. Conversely,
the laboratory personnel will expose their system to the student.
Should there be a breakdown at this point, a mechanism exists for
ending the relationship. The student can switch to a chemistry
degree at the end of the third year without severely handicapping
himself. It should be emphasized that an honest appraisal of the
student potential at this point by the professional and educator
will help assure the quality of personnel that the profession demands.

Concerning the internship itself, students take nearly all of
their science, law, and forensic science courses prior to the internship. With this background, students should be able to function in the forensic laboratory without disrupting normal laboratory operations. The potential burden that massive student internship programs could place on already overtaxed forensic laboratory facilities may discourage some forensic laboratory participation. Precautions must be taken to insure against this abuse,
since the student internship is essential to the production of
quality personnel.

The problems and respective solutions discussed to this point
have one feature in common. They all deal with basic tenets
which the profession holds dear. The proposed solutions represent
concessions to the profession which nearly every program should
make in order to be relevant.

The next problems which will be discussed are those related
to the actual preparation of students. Stated simply, these are
problems relating to the cost of the forensic science degree program, the staffing of the program, and the structuring of basic
and advanced courses within the degree program.

Restating a point previously made, "the cost of an educational program in forensic science will be one of the greatest among
the scientific disciplines taught at a college or university".
College educators contemplating a quick entry into the field to
make hay while federal dollars are available should proceed with
caution. Unless they are prepared to annually defend high cost
figures, they should reconsider their choice and elect to establish low overhead degree programs. Unless they reconsider their
actions, they may unintentionally be doing irreparable damage to
those degree programs that have realistically appraised the situation. They may in fact, be widening the gap----decreasing the
credibility----between the profession and educators!

Drawing from the experience gained in setting up this degree
program, to duplicate the basic laboratory facilities found in an

an average full service crime lab in the classroom will cost in
the neighborhood of $250,000. It should be emphasized that this
is the total cost of starting from scratch with an empty building
and equipping it with the basic tools to do the job. Should there
be laboratory rooms available for use containing appropriate lab
benches and stocked with basic glassware and chemicals, the cost
can be reduced by $70-80,000. Should there be sufficient instru-
mentation---microscopes (not only number but type), UV spectrophotometers, IR spectrophotometers, electrophoresis equipment, gas
chromatographs, centrifuges, flame spectrophotometers, and fluorescence spectrophotometers to name only the expensive items, the
total cost can be reduced by $100-120,000. If the library is up
to date and well stocked with new as well as classic forensic
books, subscriptions to the numerous forensic and related journals
and newpapers are paid, and the reference collection of instrument spectra, hairs, fibers, fire-arms and cartridges, paper and
inks, etc. are up-to-date, then the program is ready for the faculty and staff. The next job will be to justify to the administration this major investment in terms of the 5 students you will
graduate each year!

Fortunately, the FTU program was able to secure adequate
funding for the initial design of these facilities from our LEAA
SPA. It would have been impossible for the FTU program to secure
this type of facility in a reasonable time frame without LEAA
assistance. Beyond this initial advantage, the FTU program will
differ little from other existing programs. At some point in time,
hopefully in 4-5 years, administrators of this program must assess
its accomplishments in terms of meeting its stated goals, judge
its record against other science programs, and decide its future
(if the profession does not do this job by then).

The final answer to the staffing problem has no easy answer.
Ideally, the staff of a truly relevant forensic science degree
program should consist of an impressive list of experts capable of
providing instruction an almost every speciality area of forensic
science. Realistically, from a cost standpoint, this is not possible, and educationally in terms of course design, this is impractical. Each expert would feel obliged to teach a course on
his speciality and by the time each speciality was covered all the
credit hours for the degree program would have been consumed without touching the basic science and law courses. Economically as
well as educationally, a sounder approach to the problem would be
to use one or two experts with broad experience to present survey
courses which cover the basic concepts of forensic science. Such
courses would be structured much in the same manner that today's
modern general chemistry course is taught. Basic microscopy, photography, comparative evaluation of hairs, plant material, fibers,
and tool marks could be dealt with in much the same way that general chemistry is taught today. The important difference between
the two (chemistry and forensic science) would be the professional emphasis that only the expert forensic scientist could give

this course. Working in conjunction with this full-time staff,
would be a staff of adjunct faculty which could be called on as
the demand arose, to offer speciality courses in their areas of
expertise. The subject material covered in these speciality
courses would compliment the material covered in the survey
courses and would deal with problems of immediate interest or concern to the forensic science profession today.

This bi-level structuring of classes within the program seems
to offer more advantages than disadvantages. From an administra-
tive standpoint it greatly reduces the overhead expense of maintaining a large, expensive staff. From the service standpoint, it
offers the potential of being able to serve the educational needs
of the beginning student and the working professional. Upper
level specialitycourses in forensic science, if properly structured, could be utilized by both the fulltime student and the
working professional to upgrade understanding of a particular forensic speciality. In this way, the program would be meeting its
obligation to serve the educational needs of the profession.

Conclusion

It was stated earlier that the purpose of this paper was to
identify problem areas that can be expected when trying to establish a degree program in Forensic Science. To some individuals
the tentative solutions proposed for the degree program at FTU
seem obvious and/or naive. If this is the case, we ask that you
indulge our whims until the basic aspects of the relationship between the two groups become obvious. To others, the problems related to being the man in the middle of the controversy may seem
overwhelming. The previous discussion was not intended to drama-
tize the problems.

Some observers have criticized the approach taken at FTU for
following the desires of the forensic science profession too
closely. They feel that the individuality and originality---the
remoteness---of the college or university institution has been
sacrificed. Trying to second-guess a profession in a state of
flux always presents this type of problem.

Recalling that one criticism of scientific degree programs
has been   inability to keep abreast of developments within the
profession, we hope to establish a working relationship with the
profession which will reflect both the desire to interact with the
profession and the basic belief that a degree program in Forensic
Science can provide qualified personnel to the profession.

As men in the middle, educators openly solicit the involvement of forensic science professionals and college administrators
in the establishment of degree programs in Forensic Science. Of
administrators, educators ask that they provide a flexible mechanism in which to reflect changes in the degree program as they
materialize in the profession. Of forensic professionals, educators ask that they actively involve themselves with degree pro-

grams. Make their knowledge and expertise available in the classroom. Of both, educators ask patience!! An acceptable solution
to the problems can be found.

   We at FTU, wish to thank the Bureau of Criminal Justice Planning and Assistance---the L.E.A.A. State Planning agency for the
State of Florida-and the Board of Regents of the State of Florida
for actively involving themselves in the establishing of the degree program in Forensic Science. Without their respective financial and formal involvement this degree program would not have
been possible

4

An Introductory Forensic Science Course in a Law Enforcement Program

RICHARD SAFERSTEIN

New Jersey State Police, Trenton State College, and Ocean County College, N. J. 08625

ROBERT EPSTEIN

New Jersey State Police, Paterson State College, and Essex County College, N. J. 07102

The past ten years have seen a tremendous growth in the number of law enforcement or criminal justice programs offered at two- and four-year colleges. While some of these programs might be regarded as mere extensions of in-service training courses, most have been incorporated into a liberal arts program that is designed to provide the student with a knowledge of basic academic subjects while emphasizing a social science curriculum that relates to the concepts, problems and techniques of law enforcement. Often, the distinction between a training course that emphasizes vocational application and one that attempts to treat a criminal justice topic on the context of modern social problems is difficult to define. A comprehensive discussion of the philosophy, goals and accomplishments of higher education law enforcement programs can be found in recent government publications (1, 2).

While law enforcement programs have attracted numerous students who may have otherwise avoided a higher education, they have at the same time contributed to a developing educational problem; that is, how to offer meaningful and productive college level courses to a student who does not have the proper academic foundation. Nowhere has this problem been more acute and the responsive efforts more diverse than in the physical sciences (physics and chemistry). The glamour that science held in the post-sputnik era has long since disappeared in our high schools and colleges. The present-day student seems to consider a science course a better pill to swallow. In response, educators have been developing a number of palatable science courses for the non-scientist. Most of these efforts have been predicated on the overriding philosophy that science will only be comprehensible when the subject matter can be related to popular and motivating contemporary problems. Hence, courses have been devised that

incorporate and relate science to problems of modern life, for
example, environmental and health problems and space exploration
(3-6).
     In a law enforcement program, a course on Forensic Science
offers itself as an ideal vehicle for introducing the student non-
scientist to many of the basic concepts and practices of chemistry and biology while illustrating their applications to criminal
investigations, a subject that has direct relevance to the
student's vocational and/or academic interests. Such a course
has been successfully introduced into two four-year colleges and
two two-year colleges in New Jersey during the past three years.
     The forensic course has several objectives. First, to help
the student understand the role of the scientist and the crime
laboratory in the criminal justice system. The nature of physical evidence is emphasized along with the limitations that modern
technology imposes on the individualization and characterization
of such evidence. The logical procedures and methodology of
scientific inquiry with respect to the analysis of criminal
evidence is discussed. Particular attention is paid to the
meaning and role of probability in interpreting the significance of scientifically evaluated evidence. A clear distinction
is drawn between the individual and class characteristics that
physical evidence may possess. Fingerprints and tool marks
exemplify the former while a blood type or soil specimen may be
indicative of the latter. Wherever possible, discussion of the
types of physical evidence commonly encountered at the crime
scene is accompanied by statistical data that relates to its
probability of occurrence in a defined population.
     A second aim is to introduce the student to the theory and
techniques of the forensic scientist. It is here that a basic
distinction is made in the philosophy and objectives of a
forensic science course as compared to one that is soley devoted
to the techniques of criminal investigation. The student is
taken beyond a mere descriptive explanation of the analysis and
is introduced to basic biological and chemical concepts underlying the identification of physical evidence. Obviously, it is
not the intent of the subject matter to make a forensic expert of
the student. For this reason the chemistry and biology taught is
limited to the minimum core of facts and principles needed to
make the techniques of a forensic scientist comprehensible to a
non-scientist. The task is a formidable one. Experience has
shown that less than 5% of the student enrollment has had a
science course on the college level. Furthermore, any knowledge
that may have been gained from high school science courses has
long been forgotten. Any illusions that the instructor may have
had about prior student knowledge is quickly dispelled during
an introductory lecture on metric measurements. The difficulties
encountered in explaining the concept of a decimal system along
with the necessary mathematical procedures needed for converting

English system measurements into metric equivalents quickly en-
lightens the instructor to the abhorrence that the non-scientist
has towards mathematical manipulations. No prior knowledge of
scientific principles can be assumed. In our opinion, those
subjects which have not been found to be easily integrated with
chemical and biological principles are best omitted from the
first course of study. Hence, forensic photography, the polygraph, document examination and speed detection devices are
topics that are not included in the curriculum.

A third objective of the course is to emphasize the importance of the role that the proper recognition, collection, and
preservation of physical evidence has in criminal investigation.
The sophisticated techniques of the modern forensic laboratory
may be rendered meaningless if the field investigator cannot
properly present evidence to the crime laboratory. Therefore,
the correct packaging and handling of such evidence is stressed
along with adequate sampling procedures. Even more fundamental
is the development of the understanding of what actually constitutes physical evidence. As so often is the case, investigators
will collect extraneous materials at the crime scene simply out
of an unawareness of the capabilities of the forensic laboratory.
Similarly, meaningful evidence may go undetected or uncollected
because an investigator has no appreciation for the limits of
detection that accompany microscopic and instrumental techniques
of analysis. Readings of case histories are presented to further
illustrate the practical significance that scientifically
examined physical evidence may have in criminal investigations.

Course Outline

The forensic science course offered can be a four-hour
course that combines lectures with laboratory exercises or three
hours of instruction consisting of lectures and several laboratory demonstrations. A brief outline of the course curriculum
is presented for both the lecture and laboratory components of
the course.

Lectures

I.   Introduction
    A.   Definition and history of forensic science
    B.   Organization and services of our forensic laboratory
    C.   Function of the forensic scientist
    D.   Legal aspects of forensic science

II. The nature of physical evidence
    A.   Individual and class characteristics
    B.   The significance of probability in criminal
       evidence investigation

III. Physical properties of matter
 A. Units of measurement
 B. Determination of mass, volume and temperature
 C. Density and refractive index

IV. Forensic properties of glass and soil

V. Organic analytical techniques
 A. Theory and forensic applications of thin-layer and gas chromatography
 B. Theory and forensic applications of spectrophotometry

VI. Inorganic analytical techniques
 A. Theory and forensic application of X-ray diffraction, emission spectroscopy, and neutron activation

VII. Microscopy
 A. The theory and use of the compound, stereoscopic and comparison microscopes

VIII. Forensic examination of hairs, fibers and paint

IX. Forensic serology
 A. Composition of blood and semen
 B. ABO system
 C. Forensic characterization of dried blood and semen
 D. Principles of heredity

X. Forensic drug identification and toxicology
 A. Microscopic and instrumental techniques for identifying commonly abused drugs
 B. The theory and application of the breathalyzer

XI. Fingerprint identification and classification

XII. Firearm and toolmark identification

XIII. Explosives and arson investigation
 A. The chemistry of combustion
 B. The detection of explosive and gasoline residues

Laboratory Exercises

1. Measurement of the density of glass by flotation
2. Particle density distribution of soil (density gradient tube)
3. Familiarization with the compound and stereoscopic microscopes

4. Microscopic identification and comparison of hairs and
    fibers
5. Forensic presumptive tests for blood and semen - whole
    blood typing
6. Microscopic identification of marihuana
7. Color and microcrystal tests for commonly abused drugs
8. Latent fingerprint identification
9. The preparation and examination of casts and molds

Discussion

Though it is not practical to describe the depth of instruction offered for each topic covered, a brief description of the
subject of spectrophotometry can serve to illustrate the authors'
general approach to teaching a forensic science course to the non-
scientist.

The student is first introduced to the wave and particle
concepts of light. Though minimal emphasis is placed on mathematical equations, the relationship between velocity, wavelength
and frequency, as well as the correlation of energy to frequency,
is described. Those regions of the electromagnetic spectrum that
are most useful and convenient for characterizing chemical substances are emphasized.

The selective absorption of ultraviolet, visible and infrared
radiation by molecules is explained in a descriptive manner that
stresses how the noncontinuous energy requirements of chemical
substances can only be satisfied by photons that have energy
values equivalent to that of the differences in energy levels of
the molecule in question. The meaning and quantitative significance of Beer's Law is briefly discussed. The components of a
simple spectrophotometer are illustrated, accompanied by a
demonstration of the operation of a spectrophotometer in the
laboratory. Actual applications of the techniques of spectrophotometry are described during the presentation of relevent
topics, for example, in drug identification.

Unfortunately, there is at present no available textbook
which combines a discussion of the relevent fundamental chemical
and biological principles of forensic science with their
applications to the identification and comparison of physical
evidence. Paul Kirk's recent text (7) does offer a comprehensive
insight into forensic techniques. However, although the text is
an excellent contribution to forensic literature, it does not
entirely fulfill the objectives of the course we have described.
In particular, the book does not introduce the reader to the
theory and meaning of fundamental physical and chemical properties of matter that are relevent to forensic analysis.
Additionally, the book in many instances assumes prior knowledge
of many of the analytical techniques of forensic chemistry.

H. J. Walls' text (8) is a fairly recent treatment of introductory forensic science that closely parallels our course's curriculum. Unfortunately, this text is out of print and is no longer available. Therefore, the student must rely on lecture notes for reference during a significant portion of the course.

Conclusion

The success of an introductory course on forensic science for the non-scientist will be dependent on the instructor's ability to select those motivating topics that will stimulate thought and understanding of related scientific principles. Once the student comprehends the techniques and limitations of the forensic scientist, a meaningful understanding of the necessity of collecting and preserving physical evidence develops. In this manner a forensic science course serves as a vehicle for introducing the law enforcement student to scientific principles and techniques while simultaneously providing practical vocational aid to the practising or aspiring criminal investigator. It is interesting to note that results obtained from anonymous student evaluations of the course showed that more than 90% of the students felt the course fulfilled or exceeded their expectations.

Literature Cited

1. "Introducing a Law Enforcement Curriculum at a State University," U.S. Government Printing Office, Washington, D.C., 1970.
2. "Higher Education Programs in Law Enforcement and Criminal Justice," U.S. Department of Justice, U.S. Government Printing Office, Washington, D.C., 1971.
3. Cassidy, H. G., J. CHEM. EDUCATION (1971), 48, 212.
4. Fahrenholtz, S., J. CHEM. EDUCATION (1973), 50, 499.
5. Mechstroth, W. K., J. CHEM. EDUCATION (1974), 51, 329.
6. Fuller, E. C., J. CHEM. EDUCATION (1974), 51, 260.
7. Kirk, P. L., "Crime Investigation," (1974), John Wiley & Sons, New York, New York.
8. Walls, H. J., "Forensic Science," (1968), Praeger Publications, New York, New York.

5

Graduate Education and Research in Forensic Chemistry at Northeastern University

BARRY L. KARGER, JAMES M. PARKER, BILL C. GIESSEN, and
GEOFFREY DAVIES

Institute of Chemical Analysis, Applications, and Forensic Science,
Northeastern University, Boston, Mass. 02115

The continuing rise in crime has enlarged the role of law
enforcement in American society. Along with this overall growth
in the criminal justice system, the field of forensic science
has expanded as law enforcement agencies have become more reliant
on the collection, examination and interpretation of physical
evidence. This increased reliance results from at least two
factors. First, certain types of crime require physical evidence
analysis for their solution. For example, proof of drug possession can only be obtained by a chemical identification of samples
found on a suspect. Second, new and sophisticated instrumentation is becoming available in science and technology. These
instruments will continue in the future to have a major impact
on the types of samples which can be examined and the number of
analyses that can be run during any given time period. For
example, gas chromatography-mass spectrometry allows the rapid
identification of complex organic mixtures in biological samples.
As a result of these developments the forensic scientist currently has a formidable work load, with increased numbers of criminal
cases as well as increased numbers of analytical tests per case.

A forensic science laboratory is frequently requested to
assist in a broad range of investigations such as:
1) death - establishment of homicide, suicide, accidental
   or natural death
2) auto collisions - fatal and nonfatal hit-and-run cases
3) assaults - aggravated, intent to kill or maim, sexual
4) arson and explosion
5) fraud and deceit
6) burglary
7) firearms violations
8) drug abuse cases
9) poisoning and other toxicology.
Additionally, the laboratory may be required to maintain a
capability of providing crime scene examinations. The forensic
scientist must also be prepared to present expert witness testimony in court, and indeed a sizeable portion of time may be taken

up in court appearances.

In order to provide service for this broad range of investigations and responsibilities, the criminalistics laboratories have had to intensify their efforts at expansion, departmentalization and manpower specialization. Moreover, as in other technological disciplines, the forensic scientist has had to maintain a strong scientific background, as well as remain abreast with the most recent instrumental and method developments. Many of the current technical advances in forensic analysis have been discussed by Williams (1) and Curry (2). Forensic science is now at the stage where such methods as radioimmunoassay, scanning electron microscopy, and gas chromatography-mass spectrometry are used in criminalistics laboratories along with more familiar methods of analysis such as wet chemical techniques, infrared and ultraviolet spectrometry and microscopy.

Given the breadth of forensic science and the varying demands on the criminalistics laboratory, it is not surprising that there is a wide variation in the quality and capability of different laboratories. Limited analyses may be possible at the local level, whereas at regional (e.g., county, state) and federal laboratories sophisticated analytical capabilities may exist.

This brief view of present day forensic science stresses the breadth and rapid changing character of the field. Traditionally, personnel have not entered the criminalistics laboratory with college training in forensic science, rather they have possessed college education in the more standard disciplines (e.g. chemistry, biology, etc.). Expertise has been obtained by on-the-job training. Up to the present, there have been few programs of forensic science at American universities. This is now slowly changing as a result of the increased importance of forensic science and the demands of students for a more professional education at the undergraduate level. This volume has several papers dealing with recent forensic science programs at the undergraduate (3) and 2-year degree level (4). At Northeastern we have concentrated on graduate level programs and research in criminalistics. The purpose of this paper is to describe these efforts in the hope that our experiences will assist others considering introduction of similar programs.

National Criminal Justice Education Consortium

In July 1973, the following seven universities were awarded grants by the Law Enforcement Assistance Administration (LEAA) of the Department of Justice to develop and strengthen their research activities and criminal justice graduate programs.

1) Arizona State University
2) Eastern Kentucky University
3) University of Maryland
4) Michigan State University
5) University of Nebraska at Omaha

   6) Northeastern University
   7) Portland State University
The graduate programs at these schools are now coordinated
through the National Criminal Justice Education Consortium (NCJEC)
which was established in November 1973. The Consortium promotes
the exchange of ideas and experience in research and curriculum
development between its members and thereby strengthens the
resources of each school in achieving its particular goals.
   The member schools offer a cross-section of graduate programs in the criminal justice field, including corrections, rehabilitation, operations research, law enforcement, criminal law,
police training and forensic science. The consortium effort
is assisted by a program coordinator, who arranges regular
meetings of consortium members and also monitors progress in
individual programs. There are several areas in which this
consortium can be expected to have an impact on the overall
development of educational programs in criminal justice:
   1) two of the member schools have well-established doctoral
       programs; the other five can benefit greatly from con-
       sortium interaction;
   2) a duplication of effort can be avoided; member schools
       can provide special courses and services which are not
       available in individual programs;
   3) coordination of the broad scope of consortium activities
       can lead to the development of valuable operational
       guidelines for other schools interested in the develop-
       ment of criminal justice programs.

Northeastern University's Program

Institute of Chemical Analysis, Applications and Forensic Science.
   Northeastern University is the largest private university
in the nation. It has gained prominence as a leader in cooperative education, in which alternate periods of work and study
make up a student's program. This form of education fosters
close ties with the community and encourages the establishment
of degree programs relevant to the needs of society. Thus, for
example, Northeastern University has one of the largest programs
in criminal justice in the nation. Imaginative programs similarly
result in the scientific disciplines from this type of orientation. Thus, a work-study Ph.D. program in which a student spends
up to one year in an industrial setting has been established in
the Department of Chemistry at Northeastern.
   With the award of the LEAA educational development grant in
July 1973, the decision was rapidly reached between personnel in
the College of Criminal Justice and the Department of Chemistry
to concentrate development in the area of forensic science. This
decision was based on the strengths in the College of Criminal
Justice, the Department of Chemistry (especially in chemical
analysis and materials science) and the considerations outlined

in the introduction in terms of the growth and importance of forensic science.

In order to carry out development programs in forensic science, the Institute of Chemical Analysis, Applications and Forensic Science was established. This Institute, a separate organization on campus, has research and training as its main activities with special emphasis in the application of chemical analysis to forensic science. The Institute is further developing programs at the present time in pharmaceutical analysis and energy research; its overall philosophy is thus the application of chemical expertise to social problems through the team efforts of chemists and practitioners.

The Institute is organized into two divisions: (1) Organic/Biochemical Analysis (B.L. Karger), supported by faculty from the Department of Chemistry and the Colleges of Pharmacy and Criminal Justice; and (2) Materials Science/Inorganic Analysis (B.C. Giessen), supported by faculty from the Departments of Chemistry, Mechanical Engineering, and the College of Criminal Justice. Each division has a full-time senior scientist (one in mass spectrometry and one in materials science) as well as post-doctoral fellows and graduate students. We shall first describe current research activities in forensic science and then outline our efforts in curriculum development at the graduate level.

Forensic Science Research at Northeastern University

Research must be an important component of the university graduate program in forensic science. While such efforts will typically be of longer range significance than found in studies conducted in on-going criminalistics laboratories, it is necessary that the needs of forensic science be always kept in mind. This can only be accomplished by close communication between personnel in the Institute and the forensic science community.

We have found three factors to be important in the achievement of effective communication. First, we maintain liaison with practicing forensic scientists in regional and federal laboratories who have not only provided valuable advice and information but have also cooperated by offering samples for research and tests (e.g., ink standards, authenticated paper samples, gun metal samples, hallucinogenic drugs). It is our hope that this communication link will lead to field testing of useful methods developed in the Institute and the rapid dissemination of such information. Second, forensic science input is provided by personnel from the College of Criminal Justice. Here, an overall view of the impact results of research on the criminal justice system, including legal and social aspects of the work, is achieved. Third, it is necessary that one or more members of the staff are experienced as criminalists and are actively involved in common research projects with other Institute members

to provide input on the relevance of these projects to the needs
of the forensic community. One of us (JMP) worked for nine years
in the Pittsburgh-Allegheny Crime Laboratory and was actively
involved in the M.S. program in forensic chemistry jointly
operated by this laboratory and the Department of Chemistry of
the University of Pittsburgh.

While forensic science input is perhaps the most important,
relevant information from several areas such as analytical techniques, toxicology, materials science, biology, etc. is often
necessary. This means that the most effective approach is
achieved through the formation of interdisciplinary teams for
the attack on particular research problems. This interdisciplinary approach is, of course, required in any complex area involving problems of social relevance.

Specific Projects. Having discussed those components necessary for successful performance of research, we will examine some
of the projects currently in progress (or recently completed) in
forensic science.

The Organic/Biochemical Analysis Division currently has
several projects in progress. One of these involves the use of
modern liquid chromatography (LC) for the analysis of barbiturates from biological samples, e.g. blood, urine, liver. Rapid
separation of mixtures of barbiturates is achieved using a 25 cm
long column containing a small particle diameter ($\sim 10\mu$) reverse
phase packing (n-octadecyl group chemically bonded to silica) and
water-methanol solvent mixtures. A simple method has been
developed for the analysis of the barbitruates from liver specimens in which an ethyl acetate extract is injected directly into
the LC system. Figure 1 shows a chromatogram of such an extract
in which it is clearly seen that impurities do not interfere
with the analysis. With this procedure, less than 50 ng of barbi-
turate in liver can be conveniently determined. It is interesting to note that the gas chromatographic (GC) analysis of the
liver extracts involves more extensive clean-up procedures since
impurities overlap the positions of the barbiturates in the
chromatogram. This example illustrates one situation in which
modern LC is superior to GC in forensic toxicology.

A second project involves the analysis of ink dyes by
modern LC using a reverse phase small particle diameter column.
The identification of inks in handwritten signatures can be
important in the field of questioned documents. Since ink formulations are periodically changed by manufacturers, it is at
times possible to date the handwritten signature. Current practice involves punching out a small spot of the signature, followed
by extraction and thin layer chromatographic (TLC) development
(5). Use of modern LC can lead to better resolution, more sensitive detection, and where necessary, better quantitation than
TLC. We have developed a simple gradient system for the separa-

tion of classes of ink dyes with visible spectrophotometric and fluorescence detection. The combination of these two detection systems can often lead to a better characterization of the inks than simple TLC. Our method is currently being tested on standard inks kindly supplied by R. Brunelle of the Bureau of Alcohol, Tobacco and Firearms, Department of the Treasury. We plan to employ refractive index detection to examine filler materials in inks (e.g. resins).

The Organic/Biochemical Analysis Division has strengths in mass spectrometry, as well as in modern chromatographic analysis. Forensic research in mass spectrometry currently involves characterization of hallucinogenic drugs (kindly supplied by Stanley P. Sobol, Drug Enforcement Agency, Department of Justice), ink dyes (coupled off-line to LC separation), and toxicological analysis of drug metabolites. From all of the above, it should be clear that modern organic analytical techniques can play an important role in forensic science, and that university researchers can contribute to this field by developing meaningful applications.

The forensic science research of the Materials Science/ Inorganic Analysis Division is based on application of the research capabilities in these two fields, especially X-ray diffraction (diffractometers, powder cameras, single crystal equipment), scanning electron microscopy with energy dispersive X-ray analysis, transmission electron microscopy and electron diffraction, metallography and optical microscopy, metallurgical strength tests, differential scanning calorimetry, and other, conventional analytical methods.

The materials science approach to forensic science is described in detail in another chapter of this book (6), which also contains details of two comprehensive research projects presently in progress. The first of these projects concerns the recovery of obliterated serial numbers on firearms. To prevent weapons tracing, criminals frequently attempt to remove stamped identification marks by filing away the number. It is the task of the firearms examiner to try to recover these numbers by procedures such as etching. Alternate methods of recovery using the methods of materials science are under investigation. In addition, a different approach has been taken by developing a gun tagging scheme using a matrix code of laser-drilled small holes. These holes penetrate deep into the metal and can be placed in such a position on the gun that attempts at erasure may destroy the effective use of the gun (7).

A second project discussed in detail in reference (6) involves the comparative identification of paper by the study of its inorganic, mineral components. X-ray diffraction techniques and scanning electron microscope X-ray analysis provide good tests of identity. Figure 2 shows the SEM X-ray analysis spectrum of the inorganic components of a paper; the specific feature of this method is the good quality of the analytical data which results from careful ashing of the paper prior to energy dispersive

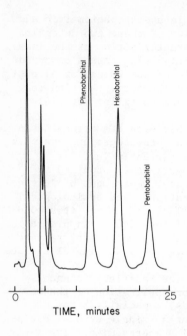

TIME, minutes

Figure 1. Liquid chromatographic separation of an ethyl acetate liver extract of barbiturates. Column: reverse phase, n-octadecyl groups chemically bonded to 10μ silica; mobile phase: methanol/water.

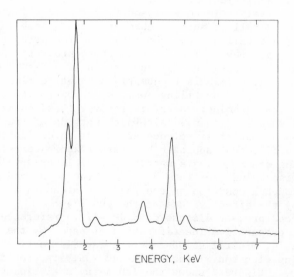

ENERGY, KeV

Figure 2. SEM x-ray energy spectrum of Eaton's corrasable bond paper, ashed at 440°C in oxygen, showing six distinct peaks corresponding (with increasing energy) to Al, Si, S, Ca, and Ti (two peaks)

analysis. In a series of 54 papers examined by this method, 98% of all pairs were found to have significantly different X-ray spectra. The application of other methods of elemental analysis such as atomic absorption and emission spectroscopy is under study.

Education Programs

Basic Considerations. The growth of forensic science programs at 2- and 4-year colleges in the last few years has been discussed above (3,4). However, at the graduate level the number of programs is small, as evidenced by Table I which lists all M.S. programs in the nation. Yet the need for graduate level trained forensic scientists is clear. First, there are ever-expanding needs for individuals properly trained at the graduate level as the criminalistics laboratory at all governmental levels increases in sophistication. Second, individuals trained both academically and practically are required for teaching in community colleges and universities. While at the present time practicing criminalists often handle courses, the necessity for having full-time personnel providing instruction is evident.

It has been argued that even though forensic science positions are available at criminalistics laboratories, a specific degree program in this area is unnecessary. In this view, it is far better to provide the student with a strong background in a science degree program (e.g. chemistry) and leave the training in forensics to the laboratory where the individual is hired. While no one can disagree with the need for a strong scientific foundation upon which to base a career in forensic science, there are still cogent reasons for having a specific degree program in this field at the universities.

First, there are a number of students interested in careers in forensics, and it is important that their interest be encouraged during their academic program. The danger exists that if such students pursue a strict scientific degree program they will become involved in other careers, as the science program may very well be oriented in directions other than forensics. Second, an appreciation of the basic foundations of the field (e.g. proof beyond reasonable doubt) and of the relationship of the crime laboratory to the rest of the criminal justice system should be studied during an individual's educational development at a university. As Turner has pointed out (8), the forensic scientist must be more than a trained analyst. Third, while some on-the-job training will inevitably be necessary, the time before an individual is a contributing member of the crime laboratory may be significantly reduced, if such a person has specific training at a university. Finally, forensic science educators can most logically be supplied by the universities.

M. S. Program in Forensic Chemistry

With these introductory comments in mind we would now like
to examine the M.S. program in forensic chemistry that is being
planned for September 1975 at Northeastern University. Personnel
from the Institute visited many of the schools listed in Table I,
as well as a number of practicing laboratories. We wish to
thank all those who freely gave advice; without their help we
would not have been able to advance to the present stage. As in
research, a team effort was made by members of the Institute in
the curriculum development. Personnel experienced in forensic
science interacted with chemists, toxicologists and materials
scientists to achieve a final program.

It was quickly realized that the term forensic science con-
notated an extremely broad subject including such areas as chemistry, pathology, psychiatry and law. In order to provide more
than a simple general background it was felt necessary to concentrate at the graduate level, and based on the available expertise,
forensic chemistry was the logical selection. This subspecialty
of forensic science represents in the view of many experts the
most important aspect of a crime laboratory's operation at the
present time. We were encouraged in this decision by the successful operation of the University of Pittsburgh Masters' program
in forensic chemistry.

The M.S. program in forensic chemistry is interdisciplinary
in nature, involving cooperation between the Department of Chemistry, College of Criminal Justice and the Institute of Chemical
Analysis, Applications and Forensic Science. The Institute is
responsible for the academic administration of the program. For
admission, an applicant must have an undergraduate degree in the
physical, life or forensic sciences including courses in: 1)
general chemistry, 2) organic chemistry, 3) analytical chemistry,
4) calculus, 5) physics. Deficiencies can be removed by taking
undergraduate courses on campus. Although not prerequisites,
courses in biology are desirable (e.g. general biology, botany,
microbiology).

Table II presents a specimen program of the full-time M.S.
degree in forensic chemistry at Northeastern which requires 1-1/4
years for completion. Part-time students take a comparable program; however, a slower pace is typically selected, with 2-1/4
to 3-1/4 years required for completion. The program is primarily
designed to offer a terminal degree for students seeking immediate forensic laboratory employment and secondarily to serve as a
source of qualified applicants for a Ph.D. degree in forensic
chemistry (see later). While it is not possible to discuss in
depth all the courses, it is appropriate to overview the program.
(Further details can be obtained by writing to Dr. B.L. Karger or
J. M. Parker.)

The program consists of four quarter-year periods of course
work and one quarter-year internship. We view the first quarter

TABLE 1

Current Masters Degree Programs in Forensic Science

School	Degree Offered	Concentration
California State College (Los Angeles)	M.S.	Criminalistics
Georgetown University	M.S.	Forensic Science
George Washington University	M.S.	Forensic Science
Indiana University	M.A.	Forensic Studies
John Jay College of Criminal Justice	M.S.	Social Science with option in Criminal Justice and Criminology
University of California (Berkeley)	M. Crim. D. Crim.	Criminology and Criminalistics
University of Pittsburgh	M.S.	Forensic Chemistry

TABLE II

Specimen Full-Time Curriculum

of M.S. in Forensic Chemistry

Fall Quarter

Modern Methods of Analysis
  with Laboratory
Forensic Materials
Administration of Criminal
  Justice
Biochemistry I

Winter Quarter

Crime Scene Investigation
Forensic Chemistry Techniques I
  with Laboratory
Concepts in Toxicology I
Elective

Spring Quarter

Forensic Chemistry Techniques
  II with Laboratory
Arson and Explosives
Seminar (or Winter)
Legal Aspects of Forensic
  Science
Elective

Summer Quarter

In-Service Training

Fall Quarter (Second Year)

Masters Paper
Biometrics
Elective

of the academic program as providing the student a foundation
in forensic chemistry, with courses in graduate level instrumental analysis (lecture and laboratory), biochemistry, basic criminal justice and forensic materials science. For example, in the
analytical chemistry course the student will learn a number of
methods such as modern liquid chromatography, gas chromatography-
mass spectrometry, scanning electron microscopy and X-ray diffraction. This basic information will then be applied in the two
lecture/laboratory quarters. These courses will involve an
examination of different classes of evidence (e.g., inks, drugs,
paints, blood stains) including the use of modern instrumentation. Forensic microscopy will also be taught in the courses.

The course on crime scene investigation will be offered by
the College of Criminal Justice and will emphasize the importance
of scene examination and evidence sampling. An improper sampling
method can invalidate the results of the forensic laboratory.
The course on toxicology will emphasize the forensic aspects of
the subject.

In the third quarter, we plan to offer a course which includes the presentation of expert witness testimony in a mock
court of law with the assistance of the Northeastern University
Law School. Practice trial sessions with student attorneys are
envisioned. The course on arson and explosives will deal with
detection of related crimes, and biometrics in the fifth quarter
will cover concepts of statistics important in forensic chemistry.

The student will take three electives during his degree program. Typically, we expect he will enroll in graduate lecture
courses in analytical chemistry (e.g., separations, optical
methods of analysis, computerized instrumentation). However, if
he is so inclined, further specialization in biochemistry, toxicology or materials science will be possible. A course on
management offered by the College of Business might also be selected, if the student wished to ultimately play an administra-
tive role in the crime laboratory.

An important feature is the three-month internship, scheduled
for the fourth quarter, in which the student devotes full-time to
work in an approved, practicing forensic laboratory. We have
made arrangements with a number of laboratories at the local and
regional level in New England and throughout the country to
accept our students. This in-service training is scheduled in
the summer quarter for two reasons. First, it comes after the
completion of the major portion of the course requirements. Thus,
a student will be able to best benefit from the work environment
on the basis of his academic training. Moreover, as a student
must achieve a grade average of at least B minus, a screening
of student quality is achieved prior to in-service training.
Second, the summer is the time of greatest need of crime laboratories for assistance because of vacation schedules. Upon completion of the degree program, we hope that many of these students will return to their in-service laboratory for full-time

employment. The Master's Paper will be written in the fifth
quarter; in many cases it will involve a write-up of a project
performed during the work period.

In the M. S. program we have tried to achieve a balance between the theoretical and practical aspects of forensic chemistry.
Fundamental principles are presented in the first quarter, and
the emphasis is then gradually shifted to the more operational
aspects of the profession, leading ultimately to the in-service
training period. Some flexibility is built into the program
through the electives and by the type of position taken in the
crime laboratory during the three-month work period.

How great is the student interest in such a program? While
we have no firm statistics, we have reason to believe that it
will not be difficult to fill available positions (ca. 15 - 20
full-time) with qualified candidates. Information from existing
M.S. programs in forensic science indicates that there are many
more applicants than positions available, and we have had
inquiries from over 40 students and 20 universities even at this
early stage of our program. Student interest in careers in
forensic science undoubtedly follows the national trend toward
professional education with social relevance (e.g. law, allied
health professions, etc.).

Financial support of student tuition through pre-service
and in-service Law Enforcement Education Program (LEEP) grants
and loans is expected. In the case of loans, the principal is
forgiven at the rate of 25% for each subsequent year of service
in the criminal justice system. Some students may also be
eligible for graduate teaching assistantships or fellowships.

The final point to consider is the job of placement of the
individual with an M.S. degree in forensic chemistry. We have
already pointed out the clear need for such trained people, but
does this translate into positions? Experience such as that at
the University of Pittsburgh is encouraging, where most of the 15
students in a class have secured positions well before graduation.
There are more than 200 forensic laboratories in the nation,
including some very extensive facilities (e.g. the FBI and DEA
laboratories). In addition, positions also exist with private
criminalists and university, toxicology and medical examiner
laboratories. Considering these possibilities for employment
as well as the growing importance of criminal justice in society,
it is reasonable to expect a firm job market for a number of
years to come, especially considering the small number of M.S.
forensic chemists being graduated.

Firm statistics on employment opportunities are currently
being assembled by the Forensic Science Foundation of the American Academy of Forensic Sciences under a grant from LEAA, as
discussed by Dr. Peterson in this volume (9). The results of this
study will be invaluable in quantifying future employment trends
in forensic science.

Ph.D. Program

As part of the LEAA educational development grant, it is our goal to develop a Ph.D. program in forensic chemistry. Since this program is only in the planning stage, it is not appropriate to discuss it in detail. However, it may prove useful to the reader to present some broad guidelines.

We believe that achievement of the doctoral degree in forensic chemistry requires a strong chemistry background with a good measure of subsequent specialization. We would expect that most students entering the doctoral program have obtained an M.S. degree in forensic chemistry (or forensic science) or offer comparable experience. Students with an M.S. degree in Chemistry may be eligible but would have to make up those parts of the forensic chemistry M.S. program not covered in their education so as to earn this degree during their residence. For the pre-service individual we look toward an in-service training period of roughly one year and hope to involve large regional and federal laboratories. For those in the Northeastern M.S. program wishing to continue for a Ph.D., there may be some combination of the three-month and one-year work periods. The in-service training period would be waived for entering students with extensive forensic experience.

We anticipate that the Ph.D. in forensic chemistry will again be an interdisciplinary degree involving the previously mentioned academic entities for the M.S. program. The Ph.D. thesis research should involve the same rigor as imposed on a regular chemistry or other science degree. Undoubtedly, much of the research will be performed within the Institute; however, there may be certain cases in which research under strict supervision at a well-qualified forensic laboratory might be accepted. The conditions under which this latter approach might occur have yet to be worked out.

Conclusion

This paper has outlined activities in forensic science over the past several years at Northeastern University. The establishment of the Institute of Chemical Analysis, Applications and Forensic Science has greatly aided in the development of forensic research and educational programs. Several years ago Bradford and Samuel (10) recommended the establishment of forensic science institutes to provide service to the profession. While we have not exactly followed their ideas, there are similarities between their recommendations and our activities. As time progresses, it is hoped that research and education at this Institute will make significant contributions to the field of forensic science.

Acknowledgment

The authors wish to thank the Law Enforcement Assistance Administration for the support of the programs in forensic chemistry at Northeastern through an educational development grant. In addition, acknowledgment is given to those practicing forensic scientists who have given us the benefit of their experience. The development of our program at Northeastern has been greatly aided by the encouragement of these individuals.

Contribution #2 from the Institute of Chemical Analysis, Applications and Forensic Science.

Literature Cited

1. Williams, R.L., Anal. Chem., (1973), 45(13), 1076A.
2. Curry, A.S., Nature, (1972), 235, 369.
3. Turner, R.F., Fox, W. and McGee, W.W., this volume.
4. Saferstein, R. and Epstein, R., this volume.
5. Brunelle, R.L. and Pro, M.J., J. Assoc. Official Anal. Chem., (1972), 55, 823, and paper by Brunelle, R.L. and Cantu, A., this volume.
6. Giessen, B.C., Polk, D.E., and Barnard, J.A.W., this volume.
7. Polk, D.E. and Giessen, B.C., J. For. Sci., in the press.
8. Turner, R.F., this volume.
9. Peterson, J.L., this volume.
10. Bradford, L.W., and Samuel, A.H., in "Law Enforcement Science and Technology", Academic Press, New York, 1970, Vol. III, p. 465.

LEAA's Forensic Science Research Program

JOSEPH L. PETERSON

John Jay College of Criminal Justice, New York, N. Y.

The goal of the Law Enforcement Assistance Administration (LEAA) is to reduce crime and delinquency while continually improving the quality of criminal justice. The responsibilities of the National Institute of Law Enforcement and Criminal Justice (NILECJ), the research arm of LEAA, include research and development efforts in the prevention of crime, in the detection of criminal acts, in the identification and apprehension of offenders, and in the swift and fair adjudication of suspects who are arrested and charged. The basic rationale of this research is that by increasing the likelihood of arrest and conviction, the risk associated with the commission of crimes is also elevated. If the risk of criminality becomes sufficiently high, there will be a proportional reduction in the volume and impact of criminal activity.

Within the past decade the methods of science and technology have assumed increasingly important roles in efforts to prevent, control and detect crime. One element of the total scientific effort within the criminal justice system assists in establishing that a crime has indeed been committed, in reconstructing the crime, in identifying likely suspects, and in eventually proving or disproving the involvement of a suspected offender with a particular criminal act. This is forensic science.

The creation of LEAA followed from the President's Crime Commission Report of 1967 which also recommended the greater utilization of physical evidence in the administration of criminal justice. The greatest proportion of LEAA funds in the forensic science area has been channeled down through the various state planning agencies in the form of block and discretion-

ary grant awards. These awards have resulted in the
creation of many new laboratories around the country
and in the improvement of existing facilities through
the acquisition of badly needed equipment and personnel
positions. LEAA funds have enabled state and local
criminalistics laboratories to provide scientific
service to jurisdictions where none was available
before, to keep pace with the skyrocketing increase
in drugs requiring analysis, and to accommodate the
increased flow of other forms of physical evidence.
Federal funds also have been instrumental in the
development of state-wide crime laboratory systems
and comprehensive long-range plans.

Over the past five years at the national level,
NILECJ has funded a number of significant research
projects in the forensic science area. Many of these
projects have included the refinement or development
of new techniques and instrumentation to facilitate
the examination of physical evidence. Research also
has examined the operations of laboratories and the
manner in which they interface with other components
of the criminal justice system. Other research has
contributed to the development of completely new fields,
such as voiceprint identification, which are now outside the scope of most forensic laboratory capabilities.

Research In-Progress

In FY 1973, select categories of research were
designated as high priority areas: forensic science
manpower needs, management and evaluation practices,
and laboratory technique development. Several of the
projects funded are nearing completion, or have been
completed, and merit a brief review.

Personnel. On July 15, 1973, the Institute
awarded a grant to the Forensic Sciences Foundation,
which is an adjunct to the American Academy of Forensic
Sciences. The Foundation, the research arm of the
Academy, is tackling a problem at the very heart of the
entire forensic science profession: the availability
and qualifications of scientific personnel. The
qualifications of individuals practicing in the forensic
disciplines range from poor to excellent and reflect
their innate abilities as well as their education and
training.

With perhaps the exception of forensic medicine,
individuals practicing in this field are normally prepared through in-service training. There are few
university level programs in the country offering

specialized training in any of the forensic sciences.
Even students who do graduate from such programs must
undergo months or years of additional training and
experience prior to qualifying as expert witnesses.
Other training courses are offered occasionally by
scientific institutes or law enforcement agencies
which serve the objective of continuing education in
the forensic sciences. Virtually no information exists
concerning the objectives, content and value of these
divergent education and training programs.

This project, therefore, will serve as an initial
assessment of the forensic science profession:
specifically, its personnel (professional and para-
professional), their education and training. The
Foundation project staff is gathering descriptive data
on the individuals within the profession, on the
scientific laboratories in which they function, and on
all the relevant education and training programs in
the country. Information on crime scene evidence
technicians and training courses will be included in
this phase of the project.

Based upon the analyses of these data, recommendations will be made regarding manpower deficiencies
within the profession, the nature of educational
programs required to train qualified personnel, and
other improvement programs to increase the contribution
of the forensic sciences to the criminal justice system.
Specifically, the following reports will be prepared
by the grantee:

- A report on the Personnel Background and
  Qualifications of scientists and paraprofess-
  ionals in the forensic science field;
- Personnel Shortages or Other Crises in the
  forensic science profession;
- The Identification and Description of Major
  Forensic Science Education and Training Centers;
- A report on Forensic Scientist and Evidence
  Technician Recruitment, Selection and Train-
  ing Practices.

This project constitutes a necessary first step
in a program to yield personnel who are more qualified
to perform their jobs, leading to increased quality
and productivity of such personnel. Final reports are
anticipated by November, 1974.

Management and Evaluation. A second major area
of research in which projects are nearing completion
addresses the problems of managing and evaluating

forensic science laboratories. It has become increasingly apparent that there is an acute absence of
management information regularly gathered by the
nation's crime laboratories. Very few laboratories
keep information on their operations in a similar
fashion; for that matter, there is no accepted definition or description of a crime laboratory. Each state
or local laboratory has developed in its own unique
fashion, primarily reflecting the special requirements
of the jurisdiction it serves and the interests and
capabilities of the crime laboratory director and the
chief executive of the local law enforcement agency.
    Up to this time there has been no accepted nomen-
clature used to describe the activities and output of
forensic laboratories. This absence of uniformity in
basic record keeping has prevented the collection of
data from more than a single jurisdiction and the
compilation of national statistics and assessments.
There is little way of knowing if the allocation of
federal funds into the forensic science field in the
past several years has been worthwhile without such
data. Management reporting models are needed so that
they can be implemented and objective evaluations can
be periodically performed to measure the performance
and effectiveness of various laboratory configurations
and operations.

    Measures of performance. In the fall of 1973,
three crime laboratories (Contra Costa County,
California; Dade County, Florida; and Columbus, Ohio)
were selected as representative sites for the
development of measures of performance and effectiveness. The Planning Research Corporation, with Mr.
Lowell W. Bradford as Project Director, was awarded the
task of developing a conceptual criminalistics laboratory model and methods for measuring the performance of
such laboratories. Teams of researchers each spent two
months collecting data on the operations of the three
previously mentioned laboratories. Data were gathered
on the forms of physical evidence submitted and the
types of crimes from which the evidence had been
recovered. Evidence and cases were traced through the
laboratories as examinations were performed and results
were formulated.
    The project involved the development and applica-
tion of techniques for determining the requirements of
crime laboratories in terms of personnel, facilities,
equipment and procedures. A state-of-the-art
conceptual model was designed to be flexible enough for
adaption to jurisdictions with dissimilar populations

and demand characteristics. The model is consistent with the recommendations published in the crime laboratory section (Standard 12.2) of the volume, <u>Report on Police</u>, prepared by LEAA's National Advisory Commission on Criminal Justice Standards and Goals.

The other primary component of the study was the development of laboratory performance measures, focusing on three primary factors: quality, quantity and response time. The most sensitive performance measure was quality, which refers primarily to analytical controls built into a laboratory operation and provisions for preserving the integrity of the evidence and reports. A "performance index" was developed which should enable any laboratory to undertake its own evaluation and to predict the impact of proposed improvements to the laboratory prior to their actual implementation.

The performance measures report is to be published in the near future and will be disseminated to all criminalistics laboratories. The report, although an initial inquiry into a very complex problem, is a major contribution to the literature and should be carefully examined and critiqued by all crime laboratory professionals. Hopefully, it will serve as the basis for future research and refinement of performance models and measures.

<u>Measures of effectiveness</u>. Concurrent with the research to develop measures of performance, the Calspan Corporation has been developing techniques for measuring the effectiveness or impact of crime laboratories on the criminal justice system. Prior to this study the various uses of criminalistics in criminal justice operations have not been evaluated quantitatively and on a crime-specific basis. Even though crime laboratories have expanded and increased in number in recent years, there is little information which shows that the quality and scope of laboratory output is satisfying the practical needs and expectations of investigators, attorneys and the courts.

The Calspan study, which is scheduled for completion in October, will thoroughly describe the role of criminalistics operations in criminal justice systems. Methods for measuring the effectiveness of criminalistics operations are being developed and validated. A series of recommendations will be drafted based upon data collection and observation in the three locations. These suggestions should serve to improve the utilization of criminalistics not only in the study sites, but in all forensic laboratories throughout the country.

Laboratory Techniques. In addition to the
previous research programs which address the personnel
and management information needs of forensic science
laboratories, the National Institute is funding
research to improve instrumentation and analytical
techniques applied to the analysis of physical evidence. The Aerospace Corporation of El Segundo,
California, and the Law Enforcement Standards Laboratory of the National Bureau of Standards (NBS) have
served as prime contractors to the Institute in the
laboratory technique area. Although space does not
permit a complete discussion of all projects underway
at Aerospace and NBS, I will describe two project areas
which are of great interest to forensic science
practitioners and researchers.

Blood and bloodstain analysis. The Aerospace
Corporation has completed a survey and technical
assessment of the state-of-the-art of forensic serological practices in the United States. Problems have
been defined which currently limit the utilization of
blood characterization techniques, and approaches have
been identified which have the potential of solving
these problems. This assessment was accomplished
primarily through contacts with criminalistics laboratories, blood banks, industrial organizations which
manufacture instrumentation and reagents for blood
identification, and through an extensive search of the
literature.

It has been determined that although human blood
is one of the most common clue materials found at crime
scenes, laboratory analysis procedures are comparative-
ly undeveloped in the United States. The major
limitations appear to be the unavailability of simple
and rapid methods of analysis, the lack of high quality
antisera prepared specifically for dried bloodstain
analysis, and the absence of blood frequency distribution data for the population of the United States. The
LEAA-sponsored program at Aerospace, therefore, is
intended to improve the methods for the detection of
genetic variants in dried blood, to expand the data
base concerning frequency of distribution of these
variants, and to design a structure for the future
collection and dissemination of such data.

The problems associated with the purity and
specificity of antisera may be solved by providing
special inducements to manufacturers to go through the
added expense of producing such antisera for the
limited market of forensic laboratories. A cooperative
relationship between the government and public and

private institutions will be needed to accumulate the
data base needed for establishing the uniqueness of
any bloodstain. In some cases genetic research and
medical testing organizations are or have the potential
of collecting useful population frequency data, but
until this time have not kept adequate records or do
not have the information in a form accessible to
forensic laboratories. The development of more
straightforward and less expensive methods would
certainly contribute to the generation of such data.

From what has been learned over the past year
during this assessment phase, The Aerospace Corporation
and its subcontractors will be concentrating now on the
development of better blood identification methodologies. Improved immunological and electrophoretic
methods, as well as combinations of these and other
new methods, are being explored for application to the
forensic serology problem. Other new blood systems
with even higher discrimination capabilities are known
but have yet to be adapted for use with dried blood.

Criminalists play an extremely important role
in this bloodstain research program. The needs of the
user community of criminalists are well-represented by
individuals acting either as consultants to the contractors or as advisors to the Institute. As new
prototype equipment and methods of analysis are
developed, crime laboratories will be invited to
participate in their field testing and evaluation.

It should be noted that a comparable survey and
assessment task in the gunshot residue detection area
recently has been completed by Aerospace. The long-
range objectives of this research program are to
develop rapid, reliable and inexpensive techniques and
equipment for use by crime laboratories in the detection of gunshot residues on the hands of suspects.
As this research progresses, the findings will be
disseminated to the criminalistics community.

Standard reference collections. The Law Enforcement Standards Laboratory of NBS has been investigating
the needs and uses of standard reference files or
collections of select groups of forensic materials.
A tentative data base has been established based upon
surveys and interviews with criminalists, educators,
scientists and manufacturers. Existing forensic
material collections and data files have been located
and evaluated. New proposed forensic material
collection specifications have been developed including
recommendations relating to size, scope and costs of
development. The report, although not yet published,

is being utilized by the Project SEARCH Crime
Laboratory Information System Project Committee and
should prove valuable in future reference standard
research.

Two standard reference collections have been
constructed and are in the process of being distributed
to crime laboratories in the United States. The first
is a set of auto paint color chips for 1974 domestic
vehicles. Each set contains samples of approximately
140 colors plus information concerning the makes and
models of automobiles on which each color was used.
The actual color samples are in the form of 1"x1½"
coated metal chips, housed in hinged plastic holders.
While this reference collection is intended for color
comparisons only, it is hoped that future research will
allow for the distribution of corresponding chemical
analysis data.

Standard samples of refractive index glass are
being distributed at nominal cost to interested forensic laboratories. Blocks of glass having properties
similar to glass used in auto headlights have been cut
and polished for use as refractometer calibration
standards; ground glass blocks for use as standards
with the liquid immersion technique also have been
prepared. Samples of two liquids have been obtained to
study their suitability as liquid refractive index
standard reference materials. NBS is also continuing
work in the development of a compendium of auto head-
light characteristics which will contain information on
refractive indices and trace element constituents, as
well as photographic reproductions of various manufactured lenses.

Computerized Information System. The Project
SEARCH Criminalistics Laboratory Information System
(CLIS) Committee is another LEAA funded project.
Approximately fifteen criminalists are serving on the
CLIS Committee which is conducting a requirements
analysis for a nationwide computerized crime laboratory
information system. With the assistance of a technical
subcontractor, PRC Public Management Services, Inc.,
the committee has determined the "user needs" for such
a data system, a conceptual design of a computer system
to meet these requirements, and an assessment of
different organizational and equipment alternatives for
the system. The most recent task reports and implementation plan have been completed and submitted to the
advisory committee for final review. Copies of the
final reports should be ready for dissemination in the
very near future.

New Projects

While the National Institute always has attempted
to be responsive to the practical needs of the professional community in the research it funds, criminalists
have had a much stronger voice in the definition of
priority areas and the actual selection of projects in
FY 1974 than at any previous time. It is anticipated
that this input will continue in the future with
criminalists playing important roles in the design of
new projects and the monitorship and evaluation of
programs already funded.

At the LEAA-sponsored FBI National Symposium on
Crime Laboratory Development held in December, 1973,
crime laboratory directors from around the country
selected several priority research areas. The Institute has been able to respond to most of the high
priority areas in the form of new grants addressing
blood, semen and hair characterization.

At the February meeting of the American Academy of
Forensic Sciences in Dallas, Texas, the Criminalistics
Section supported a resolution that the Forensic
Sciences Foundation develop a concept paper for a
national system of crime laboratory proficiency testing.
This, subsequently, resulted in a grant award to the
Foundation for an eighteen-month study which will test
the feasibility of regular proficiency testing in the
nation's forensic laboratories.

The Institute also established an informal criminalistics advisory board which offered considerable
assistance in the review and evaluation of concept
papers and proposals submitted for funding. This panel,
composed of six leading criminalists, researchers and
educators, served as an independent source of technical
expertise and practical experience in the field of
criminalistics. In addition to this group, a panel of
forensic scientists from several federal law enforcement agencies was formed and has met periodically to
discuss important issues in the administration of
research projects.

The four principal new grants awarded are the
following:

```
Grant Title:   Variant Polypeptides in Hair
Grant Number:  74-NI-99-0032
Grantee:       Howard P. Baden, M.D., Massachu-
               setts General Hospital, Boston,
               Massachusetts
```

This project is a study of the genetically

determined variants in the structural proteins
of human hair. The grantee has recently discovered a variant of hair protein and it is
anticipated this award will enable him to find
others which will make the individualization of
persons more precise. A limited survey will be
conducted to determine the incidence of the
protein variations in the population. Finally,
the present electrophoresis analysis techniques
will be scaled down so that they may be used
with single strands of hair.

Hair is a common and important type of
evidence since it is durable to the environment
and more resistant to degradation than most
other human tissues. However, present analysis
methods depend largely on morphological criteria
which do not differ sharply between different
individuals and also show great variability
in a single individual. Chemical methods of
analysis are mainly concerned with the trace
metal content of hair which is greatly affected
by environmental factors either by contamination
from the outside or by ingestion. Genetic
markers, on the other hand, are characteristic
of the individual, do not show change with age
or environment and are found in all hair of a
single person.

Grant Title: Characterization and Individual-
                 ization of Semen
Grant Number: 74-NI-99-0041
Grantee: George F. Sensabaugh, D.Crim.,
                 University of California, Berkeley

The purpose of this project is to provide
the theoretical and practical foundation for
the improved analysis of semen in the context
of rape investigations. The research has two
primary objectives: 1) Improvement of procedures for the identification of semen; and
2) Improvement of the ability to individualize
semen. These objectives will be accomplished
through an analysis of acid phosphatase and
other proteins to determine whether the forms
which are found in semen are unique to semen
and whether they display genetic polymorphisms.
A similar analysis will be done of the protein
markers in the sperm cell membrane.

Improvement in procedures and advances in
knowledge in the analysis of semen benefits

investigation and prosecution by providing
independent and scientific corroboration of
information. The potential of semen individualization in particular shifts the burden
of identification from the victim to the
physical evidence.

Grant Title: Individualization and Identi-
                  fication of Forensically
                  Important Physiological Fluids
Grant Number: 75-NI-99-0011
Grantee: Charles A. McInerney, Pittsburgh
                  and Allegheny County Crime
                  Laboratory, Pittsburgh, Pa.

This grant proposal was selected for
funding under the Institute's Innovative
Research in Criminal Justice Program which
was initiated this past winter. The purpose
of this project is to improve the capability
of crime laboratories to characterize and
individualize bloodstains through the use of
genetic markers. The project is divided into
three sections, the first of which addresses
the need for population frequency data on the
newer blood systems, including: Phosphoglucomutase (PGM), Erythrocyte Acid Phosphatase (EAP),
MN and Haptoglobin (HP). Over 2,000 blood
samples from the Greater Pittsburgh Blood
Bank will be processed for these factors
during the fifteen-month grant period.
The second part of this project will
investigate the applicability of the isoenzyme systems Glutathione Reductase and
Peptidase A to dried blood analysis. The
grantee proposes, also, to incorporate the
Gm and Inv allotypes into routine use. Techniques for identifying these genetic markers
are well-established for whole blood but must
be adapted for dried blood analysis. Per-
sistence studies will be undertaken to determine
the viability of these different systems upon
drying, to determine the effect of aging, to
document the effect of various substrates,
and to devise a practical system to type the
isoenzymes and allotypes in dried blood.
The final objective will be directed
toward the determination of the sexual origin
of bloodstains by measuring the levels of
testosterone and estradiol in dried blood.

This research will determine the suitability
of radioimmunoassay techniques for such tests
and will establish experimental limits for
making sexual determinations based on the
ratio of testosterone and estradiol in a
bloodstain.

The above project is being closely
coordinated with the bloodstain research
program being carried out by the Aerospace
Corporation.

Grant Title: Laboratory Proficiency Testing
Grant Number: 74-NI-99-0048
Grantee: Kenneth S. Field, Forensic
                Sciences Foundation, Inc.,
                Rockville, Maryland

The purpose of this project is to conduct
a nationwide criminalistics laboratory proficiency testing program. The objectives of
the project are:

· Through the use of voluntary, anonymous proficiency testing, assess
  the analytical accuracy of criminalistics laboratories in the processing
  of selected physical evidence;
· Make statistical studies of laboratory
  proficiency in the processing of test
  samples and of the accuracy and precision of the various analytical
  methods used;
· Establish the basis for the design
  of educational programs in the area
  of analytical methods which will
  assist the criminalistics profession
  in the attainment of higher levels
  of proficiency.

The first step in the project will be
the organization of the Project Advisory
Committee consisting of several nationally
known criminalistics authorities to serve
as advisors on all facets of the program.
Other critical steps in the project involve
the selection and manufacture of typical
evidence according to exact specifications
and its distribution to each criminalistics
laboratory in the United States, its posses-
sions, and to a group of laboratories in

Canada. On a strictly voluntary basis, each
laboratory will submit its analytical findings
concerning each item which will be treated in
a confidential manner. The findings will be
compared with those from a group of referee
laboratories and the resulting data will be
analyzed for long-range study purposes.

Future Directions for Research

This leads to a brief discussion of the Institute's FY 1975 research plans. Several of the
projects described earlier will be continued through
to completion. Ideas for new research are being
considered. Above all, the Institute intends to
continue the development of a nationally coordinated
program of research which will maximize the contributions of the forensic sciences to the criminal
justice system and society in general.

Of the research options available in FY 1975,
the Institute currently feels two areas merit
serious consideration.

Demonstrating Crime Laboratory Effectiveness.
NILECJ is directing increased attention in all criminal
justice program areas to projects which have strong
evaluation components. In very basic language, the
Institute needs to know "what works and what doesn't
work." An attempt is being made to identify programs
nationally which are making substantial contributions
to achieving the goals of the criminal justice system,
to describe and evaluate those projects, and then to
offer these successful programs to all jurisdictions
in the nation for possible adoption.

Crime laboratory operations of high quality are
candidates for such evaluations. As described earlier,
the Institute has funded research projects to develop
candidate management evaluation techniques. Such
measures should be very helpful to all crime laboratories in evaluating their performance and effectiveness. These measures have already been tested in
three sites and baseline data have been collected
for a period of several months in these same locations.

The Institute is now considering the merits of
going into those and other laboratory systems to
measure the impact of the crime laboratory on the
activities of local investigators, prosecutors,
defense attorneys, judges and jurors. Because the
crime laboratory currently becomes involved in Part I
crime investigations so infrequently (less than two

per cent of such crimes in many jurisdictions), the
project would involve the introduction of added crime
scene search and laboratory analysis resources for the
study period to increase the ratio of crimes in which
physical evidence is collected and analyzed. In so
doing, data could be collected which would demonstrate
the effectiveness of a crime laboratory in an area
where a reasonably high ratio of crime scenes were
being processed for physical evidence and the evidence
was receiving a thorough analysis by qualified
criminalists.

    Such studies would generate information which
could be presented to those who are skeptical of the
value of crime laboratories. The hypothesis that
forensic science laboratories can contribute much
more to the identification of offenders and the
solution of crimes, if they were only used more,
should be thoroughly tested.

    Court Acceptance of Scientific Techniques. There
continue to be problems over the admissability of new
scientific tests and procedures in court. Basically,
judges still employ the criteria used in Frye vs.
United States 293 F. 1013 (D.C. Cir. 1923), which
required that new tests must gain general scientific
acceptance before they can be admitted into court.
While there is no fundamental problem with such
criteria, difficulties do arise when an individual
scientist or expert presents information to a single
judge or court. Quite apart from the test itself,
the decision by the court is influenced by such
variables as the preparation and delivery of the
expert, the competence of the prosecutor and defense
attorney, and the abilities of the judge making the
ruling. The judge is often placed in a difficult
position because he is without adequate knowledge to
decide if any particular technique has gained "general
scientific acceptance."

    There appears to be a need for an established
procedure for evaluating new techniques and data for
use in court, from both scientific and legal perspec-
tives. Such a procedure should reflect the thinking
of both professions because the expert possesses the
scientific understanding of the test and the jurist
will be making the ultimate decision of admissability.
Criteria should be developed which meet both legal
and scientific acceptance, and procedures should be
proposed by which any new test or set of data could
be evaluated.

    One possible means for establishing such criteria

and procedures would be in the form of a standing
committee composed of leading judges, attorneys and
scientists. This committee eventually could issue
recommendations regarding the suitability of any
scientific technique for court use. Although not
binding on any court, the findings would constitute
an impartial and comprehensive appraisal of the test
in question and probably would be welcomed by most
courts in the nation. Problems such as those
encountered in recent years over voiceprint techniques
might be avoided and all the courts in the country
would have the benefit of using an unbiased
evaluation meeting both legal and scientific demands.

Conclusion

The above discussion has highlighted the forensic
science program activities of the National Institute
of Law Enforcement and Criminal Justice. Current
research projects are addressing several critical
problem areas, including the education and training
needs of scientific personnel, the management and
evaluation of laboratory operations, and the
characterization and individualization of physical
evidence. Efforts are being made to establish
programs which address the most serious problems in
the field and which reflect the best judgments of
forensic practitioners, educators and researchers.
All forensic scientists are encouraged to maintain
an active interest in the programs of the Institute
and to bring critical problem areas and new concepts
for research to its attention.

7

The Application of Materials Science Methods to Forensic Problems—Principles, Serial Number Recovery, and Paper Identification

BILL C. GIESSEN, DONALD E. POLK, and JAMES A. W. BARNARD

Institute of Chemical Analysis, Applications, and Forensic Science, Northeastern University, Boston, Mass. 02115

Materials science is a relatively young discipline which emerged in the 1960's to provide a comprehensive view and approach to the study of materials. It includes aspects of solid state physics, chemistry, metallurgy, ceramics and other fields of science and engineering.

Recent work has shown that materials science can make a substantial and growing contribution to criminalistics. As a result, forensic materials science may become a field of its own in the future.

In the following sections, we outline the possible scope of this new field and we illustrate the use of materials science methods in criminalistics by discussing two examples: the recovery of erased serial numbers and the identification of papers from their inorganic components.

The Scope of Forensic Materials Science

All objects of forensic investigations are materials of some kind, ranging from traces of evidence substances to large items that must be identified. Therefore, proper characterization for forensic purposes requires more than a mere determination of the most obvious chemical properties, such as elemental composition or density; instead, it must include a thorough understanding of these substances as materials.

From the standpoint of the materials scientist such an understanding would result from adopting an integrated view of the many aspects of a material; it would be based on the interpretation of data from many additional tools of investigation, some of which will be discussed below. The increase in the number of characterizing methods has two consequences:

  1) a direct effect is that more distinguishing parameters become available for the purpose of forensic examination. In some cases where no other means of identification exist, this may provide a new, sole means of identification of items of evidence capable of establishing rela-

tive or absolute identity. In cases where traditional chemical means of identification exist, additional methods may increase the certainty and hence evidence value of this identification.

2) a more long range effect of adopting the integrated view of materials in forensic examinations consists of producing a broader and deeper expertise in concerned forensic scientists. This gives them a greater flexibility in performing current tasks and an ability to contribute to future developments beneficial to the field.

Personnel and Personnel Training. The goals discussed here lie in the future, when a closer liaison between criminalistics and materials science will have been brought about by building up personnel with thorough training in both fields and by establishing appropriate research projects. At present, the list of active criminalists includes several metallurgists, scanning electron microscopists, X-ray diffractionists, solid state physical chemists and others; however, with a number of notable exceptions, few workers in the criminalistics field have had an orthodox advanced training as materials scientists. Possible remedies to this situation lie in academic programs in "Forensic Materials Science" on several levels, which will be discussed elsewhere (1). A continued supply of professionals with dual training (analogous to that of the forensic chemists now being educated) is, however, certainly long removed.

In this context we note that the curriculum for the planned M.S. program in Forensic Chemistry at Northeastern University which is discussed in detail in Reference 2 will contain a new course entitled "Forensic Materials" as a step in the direction indicated above. The abstract of this course is as follows:

Forensic Materials (2 Quarter Hours): Fundamental types of solids, such as metals, ceramics, minerals, organic solids, including drugs, polymers, plastics, fibers; their properties and determination by modern methods. Forensically important materials such as alloys, glass, soils, fibers, wood, paper, rubber, dyes, paints, ink, and their determination. Illustration of various materials as associative or dissociative items of evidence.

Typical Areas of Forensic Materials Science. In the following, some types of forensic materials and tasks involving them which arise in a crime laboratory are listed, and possible applications of the materials scientific approach to these substances and tasks are briefly described.

1. Metals. In forensic practice, metallic objects are investigated primarily by the firearm and toolmark examiner; typical examples are weapons, bullets, cartridge casings and hand tools. Metals are also encountered in cases of failure analysis (frac-

ture by fatigue or impact). The characterization of metallic
samples to ascertain sample identity and origin is also often of
importance (the following discussion refers principally to this
case). Depending on the type of alloy encountered, various characterization techniques could be used (see, e.g., refs. 3-5).
Study of a metallic object might involve the following determinations: (a) major and trace metal content by chemical analysis;
(b) microstructure by quantitative optical or electron microscopy,
as well as phase analysis by X-ray diffraction or Mossbauer spectroscopy, e.g., for retained austenite (γ-Fe solid solution) in
iron alloys; (c) preferred orientation (texture) by X-ray diffraction; (d) degree of cold-working by dislocation density measurement or differential scanning calorimetry; (e) nature and distribution of impurities by electron microscopy, including selected
area electron diffraction, electron or ion microprobe analysis,
chemical separation coupled with X-ray diffraction microanalysis,
and perhaps small angle scattering and high precision density
determination; (f) fractography by scanning electron microscopy
(SEM) or scanning ion microscopy; (g) lattice impurity level by
low-temperature electrical resistance and other mean-free-path
dependent measurements; (h) short or long range order (e.g. for
brass); (i) domain size or magnetic properties for ferromagnetic
alloys; and (j) surface structure by SEM, scanning Auger spectroscopy or low energy electron diffraction. A few of these methods
are in current forensic use, but most are not. While a majority
of the proposed methods, taken alone, will not yield unique specimen identification, some may provide additional parameters for
determining materials origin or sample identity, e.g., for wires
used in explosive devices. In such cases, the integrated method
of material characterization may turn out to be of considerable
value. A forensic application to a problem that occurs primarily
with metallic objects, namely the recovery of erased serial numbers, is dealt with in a separate section below.

    2. Nonmetallic Inorganic Solids. This category includes
many items of forensic importance: ceramic and glasses; naturally occurring substances such as building and insulation materials
and soil components; additives to papers, paints, explosives,
drugs and many other materials. In contrast to metals, even the
task of basic material identification often requires considerably
more than the overall chemical analysis for these substances.
X-ray powder diffraction data may be helpful but are often hard to
interpret for complex mixtures; use of computer data file search
programs (6) and microcamera methods for single particle analysis
(7) may be useful for identification. Comparative sample identification is generally less often possible than for metals since the
latter are manufactured while the nonmetallic inorganic solids
are often unprocessed materials with large property variations.
However, where applicable, the following are some examples of
determinations which might be made: (a) particle size by microscopy; (b) microstructure and sub-microstructure characterization

e.g., for minerals, by the methods described above; (c) impurity
trace analysis by particle extraction and analysis (see the
corresponding methods listed above for impurities in metals); (d)
crystal perfection, mosaic size and misorientation, e.g., by
X-ray microscopy such as the Berg-Barrett or other topographic
techniques (3) or transmission electron microscopy; (e) atomic
order by X-ray diffraction (especially for minerals such as sili-
cates); (f) identification of heteroatomic defects by electrical
resistance measurements, optical property studies or spin reso-
nance techniques; (g) concentration of point or line defects, e.g.,
by density studies; and (h) thermal and, where applicable, magnetic
properties. Current efforts in forensic science have made some
use of the above concepts. For example, the possibility of detecting small local differences in the atomic environments in glasses
by monitoring luminescence which is sensitive to the atomic environment has been demonstrated by Jones (8).

3. Organic Solids. Materials in this category are: plastics and polymers, especially fibers; drugs and dyes; some natural
products, such as wood and natural fibers, and many others. Here
also, the elemental chemical analysis is generally not sufficient.
However, the use of infrared analysis, mass spectrometry, X-ray
crystallography, chromatography and other methods to supplement
the compositional analysis data is well known for organic product
characterization, especially in the determination of the chemical
compounds present. In addition to these chemical analytical
methods, typical materials science approaches could be used for
sample identification. Thus, drugs could be further character-
ized by: (a) particle morphology (by microscopy); (b) crystal-
lite perfection (by X-ray diffraction or electron microscopy),
or (c) trace impurity level (found as a second phase in crystalline materials by transmission or scanning electron microscopy
and identified by electron diffraction and emission spectroscopy).
The recent application of luminescence properties is described
in Reference 8. Polymers have a number of exploitable properties
(thermal, mechanical, thermomechanical (9), rheological, structural (chain length), NMR and ESR, optical, electrical and surface) that are not used or, at least, not commonly used for forensic identification at present (10).

4. Organic-Inorganic Composite Products. In this category
we include here only paper, rubber and certain building materials.
Many methods suggested above for organic and inorganic solids may
be useful. Some applications for the identification of paper,
one of the forensically most important products in this category,
are discussed in detail below.

The list of new methods given above is incomplete and is intended only as a guide to the techniques that the forensic materials scientist may introduce into the field. For most of the
materials properties we have considered here the establishment
of reference libraries listing characteristic values and their
variation through the population would be necessary to make any

new methods acceptable in the field. The question of cost-effec-
tiveness would also have to be considered for each proposed inno-
vation; the use of regional or other service laboratories would
be advantageous from equipment and manpower considerations.

The Recovery of Erased Serial Numbers

A common criminalistics problem to which materials science
technology is applicable is the recovery of serial numbers which
have been obliterated from metal items. We discuss here the metallurgical background of serial number obliteration and recovery,
the theory and practice of chemical or electro-chemical methods
which form the bulk of the presently employed methods, some techniques based on alternate approaches that are mostly experimental
or have been proposed and, lastly, a recently developed serial
number marking technique capable of producing more permanent
markings.

Metallurgical Background. Generally, the obliterated numbers
dealt with in the crime laboratory have been produced by stamping,
i.e., striking the item with a die with a force sufficient to de-
form the metal so as to leave behind an impression of the tip of
the die.

The metals of interest are polycrystalline; the atoms have a
three-dimensionally periodic arrangement within local regions of
0.01-0.1 mm size which are called grains by metallurgists. Permanent deformation, or plastic flow, occurs in these materials by
the motion of line defects, called dislocations, through the crystalline array. The movement of dislocations through the periodically arranged atoms in a grain causes one part of the grain to
move relative to the other part so as to give a macroscopic
change of shape. This is represented schematically in Figure 1.

As a force is applied to the item through the die, the metal
first becomes elastically strained and would return to its initial
shape if the force were removed at this point. As the force
increases, the metal's elastic limit is exceeded and plastic flow
occurs via the motion of dislocations. Many of these dislocations
become entangled and trapped within the plastically deformed
material; thus, plastic deformation produces crystals which are
less perfect and contain internal stresses. These crystals are
designated as cold-worked and have physical properties which
differ from those of the undeformed metal.

As shown schematically in Figure 2, each stamped number thus
consists of a visible indentation, a plastically deformed region
surrounding and defining the indentation, and an elastically
strained region bordering the plastically deformed area. Typically, serial numbers are removed illegally by filing or grinding
until the visible indentation has been removed, often leaving
behind the plastically deformed metal which was present beneath
the indentation (See Figure 2). All serial number recovery tech-

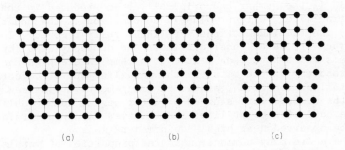

(a)   (b)   (c)

Figure 1. Two-dimensional schematic of the motion of a disloca-tion through a crystalline array of atoms which causes a change in the shape of the crystal and contributes to change in the macro-scopic shape of a metal item. The dislocation, visible at the left center of (a), is centered at the trapezoid connecting five atoms and is due to an extra vertical line of atoms in the upper half of the crystal. A shearing force which pushes the top half of the crystal to the right relative to the bottom half causes the disloca-tion to move from its position in (a) across the crystal, as shown in (b) and (c). This leads to the change in shape apparent by comparing (a) and (c).

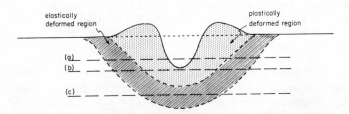

Figure 2. Schematic of the cross section through a number stamped into metal. Removal of metal down to level (a) results in incomplete obliteration although the number may no longer be readily visible because metal has been smeared into the groove forming the number; recovery is easiest in this case. Removal of metal to level (b) leaves behind plastically deformed material; this is the situation for which recovery techniques, e.g., etching, can bring out the obliterated numbers. Removal of metal down to level (c) removes all metal plastically deformed during the stamping of the number; in this case, recovery is impossible.

niques aim at detecting the location of this remaining plastically deformed metal.

As a consequence, no recovery technique can possibly be successful if the number had originally been produced in the item by casting (i.e., without plastic deformation of the underlying region) and the indentations were later fully removed. In addition, recovery is at least difficult and probably also impossible for items which have been heated to a temperature high enough to cause recovery of the metal by the annealing out of defects or recrystallization (i.e., atomic rearrangement forming new grains) after the numbers were stamped or after serial number obliteration. (In the case of recrystallization, however, abnormal grain growth might be observed near highly deformed regions.)

There are many commonly measured properties of metals which are known to change upon cold-working. The best known effect is an increase in hardness. Additionally, the resistivity increases and the thermal conductivity decreases; the electronic work function is changed; the X-ray diffraction pattern is broadened. Each of these property changes can be considered as the basis of a method to detect plastically deformed regions left behind after the visible indentations of serial numbers have been removed.

Chemical or Electrochemical Serial Number Recovery Methods. These methods form the bulk of the procedures in current practice in crime laboratories; they are therefore discussed here in more detail than other, still experimental techniques.

1. Etching. It is well known to metallurgists that metal in the vicinity of a grain boundary or dislocation or from a region of localized elastic stress is more electrochemically active, i.e., it can be made to dissolve preferentially in a suitable acidic solution. This occurs because the metal at these locations has a higher chemical potential than in the rest of the substance due to the stored energy of cold-working, i.e., the region containing the defect is more negative in the EMF series. This effect is the basis for the visualization of metal defects by etching. Many years of empirical testing have resulted in lists of etchants suitable for particular metal studies (11,12); the desired result of etching generally consists of a local change in the light reflectivity. This change may be due to preferred attack at crystal defects, a change of grain surface orientation to expose crystal planes with a lower rate of attack or variations in the rate of attack for grains with different crystal orientations. Various etchants suitable for serial number recovery and the procedures to be followed have been discussed in the literature (13-15). Here, we give a brief review of the process used for steels and add some observations made in our laboratory.

An important first step involves proper surface preparation. The area to be treated must be smooth for optimal application of this recovery process. A smooth finish to remove all grinding and filing scratches is required as the shallow cold worked

regions associated with the grinding or filing scratches also
produce contrast effects and thus interfere with number recovery.
(Obviously, care must be taken not to remove more metal than is
necessary so as to conserve the plastically deformed metal beneath the number.) We believe that careful polishing can be done
without decreasing the probability of successful recovery since
generally the cold worked regions beneath the serial number im-
prints are deeper than those under the scratches; under these
conditions, the elimination of interference from the scratches
by polishing outweighs the advantages of retaining the additional metal. Thus, we have polished metal specimens by using a 240
grit paper to polish in a direction perpendicular to grinding
scratches just until they disappeared. Then 320, 400 and 600
grit papers were used in turn, again polishing perpendicularly
to the previous scratches until they disappeared. The specimen
being polished was kept wet; the final surface had a mirror-like
reflectivity. There may be advantages to going even further and
producing a microscopically smooth surface finish (scratch width
< 0.001mm) which can be obtained by polishing with alumina slur-
ry or diamond paste; this area is being explored in our laboratory.

The acid is then applied to the surface, either by immersion
or swabbing. The acidic solutions which are recommended for
steels (13,15) and have been found to work well for number recovery are aqueous solutions of HCl and $CuCl_2$ (which sometimes contain an alcohol). Specific etchants of this type are known as
"Fry's reagent" and are known to make visible strain lines due
to cold work (12).

A preferred reagent (12,13) is a mixture of 5 gm $CuCl_2$, 40 ml
HCl, 30 ml distilled water and 25 ml ethanol. Swabbing of the
surface with this solution has been found to restore the number
on steel samples, where the indentations have been fully ground
off and which were then polished, within 5-20 minutes. This
etchant dissolves away the plastically deformed regions more
rapidly, forming etchpits which become visible because of differences in light reflectivity.

The etching process depends on properties studied in different subdivisions of materials science and chemistry: stored
energy and the nature of the defects (physical metallurgy), local
electrolytic action (electrochemistry), boundary layer effects
on etching (surface science), and the nature (e.g., type of complex) of the solute present in the liquid (inorganic solution
chemistry). Fundamental understanding of the participating processes would be required to optimize etchant compositions or
find new, better etchant combinations; however, the mechanism of
this differential attack does not appear to be well understood.
The mechanism of attack must be dependent on the types of copper-
chloride complexes which are present since a reagent solution
without copper does not show a very pronounced differentiation in
attack while a $CuCl_2$ solution containing more dilute HCl results
in copper precipitation on the steel. It is not known whether

the differential attack is kinetically as well as thermodynamical-
ly controlled, and no study of the nature of the surface structure
modification upon etching has been reported.
   2. Electroetching. The etching can be speeded up by
applying an electric field to the specimen (13,15,16). Current
practice in some crime laboratories is to use an applied D.C. voltage, but it appears that the potential of this approach has not
yet been exploited fully. Electroetching has the potential for
a fine tuning of the applied voltage so that the difference in
reaction rate between the deformed and undeformed material can be
maximized, resulting in faster and possibly better number recovery.
   3. Other Chemical or Electrochemical Methods. Of interest is a specialized procedure for aluminum which has been reported (17). A thin coating of mercury is used to catalyze the oxi-
dation of aluminum by air, possibly by breaching the protective
aluminum oxide layer. The number presumably becomes visible because the plastically deformed regions oxidize faster than the
surrounding material, thus again making use of the electrochemical difference between deformed and undeformed regions.
   Another electroanalytical technique is being considered.
If a heavy metal, e.g., Au, were preferentially plated out over
the deformed region in the form of a thin layer, (e.g., in an
electrochemical cell or simply by immersion in an appropriate
solution, the resulting replica of the serial number could be
made visible in the scanning electron microscope by elemental
mapping of Au, where the location of the Au is displayed by
analyzing for fluorescent Au X-radiation. This approach has yet
to be examined experimentally.

   Restoration Methods Based on Alternate Approaches. Other
property changes occurring in the plastically or elastically
deformed regions may be considered for utilization in serial number restoration; their identification and exploitation for field
use is a genuine challenge to the materials scientist.
   1. Hardness. The increase in hardness of a metal upon cold
working (work hardening) is well documented. Direct detection
of the deformed regions using local micro-hardness measurements
over the surface appears impractical because of the fine resolution and, hence, time required to recover a series of numbers.
   Methods which would produce a surface morphology dependent
on the local hardness might, however, be applicable. One such
experimental technique uses ultrasonic cavitation to detect hardness differences (18). The sample and an ultrasonic transducer
placed near the surface to be studied are immersed in a liquid.
The ultrasonic excitation causes small bubbles to form in the
liquid; the collapse of these bubbles causes abrasion of the
surface. The hardened regions are not damaged as much as the
surrounding matrix (in contrast to the chemical method described
above!) and thus become visible because of differences in light
reflectivity. This method is especially effective in removing

metal which was smeared into the grooves forming the number, i.e.
in situations involving an incompletely obliterated serial number. Its effectiveness has not yet been quantitatively compared
with the chemical methods described above.

    2. Magnetic Methods. The preceding methods are destructive
tests in that the restoration technique permanently alters the
speciman. If improper conditions are applied in destructive
tests, there is often no second chance to recover the number.
Nondestructive methods are therefore especially attractive. Several promising, nondestructive approaches for serial number recovery from ferromagnetic alloys are based on the magnetization
behavior of the metal. The potential of this method has been
realized (15) but appears not to have been fully exploited.

    Cold working of magnetic steel changes its magnetization
behavior. When the steel is magnetized by being placed in a
magnetic field, the cold worked regions do not magnetize as readily as the undeformed material. This is due to the presence
of the defects described above which inhibit the rearrangement
of the ferromagnetic domains existing in a disordered arrangement
prior to magnetization of the metal. Conversely, the deformed
regions do not demagnetize as readily as the undeformed regions
on removal of the field. The different degrees of magnetization
can be displayed by applying a magnetic powder to the surface.
Differences in residual magnetization can also be detected by
scanning the surface with a magnetic probe. A third approach,
which is in the experimental stage at this laboratory, is based
on the possibility of displaying magnetic domains directly in
the scanning electron microscope.

    3. Electrical Resistivity. Differences in electrical resis-
tivity and magnetic permeability are utilized in another potentially useful, nondestructive technique, the eddy current method
(19). In this technique, the surface is scanned at close dis-
tance with a small coil carrying alternating current. The magnetic field of the coil induces eddy currents in the nearby sample;
the magnitude of the eddy currents depends on the local electrical conductivity and on the permeability of the sample. These
eddy currents in turn set up a magnetic field which opposes the
field from the coil and thus changes the apparent impedance of
the coil. Since the electrical resistivity and magnetic permeability are changed by deformation, the regions underneath the
indentation can be detected by scanning with a suitably small
probe so as to record the apparent impedance as a function of
position.

An Improved Serial Number Marking System

    Since recovery of obliterated stamped numbers cannot always
be accomplished, a marking system which produces tagging more
resistant to removal would be desirable. In such an improved
system, the marking effect must extend well into the item rather

than being a surface effect such as results from stamped numbers.
For specific items, the marking should be compatible with locations such that its removal would make the item useless.

One possible marking system which has such features has been
developed at this Institute (20). This marking system is based
on the drilling of an array of holes into the item; an encoding
system is utilized such that the serial number is represented by
the relative placement of the holes.

In each case, the holes would have to be small enough so that
they would not interfere with the function of the item. For this
reason and so that the number can be recorded in a small region,
very small holes having a diameter of several thousandths of an
inch are desirable. Such holes can be produced by using a high
powered laser. A pulse of light from the laser is focused to a
very narrow beam which then boils off the material which it
strikes. For example, holes with a diameter of 0.005" and a
depth of 1/8" can be drilled into steel within a second.

Various encoding systems can be envisioned; one possible
encoding system using laser holes is shown in Figure 3. In this
example, the number 5488159066 is represented by 10 holes located
on a 10 x 10 grid. Each individual digit of the serial number
is represented by one hole in its column; the uppermost location
corresponds to a 1, the next lower to a 2, etc. The three holes
flanking the grid are reference points which define the grid
since the grid shown in the drawing of Figure 3 would not appear
on a marked item. Thus 13 holes can be used to distinguish 10^{10},
or 10 billion, different items. Some of the digits could be used
to signify the model number of the item.

Using a grid having points 0.010" apart, this pattern can be
recorded within a surface area of 1/8" square. A drilled array
using the code described above and representing the number
5383158068 is shown in Figure 4. Next to it is a 1/8" digit
typically used for serial numbers on guns, shown for comparison
of size.

As has been stated previously, many different encoding systems and modifications of this method can be envisioned (20).
Miniaturization is especially useful to record the number in a
critical area of a small item. The proposed marking system
appears ideally suited for firearms where it would be desirable
to locate the marking in an area such that its removal would
make the gun inoperable. For items not having critically important regions, the hole pattern could be spread out over a large
part of the surface. Drilling of somewhat larger holes with a
different encoding system could be used to produce a pattern which
could be read by the unaided eye.

The laser drilling based marking system is commercially
feasible and could be fully automated for a production procedure.
It could also be used to tag individual items. If desired, the
holes could be fully hidden by a treatment of the surface after
drilling. Further work is in progress to evaluate the potential

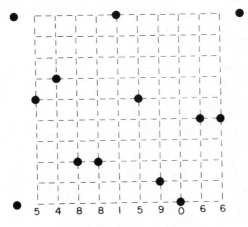

Figure 3. *An example of a pattern of 13 holes that can be used to represent a 10-digit serial number. The three holes flanking the grid are reference points which define it. Each digit is determined by the position of the hole in the column associated with it.*

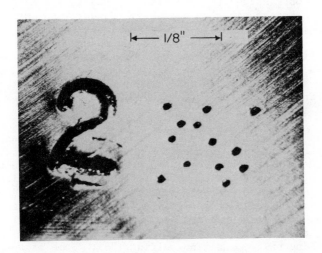

Figure 4. *A photograph of a pattern of laser drilled holes in steel representing the number 5383158068. Also shown is a ⅛" stamped digit for the purpose of size comparison.*

of the method for the marking of firearms.

Paper Identification

Paper is one of the more common evidential materials encountered in crimes such as forgery, conspiracy, threatening letters
and kidnapping; its examination is therefore frequently required
in the forensic laboratory (21). (Another aspect of document
examination, viz., ink analysis, is treated in another chapter of
this volume (22).) As with other forensic materials, two questions commonly arise:
1. Are two samples of paper identical?
2. What is the origin and history of the paper, especially,
   what is its date and place of manufacture?
The methods currently used in forensic science laboratories
(23,24) are based, in general, on those developed by the paper
industry for its own uses (25). The main objectives of the industrial tests are to monitor and detect faults in the manufacturing process and to improve product quality and uniformity; as the
origin of the tested paper is known, questions of identification
do not arise and some tests are therefore not very helpful in
differentiating papers. Industrial criteria which have been used
in the forensic situation are: surface and macrostructural
characteristics of the papers such as wire marks and watermarks;
thickness; weight per unit area; elemental analysis using spec-
trography or chromatography; relative amount of different fiber
types in the sample.
Recently, the possiblity of improving the elemental analysis
of paper by a quantitative determination of metals and trace metals using neutron activation analysis has been investigated (26,
27). This work showed the potential of NAA in attempting to
answer the two questions posed above. However, the method involves equipment available to very few laboratories.
An alternative, materials-oriented approach involves the
quantitative identification of the constituents of the paper.
This would include the determination of their compositions, structures and morphologies, as well as their amounts. A study of this
approach involving the inorganic components of paper has been
initiated in this laboratory.

X-ray Diffraction Analysis. The inorganic components of paper are the most suitable ones for quantitative X-ray diffraction
analysis. Most of these compounds are minerals and are present
as fillers, coatings and pigments (often whiteners) which are
added to improve the properties of the paper. Examples of compounds commonly added to paper are alumina, aluminum silicate,
barium sulfate, calcium carbonate, calcium sulfate, calcium sul-
foaluminate, iron oxide, magnesium silicate, silica, titanium
dioxide, zinc oxide, and zinc sulfide (28). Some of these, e.g.,
calcium carbonate and titanium dioxide, may be present in any of

several crystalline modifications.

In the paper industry, these inorganic components are determined primarily by microscopy, which is time-consuming and qualitative rather than quantitative. X-ray diffraction has been recognized as a possible method of analysis and a number of inorganic components are described as having been easily identified at concentrations down to 0.5 to 2% of the paper weight (29). While this method is not ideally suited to the quality control needs of the paper industry and has not been put into practice, it appears promising for the purpose of forensic identification. An investigation of the possible value of X-ray methods is now in progress using both untreated and ashed paper samples.

If untreated paper samples are examined, the X-ray diffraction method appears presently to be limited to the determination of those major inorganic components constituting more than about 0.5% of the paper. This is caused by the swamping of the less intense sharp line patterns from the inorganic crystals by the intense, diffuse reflections from the cellulose which constitutes the bulk of the paper material. Thus, sensitivity considerations limit conventional X-ray diffraction to papers having sufficient quantities of inorganic components and, even for these papers, precludes the examination of minor components present with lower concentration.

Two complementary approaches can therefore be utilized.

1. Untreated Paper. One approach is to use a modified X-ray diffractometer with an increased signal-to-noise ratio, (e.g., employing slow scanning or step scanning, high quality solid state electronics, and single or double-monochromated radiation) to examine untreated paper samples. Advantages of this method are that it is non-destructive and that the use of a diffractometer makes possible the examination of inch-size samples; data output from the diffractometer may be in digital as well as chart form and is thus directly usable for computer treatment, e.g., in connection with a file-search program (6). The simultaneous input of elemental composition data (see following section) into the computer treatment of the X-ray data substantially facilitates the powder pattern identification.

2. Ashed Papers A second approach starts with the ashing of the paper. This is also done as a standard characterization technique which determines ashed weight as a percentage of original weight. Ashing could lead to a change in the crystal structures of some of the inorganic components and possibly also to their decomposition. Although the method would not be ruled out if such changes were found to be reproducible, precautions should be taken to minimize these effects; ashing in oxygen at a lower temperature than usual has therefore been introduced. The ash is then studied in a powder camera; here the modifications recently proposed (7) for the examination of microsamples (small camera radius, vacuum, monochromated radiation) may be employed. Photometry yields relative intensities of the component reflec-

tions and hence information on the relative abundance of each
component is obtained.

3. Paper Separations. The separation of the inorganic components from the remainder of the paper by differential centrifu-
gation of a suspension of the paper dispersed in a fluid before
X-ray examination may also be useful. Insoluble components
could be obtained directly, while soluble components would have
to be extracted and isolated by evaporation. However, this dispersion process would probably lead to a modification of the components or their structures. The same is true for the possible
removal of the cellulose by hydrolysis in the presence of commercially available enzymes.

Scanning Electron Microscopy of Paper. The surface morphology of papers is a natural area of application of the scanning
electron microscope (SEM) because of its depth of focus. Surveys
have been made, and an excellent atlas of paper structures exists
(28).

Attachments for wavelength or energy dispersive analysis of
fluorescent X-rays on the SEM allow the elemental analysis of
selected particles; this can be done especially rapidly if a
high-resolution energy-dispersive semiconductor detector system
(30) is used. Particle identification is often possible (29).
This type of analysis would be helpful in the identification
stage of the quantitative X-ray diffraction analysis method described in the previous section; however, it appears that, by itself, X-ray microanalysis only of isolated particles will not
in general yield a quantitative, identifying analysis of the paper
because of sampling considerations related to the microscopically
inhomogeneous distribution of these particles.

An alternative approach is to do the SEM X-ray analysis over
a representative area of the paper to produce proper averaging
(31). However, the presence of a large Bremsstrahlung background
in the fluorescence spectrum due to the cellulose makes the
counting statistics for the inorganic component unfavorable,
especially for elements with low abundance in paper.

A representative elemental analysis, however, may be obtained
by subjecting ashed paper to SEM X-ray analysis; this method,
which is presently under study, avoids the disadvantages noted
above and will be reported upon shortly (32).

The Fluorescence Properties of Paper. Luminescence properties provide highly distinctive forensic characteristics, as
shown by Jones (8). In a current study in this Institute, the
fluorescence properties of several types of paper were determined
under excitation with Hg radiation, and this work will be reported in greater detail elsewhere (33). We note here that quantitative fluorescent emission spectrometry is not, per se, sufficient
for forensic paper identification; almost all papers that show
any significant fluorescence emit a similar spectrum due to a

small number of active organic compounds. While there are significant intensity differences in different papers, the samples do not show sufficient dispersion of the intensities for the method to be useful as a prime measurement for forensic identification. Lifetime studies have been made, but the very short lifetimes of <1 nsec can be measured accurately only with special equipment and are not expected to provide variations of the kind found, e.g. for the fluorescence of the active molecules in human hair (8). In summary, fluorescence does not appear to have promise as a prime forensic tool for paper identification at present.

Acknowledgment

The authors thank the LEAA for support under the National Criminal Justice Educational Consortium grant. They are pleased to acknowledge helpful discussions with A. Attard, R. L. Brunelle, G. Davies, B. L. Karger, C. Majeskey, J. Parker and S. G. Young.

Communication No. 3 from the Institute of Chemical Analysis, Applications and Forensic Science.

Literature Cited

1. Giessen, B.C. and Polk, D.E., to be published
2. Karger, B.L., Parker, J.M., Giessen, B.C. and Davies, G., this volume
3. Barrett, C. and Massalski, T.B., "Structure of Metals" Third Edition, McGraw-Hill Book Co., New York, 1966
4. Cahn, R.W., Ed., "Physical Metallurgy" Second Edition, American Elsevier Publishing Co., New York, 1970
5. Sharpe, R.S., Ed., "Research Techniques in Nondestructive Testing", Academic Press, New York, 1970
6. Program available from Joint Committee on Powder Diffraction Standards, Swarthmore, Pennsylvania
7. McCrone, W.C. and Delly, J.G., "The Particle Atlas" Vol. I, Second Edition, Ann Arbor Science Publishers, Ann Arbor, Michigan, 1973, pp.119-129
8. Jones, P.F., this volume
9. Hall, J.H. and Cassel, B., this volume
10. Billmeyer, F.W., Jr., "Textbook of Polymer Science" Second Edition, Interscience Publishers, New York, 1971
11. Kehl, G.L., "The Principles of Metallographic Practice," McGraw-Hill Book Co., New York, 1949, pp.409-448
12. Metal Progress, (1974), 106, mid-June, 201-209
13. Mathews, J.H., "Firearms Identification," University of Wisconsin Press, Madison, Wisconsin, 1962, p.77
14. Nielson, B., AFTE Newsletter, (1972), 20, 32
15. Cook. C.W., "The Restoration of Obliterated Stamped Markings on Metal," Colorado Bureau of Investigation, Denver, Colorado

16. Miller, K.E., AFTE Journal, (1972), 4, 38
17. Chisum, W.J., J. For. Sci. Soc., (1966), 6, 89
18. Young, S.G., "The Restoration of Obliterated Stamped Serial
    Numbers by Ultrasonically Induced Cavitation in Water,"
    NASA TM X-68257, 1973
19. McGonnagle, W.J., "Nondestructive Testing," McGraw-Hill
    Book Co., New York, 1961, p.346
20. Polk, D.E. and Giessen, B.C., J. For. Sci., in press
21. Grant, J., J. For. Sci. Soc., (1973), 13, 91
22. Brunelle, R.L. and Cantu, A., this volume
23. Browning, B.L., "Analysis of Paper," Marcel Dekker, New York,
    1969, pp. 319-326
24. Martin, E., in "Methods of Forensic Science" Vol. II, Inter-
    science, New York, 1963, pp.1-33
25. ASTM Standards Part 15: (A) Standards for Paper and Related
    Products; (B) Paper and Paperbond Characteristics, Nomencla-
    ture and Significance of Tests, Spec. Tech. Publ. 60-B,
    ASTM, 1916 Race Street, Philadelphia, 1963
26. Lukens, H.R., Schlesinger, H.L., Settle, D.M. and Guinn, V.P.,
    USAEC GA-10113, 1970
27. Brunelle, R.L., Washington, W.D., Hoffman, C.M. and Pro, M.J.,
    JAOAC, (1971), 54, 920
28. Parham, R.A. and Kaustinen, H.M., "Papermaking Materials-An
    Atlas of Electron Micrographs," The Institute of Paper Chemis-
    try, Appleton, Wiconsin, 1974
29. Parham, R.A., in "Scanning Electron Microscopy/1975," IIT
    Research Institute, Chicago, in press
30. Woldseth, R., "X-ray Energy Spectrometry," Kevex Corp.,
    Burlingame, California, 1973
31. Sabo, J., Judd, G. and Ferris, S., this volume
32. Barnard, J.A.W., Polk, D.E. and Giessen, B.C., in "Scanning
    Electron Microscopy/1975," IIT Research Institute, Chicago,
    in press
33. Barnard, J.A.W., Halpern, A.M. and Giessen, B.C., to be
    published

Examples of SEM Analyses in Forensic Evidence Applications

JOHN SABO, New York State Police Scientific Laboratory, Albany, N. Y. 12226
GARY JUDD, Materials Division, Rensselaer Polytechnic Institute, Troy, N. Y. 12181
STARK FERRISS, New York State Police Scientific Laboratory, Albany, N. Y. 12226

The scanning electron microscope (SEM) has been shown to be an effective instrument for the analysis of physical evidence materials. Both topographical, i.e. surface characterization, and compositional, i.e. elemental constitution, analyses have been successfully reported in several recent studies (1-8). The utilization of this instrumentation has widely increased. Several forensic laboratories in the United States and in other countries have SEM facilities, many of which are equipped for energy dispersive compositional analysis (EDA). This paper will describe selected actual recent applications of SEM-EDA techniques performed at the New York State Police Scientific Laboratory and Electron Microanalysis Laboratory at Rensselaer Polytechnic Institute.

Experimental Procedure

Physical evidence obtained from criminal investigation was introduced into the scanning electron microscope[1]. The topography of the samples was initially examined in the SEM to determine areas of interest and whether or not EDA would be required. For conductive samples and also for samples in which charging was minimal, SEM topographical and EDA[2] compositional

---

1. AMR 1000 Scanning Electron Microscope, AMR, Burlington, Mass.
2. Edax 700A Energy Dispersive Analyzer, EDAX, Prairie View, Ill.

analyses were performed simultaneously. For samples displaying
charging, the energy dispersive analysis was performed first.
These samples were then coated with a thin layer of gold[1] and
viewed in the SEM for topographical analysis. All images were
recorded using Polaroid P/N Type 55 film and the negatives were
used in those comparison procedures where the highest resolution
images were required.

For reporting convenience the results were catalogued in
terms of topographical analysis, compositional analysis, and
coupled analysis.

Results and Discussion

A. Topographical Analyses. The SEM allowed for the
analysis of several cases by virtue of topographical information
that could not have been acquired as readily, or with as
convincing an opinion, using other available techniques in the
crime laboratory. Examples are presented in the paragraphs
that follow.

In an auto theft case, the vehicle information number tab
(VIN) had been removed and a second one welded on to replace it.
The VIN tab was examined in the SEM and the weld, the remaining
fracture surfaces, the grinding marks and the swarf remnant from
the grinding were easily identified and photographed. These
features are shown in Figure 1. Metallographic procedures were
also used after the SEM analysis to confirm the fact that a
welding operation had been performed.

The firing pin impression on two cartridge casings, one
casing that had been taken from the scene of a homicide, and one
casing that had been fired from the suspect weapon at the
laboratory, are shown in Figure 2. The unusual aspect of this
case is that after the homicide, the weapon was thrown into a
river. Until it was retrieved by police divers, sufficient time
had elapsed to alter the compression of the firing pin. This
resulted in a variation in depth between the evidence firing pin
impression and the laboratory test firing pin impression. This
made comparison using optical techniques nearly impossible.
However, using the significantly larger depth of field of the
SEM, a positive comparison could be made employing persistent
features in the firing pin impression and the angular spacings
between them (Figure 3).

B. Composition Analysis. Comparison of elemental
composition present in physical evidence has been facilitated
with the advent of SEM-EDA instrumentation. A paint chip
comparison between a minute chip taken from the clothing of
a hit-and-run victim and the suspect's car is shown in Figure 4.
The analysis of safe insulation taken from the scene of a safe

1. Film Vac EMS-41 Mini Coater, Film-Vac Inc., Englewood, N.J.

Figure 1.   SEM photomicrographs of the filler metal and grinding swarf on a Vehicle Information Number (VIN) Tab (275×)

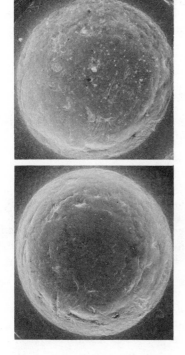

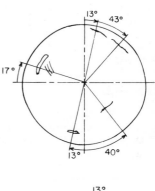

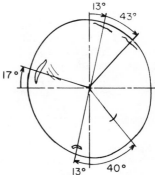

Figure 2.   Firing pin impressions from (a) evidence (b) control firings

Figure 3.   Schematic and angular representation of selected details observed in the firing pin impressions shown in Figure 2. (a) evidence (b) control.

breaking, the clothing of a suspect, and from a tool (crow bar) taken from the suspect car is shown in Figure 5. The spectra from paper used to wrap marijuana and from paper taken from a suspect's "workshop" is shown in Figure 6. In addition to the EDA of the paper other standard physical paper analyses were performed (fibrillation tests, density, thickness, basis weight, and infrared analysis) which also confirmed that the papers were from the same batch.

C. Coupled Analyses. In a malicious mischief case, an unknown substance wás found in the gas tank of a fleet of trucks. The topography revealed that the substance had a characteristic cube-like shape. The chemical spectrum indicated that elemental make up of the particle was sodium and chlorine (Figure 7). The same examination was performed on table salt and the results showed that the foreign substance was indeed common salt.

In a grand theft case a critical aspect of the case involved the matching of lacquered wood which was an integral part of the stolen merchandise with wood found at the suspect's work area. The composition comparison of the lacquer is shown in Figure 8. The topographical comparison of the wood (coniferous) is shown in Figure 9. The positive comparison obtained in both independent analyses was confirmed by IR techniques.

Conclusions

The SEM has proved to be an invaluable instrument in its application to forensic evidence materials. Several widely different successful applications of the SEM-EDA instrumentation to actual criminal cases have been presented.

Acknowledgment

The work in this paper was supported by a Federal grant (FORSEM II - NYSP C-55708) distributed by the New York State Office of Criminal Justice. The studies were conducted at the New York State Police Scientific Laboratory and in the Electron Microanalysis Laboratory in the NASA Interdisciplinary Materials Research Center at Rensselaer Polytechnic Institute.

Literature Cited

1. MacQueen, H. R., Judd, G., and Ferriss, S., Journal of Forensic Science,(1972), 17, 645-658.
2. Wilson, R. and Judd, G., Advances of X-ray Analysis, (1972), 17, 19-26.
3. Grove, C. A., Judd, G., and Horn, R., Journal of Forensic Science, (1972), 17, 659-667.

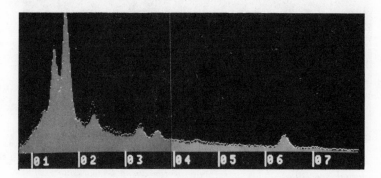

Figure 4. *EDA spectra comparison of paint chips. The solid spectrum is from the evidence, the dotted is from the control. The major peaks are Al, Si, S, Cl, K, and Fe.*

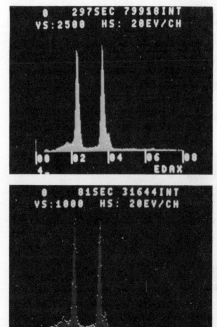

Figure 5. *EDA spectra comparison of safe insulation. The upper comparison is between contaminant particles on the clothing and the control specimen. The bottom comparison is between contaminants on a tool and the control specimen. The dotted spectrum in both cases is the control and the solid spectrum is the evidence. Major peaks are S and Ca.*

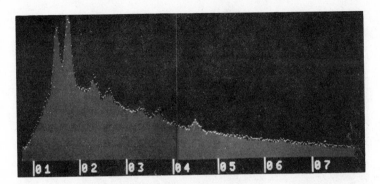

Figure 6. EDA spectra comparison of paper used to wrap marijuana (dotted spectrum) and paper found at the suspects workshop (solid spectrum). Major peaks are Al, Si, S, Cl, K, Ca, and Ti.

Figure 7. (a) Sodium chloride crystals, SEM photomicrographs (155×). (b) EDA analysis of crystals showing major Na and Cl peaks.

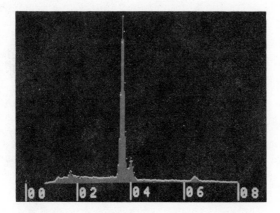

Figure 8. *EDA spectra comparison of lacquer found on evidence (dotted spectrum) with lacquer found in the suspect's possession (solid spectrum)*

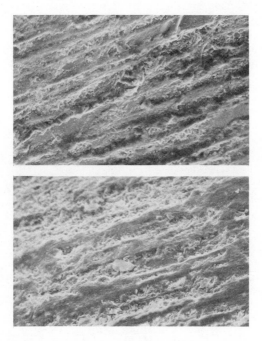

Figure 9. *SEM comparison of wood samples. (a) evidence (b) wood in suspect's possession.*

4. Grove, C. A., Judd, G., and Horn, R., to be published in
    the Journal of Forensic Science.
5. Wilson, R., Judd, G., and Ferriss, S., Journal of Forensic
    Science, (1974), 19, 363-371.
6. Williams, R. L., "An Evaluation of the SEM with X-ray
    Microanalysis Accessory for Forensic Work", 537-544,
    Fourth IITRI Symposium, 1971.
7. Siegesmund, R. A. and Hunter, G. M., "Scanning Electron
    Microscopy of Selected Crime Laboratory Specimens",
    577-584, Fourth IITRI Symposium, 1971.
8. Judd, G., Sabo, J., Hamilton, W. J., Jr., Ferriss, S., and
    Horn, R., to be published in the Journal of Forensic
    Science.

Recent Developments in Bullet Search Systems

AL JOHNSON

Ballistics Section, New York City Police Department, New York, N. Y.

Ever since the introduction of the comparison microscope into
the field of advanced firearms indentification in about 1925,
people engaged in this work have been processing ballistics evidence, bullets and shells, in exactly the same manner. This can
only be done by examining each piece of evidence separately and
individually, one piece at a time, and comparing this evidence,
again separately and individually, by the utilization of the
comparison microscope. Today, we in the field of firearms indentification still process evidence in exactly the same manner
using the same techniques and basically the same instrument
that was applied almost fifty years ago.

"Because this science is very new, it is still in the throes
of vigorous growth. Important contributations to methods and
technique are constantly being made by prominent practitioners
such as Luke S. May of Seattle, whose Magnascope may go a long
way towards eliminating the comparison eyepiece, and Captain C.A.
Petersen of Miami, Florida, whose bullet camera has a moving
film geared to the bullet stand in such a way that it takes a
single picture in the form of a long strip showing all sides of
the bullet at once. As time goes on, instruments and methods are
bound to be improved at the hands of such men" (1). This para-
graph was written over forty years ago. Time has certainly gone
by, a great deal to time, but instruments and methods are certainly
not much improved!

In the past fifty years there have been no appreciable changes
in the instruments or methods of examination employed in this
field. Improvements have been made on some of the equipment
utilized by firearms examiners. The most obvious change was made
by the updating the examiner's major piece of equipment, the
comparison microscope. From its early beginning as an instrument
consisting of a pair of compound microscopes mounted side by side
on a stand, connected by a special optical bridge fitted with a
monocular comparison eyepiece, has evolved a highly sophisticated
instrument utilizing special mechanical stages and evidence mount-
ing equipment, standard tungsten illumination or the application

of cold light sources (fiber optics). Binocular eyepieces and
turret-mounted objective lenses supply the technician with the
option of various magnifications. Other changes include the
utilization of electronic measuring devices in place of analytical
balances, and various methods of recovering test specimens have
been employed; but no real changes in the method of examining
and evaluating evidence specimens have resulted·

During this past year (1973), the New York City Police Department Ballistics Section processed 16,184 cases involving 16,850
individual firearms. In addition, personnel at this office
examined and processed evidence in 750 homicides by gunshot, 71
suicides by gunshot and 1772 felonious assaults during the commission of which firearms were used. This work involved thousands
and thousands of microscopic comparisons. This constituted a 20%
increase in workload over 1972. Evidence recovered in these
cases and tests from the firearms processed by our unit had to be
compared with an open evidence file numbering more than 25,000
specimens within a test specimen file dating back to the 1930's.
All of this comparison work was performed by six microscopists,
who, in addition to this work, made frequent court and Grand Jury
appearances to testify in these cases, performed special field
investigations, and were available for lecturing assignments.
Add to these figures the number of requests for examinations by
other police agencies across the nation and the processing of test
specimens sent in for comparison with evidence currently on file
in our office. The figures for the first half of 1974 show a
continuation in the increase in case load. The situation is the
same in firearms identification laboratories throughout the
country. Obviously, a better method must be developed for the
processing of ballistics evidence than the method currently being
used.

What is needed is some form of automated ballistics file
searching system. The computer could certainly be employed as the
storage facility for such a system. What has yet to be developed
is the apparatus that will take the information that appears on
the surface of a fired bullet, separate and identify the individual tool marks (striations) that appear within the lands and
grooves of a particular bullet, transform this information into a
language that will enable the computer to be   utilized; that
information may be classified, filed and stored, and then supplied
to the technician on demand. We need a system that will aid in
examining the enormous amount of evidence and test specimens that
have accumulated in our files, and to perform preliminary comparison work. It would be too much to expect the development of
equipment that would perform positive comparisons for us, that is
select the one test specimen that compares positively with the
evidence specimen. We are working to develop equipment that would
perform in the negative aspect of this work, to reject those test
specimens that do not closely compare with the evidence at hand,
and that would select for the examiner a certain percentage of

specimens having similar characteristics that would have to be
compared on the comparison microscope.

This automated system should also permit examiners to transmit
the information contained in the rifling markings on a bullet or
the impressions of the breech of a firearm that appear on the
head of a discharged shell to examiners in other localities, rapidly and accurately, without the worry of preserving the continuity
of the chain of evidence that becomes our primary concern when
transporting evidence and firearms.

Various proposals have been made along the lines of an automated bullet identification system based on the computer. One of
the most promising of the more recent developments was a proposal
made in 1964 for a computer-based ballistics identification system
utilizing a surface analyzer and a small computer. This unit
consisted of an electro-mechanical scanning component utilizing a
stylus, one ten-thousandth of an inch in diameter, that contacted
the surface of the bullet. The bullet revolved on its own axis
and the stylus recorded the surface irregularities on the entire
circumference. It was possible to scan a six land bullet in ten
to fifteen minutes, including set-up time. The markings picked up
by the stylus were magnified by the electronic unit and projected
as linear graphs or readouts. In concept, this operated in much
the same manner as the striagraph developed around 1951. The
striagraph was a mechanical surface analyzer connected to an optical device and prisms that directed light beams onto photo-sensi-
tive paper, producing what was then called a "shadow-graph".

Surface-analyzing (or contour-analyzing) methods are a completely different approach in the examination of firearms evidence.
They do not duplicate or replace the comparison microscope.
Instead, they give a truer representation of the surface markings
on an evidence bullet than the microscope does. The analyzer will
chart every surface characteristic, however minute, and project
a representation of that surface onto a linear, or perhaps
circular, graph. The circular graph appears as a cross-section of
the bullet.

When using the comparison microscope, the examiner observes
patterns of shadows created when a low-intensity, highly direction-
al light source is directed across an irregular, sloping, and at
times poorly reflective surface containing the minute tool marks
(or striae) and viewed through relatively low-powered optics,
usually less than 20X magnification.

Surface analyzing techniques aim at being able to reproduce
not only striae, but all surface phenomena, including ridges and
valleys whose slopes are too gradual to show up under the comparison microscope, and to be able to compare not patterns of light
and shade but actual three-dimensional surfaces.

Other data-gathering techniques have been attempted at one
time or another since then, such as the photographic recording of
ballistic evidence, followed by overlay comparison procedures, or

scanning methods employing photo-detectors. These instruments produced digitalized versions of the image from contrast information supplied by the photograph.

Replica-producing techniques have been employed using various casting materials to produce an accurate, detailed reproduction of the evidence specimen. If the replica were of a high quality, comparisons could be made using the replica in place of the actual specimen.

Techniques utilizing holographic recordings have been attempted. These holographic recordings are in the form of photographic records of certain light waves (beams of monochromatic coherent light separated into illuminating and reference beams) reflected from the evidence, and projecting three-dimensional images or replicas. It is possible to make direct measurements on holographic images of a specimen bullet.

The scanning electron microscope (SEM) has been used with some success. During the SEM process, an image is formed by scanning a fine beam of electrons over the sample surface and recording the secondary electron signal. Good results have been achieved using this method on firing-pin impressions on cartridge case heads. However, the application is limited when examining bullets. The entire surface of the bullet cannot be examined without remounting the bullet on its stage. The system is also very slow due to the necessity of creating a vacuum in the specimen chamber prior to the examination procedure, Recently, the Polytechnic Institute of New York City has extended a proposal to the NYCPD to attempt to develop this SEM system more fully.

The latest, and most current proposal for an automated bullet identification system has been made by the National Aeronautics and Space Administration. This proposal was offered to my department as a feasibility study into using an optical fourier transform technique for classifying and comparing the information that appears on the surface of bullets. In this system, a collimated coherent light beam and simple lens system are used to form a fourier transform from a photographic transparency of the specimen bullet. This study was approved by the City of New York and is underway at this time.

All of the systems previously outlined will produce acceptable results when dealing with test specimens. The 'stumbling block' is the inability of these systems to cope with the deformity of the evidence specimen. The evidence bullet, in most instances, will have suffered some deformity from the time it exited from a gun barrel until it finally comes to rest. It may be deformed in any number of ways, for example through contact with hard materials which may mutilate areas of the surface or perhaps it may suffer deformity through compression or expansion of the surface area of bullet which would make the bullet land and groove dimensions wider or narrower, compressing or expanding the pattern of striae that appear within them. As sometimes happens, evidence bullets may become so deformed as to make even optical comparison impossible. It is the bullet that does suffer from some degree of deformity, but still retains enough of its surface characteristics (striations) to make positive comparisons possible, that we should be primarily concerned with. The difficulty is in the comparison of areas of test bullets that most times will be in the form of true cylinders, with moderately, or, at times, severly deformed evidence bullets.

Everyone involved with these various proposals realizes the urgent need for a more modern system than that currently in use. The use of the comparison microscope, and the direct optical comparison in split-field observation of each and every separate piece of evidence is a tremendously time-consuming process. It also requires the physical presence of all evidence and test specimens. The circulation of evidence specimens for comparison with evidence or tests on file in other cities is also a very costly and time-consuming process, not to mention the problems that can arise in maintaining the continuity in the chain of possession of evidence. Presently, each comparison requires a manual   search through the ballistics evidence files. This requires time, personnel, and a great deal of space devoted to the storage of evidence files.

It is my hope that one of these proposals will produce successful results sometime in the not-to-distant future, and we in the field of firearms identification will reap the benefits.

Literature Cited

1. Hatcher, J.S., "Textbook of Firearms Investigation, Identification of Evidence", Small Arms Publishing Co., Planterville, S.C., 1935, p14.

10

Progress in Firearm Residue Detection

EDGARS RUDZITIS
Illinois Bureau of Identification, Joliet, Ill. 60432

MORRIS A. WAHLGREN
Argonne National Laboratory, Argonne, Ill. 60439

The concept of Neutron Activation Analysis (NAA) of barium and antimony present in primers as a means of firearm residue detection is now ten years old and it appears appropriate to point out the salient points of the development of the technique. The original work (1) and later investigation by high speed photography and autoradiography (2) conclude that Ba from primer and bullet are deposited on the back of the firing hand as discrete particulate matter. The obvious problem for the detection of firearms residue on skin is the efficiency of collection both from the standpoint of convenience and quantitation. After exploring a variety of methods, paraffin cast was suggested as the best (3) while another investigation suggests a complete hand rinse (4) as the most quantitative technique. Collodion lifts have been reported (5) and a comparison between collodion lifts and filter paper swabs concludes (2) that both techniques are about equally efficient. Sampling by moistened cotton swab has been also suggested (5,6) as a convenient technique.

While there has been considerable experimentation with sampling techniques, there have been few attempts to improve the analytical procedure. The original separation method (1) has undergone only minor changes (6-8).

There have been two attempts to optimize the radiochemical procedure and improve the accuracy by introducing Ba and Sb as tracers (9,10) and by re-exploration of Sb radiochemistry (10). A purely instrumental method has been reported (11) at the expense of excluding the determination of barium.

The bivariate-log-normal analysis of data collected by Guinn and co-workers appears to be the only comprehensive statistical treatment of firearm residue detection by NAA (11). Suspects' handswabs were interpreted in terms of accumulated firing test data and handblanks collected from individuals of different occupational backgrounds. A somewhat more empirical interpretation of the same data is also reported (12). Additional data from smaller scale collection of handblanks have been published recently (13,14).

The NAA method for the determination of firearm discharge residue has been generally accepted, but applications have been limited to just a few laboratories. In the process of establishing NAA capability for the State of Illinois crime laboratories we re-examined the standard techniques (10). In the course of our work it became clear that post-irradiation is the cause of several constraints which have discouraged a more widespread use of NAA. The inherent time limitation due to the 87 min. half-life of ^{139}Ba necessitates fast manipulations of radioactive solutions which in turn requires an experienced radiochemist. In addition to an ever present danger of overexposure and contamination, typically only a dozen samples can be irradiated per batch, which makes the method quite expensive. The developed statistical bivariate-normal analysis (11) is convenient for routine applications. With this in mind, a method was developed which: a) eliminates post-irradiation radiochemistry and thus maximizes time for analysis; b) accommodates over 130 samples per irradiation capsule (rabbit); c) does not require a collection of occupational handblanks; and d) utilizes a simplified statistical concept based on natural antimony and barium levels on hands for the interpretation of data. The detailed procedure will be published elsewhere (15).

Briefly, a cotton swab technique is employed; after swabbing, Sb and Ba are fixed on the cotton of the swab by moistening it with an aqueous solution of thioacetamide (TAA) and then with dilute sulfuric acid. The cotton of the swab is then stripped and soluble interferring materials, notably NaCl, are removed by leaching with 2N H_2SO_4 and methanol. The treated cotton is compacted into a small piece of ¼" polyethylene tubing and irradiated at a neutron flux of $5x10^{12}N/cm^2/sec$. Best results were obtained by double irradiation: 40 min. with immediate count for barium and 5 hrs with 2 day cooling for antimony. The photo peaks of ^{139}Ba and ^{122}Sb were determined utilizing a Ge-Li detector with a computerized pulseheight analysis system.

With the availability of some 50 sets of handblanks (environmental-natural levels of Ba and Sb on hands), firing tests and calibrations, we considered a different concept for the interpretation of the results. The evaluation consisted of two steps: 1) establishing that the Ba and Sb values of handblanks of the accumulated population sample followed a normal (Gaussian) distribution as statistically approximated by the t-Distribution, and 2) utilization of relatively simple statistical formalism for the calculation of the probability that the amount of Ba and Sb found on a given swab belongs to the established handblank population. (An appendix at the end of the paper may be useful to readers not normally utilizing statistics).

PRESENTATION OF DATA

Calibration

In order to test the reliability of the chemical and irradiation procedure, detection, and data reduction described in reference (15), each irradiation batch had several sets of chemical standards. In Table 1, "in" represents the amounts in nanograms, ng, of Sb and Ba standards deposited on swabs, the mean of 12 determinations each is in the "found" column and the standard deviation, "std. dev.", is given as a percentage of the "found" value. The average value in terms of CPM (counts per minute) per ng calculated from the three concentrations (5,10 and 20ng) yielded 98 CPM ± 27% for Ba and was used as a basis to calculate "found" values.

TABLE I

CALIBRATION DATA
(nanograms)

Sb			Ba		
in	found	std.dev.(%)[a]	in	found	Std.dev.(%)[a]
5	5	27	50	49	22
10	8	18	100	101	14
20	22	32	200	270	25

[a] std.dev. expressed in % of the "found" value.

Graphical extrapolation yielded linear plots through the origin within a corresponding one standard deviation range for each concentration. (Previous tracer experiments have shown a virtual 100% retention of ^{124}Sb and ^{133}Ba on cotton, (10)).

Considering the involved path from sampling through data reduction, the method appears to be sufficiently reliable to warrant a statistical analysis.

Handblank Values

Table 2 represents the mean values and standard deviations in percent of the mean value of the four separate hand swabs, right back, (RB), right palm, (RP), left back (LB), left palm (LP), collected from 30 persons. The hands of crime lab technicians and police officers were swabbed "as is" without any pretreatment. While there were occasional higher readings on palms, the found values were all represented by the means and standard deviations. In only one instance were high Ba values (less than 1:333 probability being "normal") encountered on all four surfaces. When question-

ed, the individual remembered having used a carbon-based solid
lubricant the night before, which was difficult to remove from
the hands and therefore quite likely was the origin of the high
Ba determination; nevertheless, these values were also included in
the calculation of the means. As can be seen from the table, the
mean values of the handblanks did not differ significantly in
terms of standard deviations and it was convenient to lump them
as the total hand averages of 0.4 and 7 ng of Sb and Ba respectively, with an approximated standard deviation of ± 100%, i.e.,
± 0.4 and ± 7 ng respectively. While our values are lower than
those encountered by previous workers, the relative relationships
are essentially unchanged and the data are self-consistent.

TABLE II

HANDBLANK VALUES
(nanograms)

	Antimony				Barium			
	RB	RP	LB	LP	RB	RP	LB	LP
mean (ng)	0.4	0.5	0.3	0.4	6	8	5	10
std.dev.(%)	81	116	87	110	116	87	128	93

t-Distribution of Sb and Ba Values of Handblanks

There is no a priori reason to doubt that the Central Limit
Theorem, and consequently the normal distribution concept, applies to trace element distribution, including Sb and Ba on hands
in a human population, because these concentrations are affected
by such random variables as location, diet, metabolism, and so on.
However, since enough data were at hand (some 120 samples per
element), it was of interest to test the normal distribution
experimentally by examination of the t-Distribution. The probability density plots of 0.2 and 3 ng increments for Sb and Ba,
respectively, had similar appearances. The actual distribution
test was carried out for Sb only because of better data due to
the more convenient half life of ^{122}Sb. After normalization, a
"one tail" test was carried out.
Normalization consisted of shifting the scale one standard
deviation to the left so that the origin and maximum (mean) were
superimposed. Also, the vertical scale was shifted in order to
superimpose the theoretical and experimental probability densities
at the origin. The theoretical values were calculated from the
expression $f(Z)=(2\pi)^{-\frac{1}{2}} \int e^{\frac{1}{2}Z^2}dz$ where $z=(x_i-\bar{x})/s=\bar{x}/s$ (for defini-

tions see Appendix) since x=o as a result of the shift. The
theoretical and experimental values are compared in Table 3 as
a function of weight increments of antimony. As can be seen, the
agreement is as good as can be expected for an average of 13
samples per weight increment. The experimental values show the
tail expected for a t-Distribution. Therefore, the application
of t-tests to determine the probability of a given antimony
amount of a hand swab being natural background is justified. By
analogy, the same conclusion may be made for barium levels.

TABLE 3

EXPERIMENTAL t-DISTRIBUTION VS.
NORMAL DISTRIBUTION FOR Sb HANDBLANKS

x (ng Sb)	Theoretical	Experimental
0.1	42	42
0.3	32	32
0.5	19	15
0.7	9	14
0.9	3	7
1.1	1	5
1.3	0	4
1.5		0
1.7		1

Comparison of Handblanks and Firing Tests.

Thirteen known one hand-one shot firings of both automatics
and revolvers of various calibers were selected. The means and
ranges of antimony and barium values for the firing hand are
presented in Table 4.

TABLE 4

FIRING TEST DATA[a]

	FIRING HAND BACK (FHB)		FIRING HAND PALM (FHP)	
	Sb	Ba	Sb	Ba
mean:	10.0	144	6.6	68
range:	2.5-27	27-660	0.4-26	0-223

[a] All units are ng.

If the means are taken as a characteristic test firing, it
is obvious from the range that standard deviation has little
meaning for comparison with handblanks - one of the difficulties
encountered in previous   investigations when statistics were
based on test firings (11, 12). An interesting note is that the
firing hand back, FHB, has roughly twice the amount of Sb and Ba
as the palm, FHP, which in turn shows about ten times the amounts
of a typical handblank. In order to quantatively compare the
means of the firing tests and those of handblanks, we will use
the so called Null Hypothesis in conjunction with the t-Test.
The Null Hypothesis divides the expected results into two classes,
the acceptance (true) class and the rejection (false) class, in
such a way that the probability of the rejection class when the
Null Hypothesis is true is equal to some small preassigned value
called the significance level. In this instance, the hypothesis
will be that the firing test data represent handblanks. (This
is not an unreasonable assumption, because whenever a handswab
is taken in a case it has to be assumed that the subject has a
normal handblank until proved otherwise). In other words,
because of potentially serious implications, every attempt should
be made to avoid the error of rejecting the Null Hypothesis (conclusion of abnormally large Sb and Ba amounts) when actually the
hypothesis is true (normal handblanks). Utilizing the t-Distribution tables of Bulmer's text (16) (see Appendix), the most
conservative limit was chosen, namely a 1:2000 probability of
rejecting the Null Hypothesis when actually true (i.e., rejecting the assumption of normal handblanks). The degree of freedom
was taken as 120 (actually 119) because, as Table 2 shows, the
combination of all four data for a handblank is justified.
Table 5 illustrates the t-test by comparing the mean Sb and Ba
values of firing tests and handblanks. The wide disagreement
between the calculated and theoretical is not surprising if one
considers that in a normal distribution there is a 1:333 probability that a value is outside three standard deviations, whereas in this example even firing hand palm values are approximately
10 standard deviations away in terms of mean and standard deviation of the handblanks. The improbability of matching the data
of handblanks and firing tests is made even more astronomical by
the multiplication rule of statistics because both elements, Sb
and Ba, have to be considered. A positive correlation between
back and palm values certainly should have an added statistical
significance as to the abnormally high antimony and barium
values of the firing tests.

CONCLUSIONS
    It should be reemphasized that the complete incompatibility of
firing test and handblank values are based strictly on the statistical   treatment of the two sets of data accumulated so far. A
more general applicability will hopefully emerge as more hand-

blanks are accumulated. It can be realistically argued, though,
that environmental handblanks of sharpshooters, employees of
fireworks factories, or scientist engaged in research of Sb-Ba
alloys may be significantly higher.

   While the above statistical reasoning may not yet be applied
within the present judicial system, it at least provides a back-
up for reaching decisions. After all, the correctness of the
judgment of an expert witness is also subject to the laws of
statistics.

APPENDIX

   Sample, $x_{1, 2, \ldots n}$ is a single measurement of a datum from a
population.   Mean and average, $\bar{x}$, can be used inter-
changeably. The standard deviation, s, is a useful parameter
for a reasonably large population; n, is, in effect, an absolute
average deviation from the mean. The degree of freedom is n-1
(i.e., with n=1 no statistics is possible). The probability
density is the percentage of samples within a given range.

   Normal and t-Distributions: the Normal Distribution is represented by the well-known bell-shaped curve, where the maximum is
represented by the mean, x, and the standard deviation, s, is the
width at the inflection point. The basis of its application to
many natural phenomena is the Central-Limit Theorem, which states
that the sum of a large number of independent variables will be
approximately normally distributed regardless of their individual
distributions. The theory of the normal distribution was developed from a large number of samples, which, of course, can not be
strictly applicable in most practical cases. This was recognized
early by an Irish chemist W.S. Gosset (17) who formed the basis of
of the "small sample theory" - the so called t-Distribution-in-
cluding-t-Test. The theory, in effect, states that the t-Distribution has the same shape as the normal distribution except that
the curve is flatter and has a longer tail. The t-Test, which is
an estimate of the probability by which a given sample falls into
an established t-Distribution, is represented by the formula
$t = (x_i - x/s)n^{\frac{1}{2}}$, where x_i is the value of a given sample and x, s,

and n are the parameters of a previously established t-Distribution. The calculated t-value is compared with tabulated theoretical values and the probability of fit (or misfit) is thus determined. The "One tail", in which only one half of the curve is
tested, is indicated when below-average values are not of interest
or when the sensitivity is limited (as in very low level antimony,
barium determinations).

   The "small sample statistics" is widely used and has obvious
applications in criminalistics. A number of suitable texts are
available (16,18).

TABLE 5

ILLUSTRATION OF THE t-TEST

	Sb	Ba
x_i (FHB)	10.0 ng	128 ng
x_i (FHP)	6.3 ng	68 ng
x	0.4 ng	7 ng
s	0.4 ng	7 ng
t (FHB)	190	143

Tabulated t-value (applies both to Sb and Ba) for m=120 and at a significance level of 0.0005 is 3.4; the corresponding t-value for a significance level 0.01 is 2.4. FHB=firing hand back, FHP=firing hand palm.

Literature Cited

1. Rush, R.R., Guinn, V.P. and Pinker, R.H., NUCL. SCI AND ENG., (1964), 22, 381.
2. Scott, H.D., Coleman, R.F., and Crips, F.H., UKAEA, AWRE REPORT 0-5/66.
3. Bryan, D.E. and Guinn, V.P., GULF G.A. REPORT GA-5556, (1964).
4. Krishnan, S.S., J. CAN. SOC. FOR. SCI., (1973), 6, 55.
5. Albu-Yaron, A. and Amiel, S., J. RADIOANAL. CHEM., (1972), 11, 123.
6. Hoffman, C.M., IDENT. NEWS, (1968), 18, 7.
7. Pro, M.J., INST. CRIM. POL. REV., (1970), 372, 270.
8. Hoffman, C.M., J.A.O.A.C., (1973) 56, 1388
9. McFarland, R.C. and McLain, M.E., J. FOR. SCI., (1973), 18, 226
10. Rudzitis, E., Kopina, M. and Wahlgren, M.A., J. FOR.SCI., (1973), 18, 93
11. Schlesinger, H.L., Lukens, H.R., Guinn, V.P., Hackleman, R.P., and Korts, R.F., GULF G.A. REPORT 9829, (1970).
12. Lukens, H.R., GULF G.A. REPORT GA-10245, (1970).
13. Midkiff, R.C., IDENT. NEWS, (1973), 23, 9.
14. Gerber, S.R., et. al., 6th INT. SYMP. ON FOR. SCI., Glasgow, Scotland, (1972).

15. Rudzitis, E., and Wahlgren, M.A., to be published in J.
     FOR. SCI., (1975)
16. Bulmer, M.G., "Principles of Statistics", M.I.T. Press,
     Cambridge, Mass., 1965.
17. "Student", BIOMETRIKA (1908), 6, 1.
18. Bauer, E.L., "A Statistical Manual for Chemists", Academic
     Press, N.Y., N.Y., 1974; Mood, A.M. and Graybill, F.A.,
     "Introduction to the Theory of Statistics", McGraw Hill,
     N.Y., N.Y., 1963.

A Comparison of Neutron Activation Analysis and Atomic Absorption Spectroscopy on Gunshot Residue

W. D. KINARD and D. R. LUNDY

Bureau of Alcohol, Tobacco, and Firearms, Forensic Branch,
Department of the Treasury, Washington, D. C. 20226

Several techniques have been utilized for the detection of firearms discharge residue on the hands of an individual who has recently handled or discharged a weapon. Testing for the presence of nitrates proved unreliable and was discarded. Colorimetric tests for barium and antimony from primer composition were found to lack sufficient sensitivity for general application.

Neutron activation analysis (NAA) with a rapid radiochemical separation has been the method generally used in recent years, but requires substantial investment, has high operating cost and limited availability. Modern flameless atomic absorption (AAS) instruments provide sensitivity approaching that of NAA and offer a viable alternative for the detection of firearms discharge residue.

Measurements made by both NAA and AAS on samples taken from actual firings will be compared in this paper, and the advantages and limitations of each methodology will be discussed.

Introduction

Faced with the widespread use of firearms in criminal activity, law enforcement officers have long sought an effective method to determine if an individual has recently handled or fired a weapon. A test of this type is obviously valuable in the investigation of alleged suicides, homicides, armed assaults and other violations involving the use of firearms.

The diphenylamine-sulfuric acid dermal nitrate test, introduced in the 1930's, was a method to detect the presence of nitrites and nitrates from gunpowder discharge residues. Restrictions on the use of this procedure were suggested in 1935 and again in 1940 by the Federal Bureau of Investigation (1,2). Although the limitations of this test for detecting the presence of gunpowder residues were known, its use continued, due mainly to the lack of a suitable alternative method.

In 1959, Harrison and Gilroy (3) demonstrated the detect-
ability of barium, antimony and lead in firearm discharge residue
using a specific "spot" test for each element. Inadequate
colorimetric sensitivity for barium and antimony (4) has
severely restricted the use of the method as a field tool.

The development of neutron activation analysis (NAA) as a
sensitive and specific method of trace elemental analysis led to
its application during the 1950's for the detection of firearm
discharge residue. Its ability to detect and identify very low
concentrations of barium and antimony, elements associated with
most primer compositions, was encouraging.

Neutron activation analysis is based upon the production of
radioisotopes by nuclear reactions resulting from neutron bombardment, followed by identification and measurement of the
different radioisotopes formed. Element activation can also be
carried out by bombardment with high-energy charged particles,
X-rays or gamma rays (5).

Since the development of high-flux research reactors,
neutrons, mostly in the thermal energy range, have been widely
used as bombarding particles. Most of the stable isotopes are
capable of capturing "thermal" neutrons, but with widely varying
capture probabilities. These probabilities are determined by
the elemental neutron capture cross-section. The capture of a
neutron produces an energetically "excited" radionuclide which
then may relinquish its excess energy by emission of gamma
radiation. The overall process is commonly known as an "n-gamma
reaction". Elemental identification and quantitation based on
n-gamma reactions are possible because the energy of gamma
radiation emitted by excited nuclei is characteristic of the
nuclear species and the intensity of radiation is proportional
to the number of such nuclei in the sample. Most (75% to 80%)
of the naturally occuring elements are capable of undergoing
n-gamma (n,v) reactions.

The utilization of NAA in forensic investigations began in
the late 1950's, when several potential applications were reported (6,7). Soon after, Ruch and co-workers (8) demonstrated the
suitability of the NAA method to the detection of elements
associated with firearm discharge residue. A decade of effort
by that group produced several volumes of useful information regarding the application aspects of this method(9,10). Between
1966 and 1973, the application of NAA to the detection of firearm discharge residues were examined by a number of other investigators (11,12,13), and encouraging results were obtained.

A major problem confronting forensic laboratories interested
in employing NAA is the scarcity of suitable reactor facilities.
If firearms discharge residue analysis is to be widely employed,
an alternate technique must be developed. Atomic absorption

spectroscopy (AAS) appeared to be a promising candidate. It has, for many elements, sensitivity comparable with that of NAA, and all work can be done in the forensic laboratory. The early AAS work, carried out on flame-type instruments encountered sensitivity limitations; however, such problems have decreased by the introduction of flameless units, with attendant improvements in instrumentation and optics. Although difficulties have been encountered with carbon rod techniques, the tantalum strip atomizer has afforded excellent results.

Atomic absorption spectroscopy (AAS) is based upon the absorption of light at specific and characteristic wavelengths by elements in their atomic states. Analysis for an element is accomplished by passing light of a selected wavelength through a "cloud" of free atoms and observing the amount of light absorbed. One method of obtaining the "cloud" uses a flame. The sample is dissolved and the solution is aspirated through a hot flame to atomize any metallic components. This method was first reported in gunshot residue determination by Krishnan et. al. in 1971 (14). Its sensitivity was sufficient for lead and copper but not for antimony, so antimony was determined by NAA. Green and Sauve (15) used flame atomic absorption to analyze for barium, copper, lead and antimony in gunshot residue, and found the sensitivity for barium and antimony to be quite low. Both studies showed that copper levels varied too much to be useful as an indicator of gunshot residue.

An alternative method for obtaining the sample in atomized form is termed "flameless" and uses an electrically heated carbon rod or tantalum strip. Despite several promising initial efforts (16,17,18) use of the carbon rod has encountered problems in the determination of barium (19). With the tantalum strip, on the other hand, good results have been obtained for both barium and antimony (20).

I. Experimental

A. Sample collection. A series of test firings was conducted under known conditions and hand swab samples were obtained immediately for examination by NAA or AAS. Firings were conducted indoors using a Smith and Wesson Model 15, .38 caliber revolver. This weapon was selected as being representative of weapons encountered in actual criminal cases. Ammunition used for all tests was Remington/Peters.

Each of ten laboratory staff members, engaged immediately beforehand in his normal work activities, fired a single shot, using only the right hand. Both hands of each shooter were then swabbed twice, "palm" and "back", using for each hand area two plastic-shaft cotton swabs moistened with four drops of nitric acid (5%). Immediately after use, each pair of swabs was sealed into an appropriately labelled 3" x 4" Zip-Lok plastic bag. A fifth pair of swabs (per shooter), moistened with the same amount of nitric acid but otherwiše in "new" condition, was similarly packaged for use as a "control" sample. The foregoing sample collection procedure is essentially that described a few years ago by Hoffman (21), but modified to eliminate the high "background" of barium contamination potentially associated with the use of either wooden swab sticks or glass containers (22).

B. Neutron activation analysis. Each pair of test swabs is removed from its container and inserted into a pre-numbered polyethylene envelope, tip-end first. The plastic shafts are cut off a few millimeters above the cotton and discarded. The plastic bag is heat-sealed and placed into a container for irradiation. Samples are irradiated, simultaneously with suitable standards, in the National Bureau of Standards reactor for 15 minutes at a thermal neutron flux of 5×10^{13} n cm^2 sec^{-1}. Following irradiation, the samples are allowed to decay for approx. 30 min. to reduce background radiation from ^{38}Cl. After transfer from their plastic bags to pre-labelled beakers, the samples are ready for the chemical separation of barium and antimony from interfering radionuclides. A number of separation procedures have been proposed (23,24); however, the one developed and used in our laboratory (25) has been designed to process efficiently large numbers of samples. This procedure involves acid leaching of the activated barium and antimony from the swab into 10ml of a nitric acid "carrier" solution containing 1000 ppm each of non-radioactive barium and antimony. By sequential addition of sulfuric acid (98%) and thioacetamide (sat'd. aqueous solution), barium and antimony are precipitated as barium sulfate and antimony trisulfide. The precipitate is filtered, washed and dried. A standard solution containing 5 μg each of barium and antimony (previously irradiated together with the test samples) is similarly processed. The samples and standards (which have essentially identical geometries) are counted on an 80cc Ge(Li) detector in conjunction with a 4096-channel pulse-height analyzer. Gamma ray emission at 0.166 Mev. for ^{139}Ba and 0.564 Mev. for ^{122}Sb is measured. The emission data are fed to a Nova 1200 computer containing a program (developed in this laboratory) for their reduction to weights of barium and antimony.

C. Flameless Atomic Absorption Spectroscopy. A Jarrell-Ash Model 810 Dual Monochromator Atomic Absorption Spectrophotometer was used for this work. The instrument was equipped with the Barnes Instrument's tantalum ribbon flameless atomizer and a two-pen recorder. This instrument allows a choice between the determination of two elements simultaneously and the analysis of one element with simultaneous monitoring of a selected line close to the analytical line. The latter choice permits improved accuracy of determination even in the presence of significant background. With high backgrounds occasionally being observed in the determination of antimony, the background correction feature was utilized. The sensitive 2176A$^{\circ}$ line for Sb was selected with background monitored at 2179A$^{\circ}$. For barium, the 5536A$^{\circ}$ line was used with the 5400A$^{\circ}$ Neon line as background monitor; however, in this spectral region, little background was encountered. For high levels of barium, the less sensitive 3071A$^{\circ}$ line was satisfactory with 3057A$^{\circ}$ used as reference.

The tips of the test swabs were cut off and placed in labeled plastic vials. One ml of 1M HNO_3 was added, the samples were agitated and allowed to leach for 15 min. A 10 μl aliquot was placed on the tantalum strip and the purge gas flow was started (Ar alone for Sb and Ar & H_2 for barium). The atomizer unit was automatically cycled through preset time for drying, ashing and atomization (at 2500°C). Absorbance values were recorded on the chart recorder and results were obtained by comparison with a standard curve prepared for each tantalum strip.

Operating parameters, e. g., temperatures, flow rates, etc. were previously optimized in our laboratory and reported (20).

Results and Discussion

Summarized in Tables I and II are levels of barium and antimony found by (1) Flameless Atomic Absorption and (2) Neutron Activation Analysis in swab samples taken from both hands of twenty (20) subjects after each had fired a single shot from a .38 caliber revolver.

It is evident that the recovered amounts of barium and antimony are much higher for the firing hand than for the non-firing hand. It is also evident (in the same tables) that the ranges of barium and antimony recovery values are broad. Similary broad ranges have been observed by others (8,11,20,24).

Table III shows that two quite different analytical techniques, Flameless Atomic Absorption Spectroscopy and Neutron Activation Analysis, yield equivalent frequencies of detection of firearms discharge residue.

Referring further to Table III, it is clear that not every firing of the test weapon led to a positive indication of gunshot residue. Any or all of several factors may account for the 15% incidence of "non-positives" in this study. One is variability in the spatial distribution of gunshot residue from one firing to another. A second involves non-reproducibility

Table I

Amounts of __Barium__ recovered by swabbing the firing (right) and
non-firing (left) hands of 20 subjects, firing a single shot
as measured by (1) Flameless Atomic Absorption (FAA) and (2)
Neutron Activation Analysis (NAA).

Sampling Area	A. FAA Method		B. NAA Method	
	Range (µg)*	Mean (µg)	Range (µg)	Mean (µg)
Control	0.01-0.15	0.05	0.01-0.03	0.01
Right Back (firing hand)	0.07-3.35	0.76	0.13-3.86	1.13
Right Palm (firing hand)	0.07-2.15	0.49	0.08-2.61	0.66
Left Back (non-firing) (hand)	0.01-0.38	0.11	0.01-0.11	0.05
Left Palm (non-firing) (hand)	0.01-0.30	0.12	0.01-0.36	0.11

---

*Micrograms

Table II

Amounts of <u>Antimony</u> recovered by swabbing the firing (right) and non-firing (left) hands of 20 subjects, firing a single shot as measured by (1) Flameless Atomic Absorption and (2) Neutron Activation Analysis.

Sampling Area	A. FAA Method		B. NAA Method	
	Range (μg)*	Mean (μg)	Range (μg)	Mean (μg)
Control	0.01-0.01	0.01	0.01-0.01	0.01
Right Back (firing hand)	0.06-1.20	0.43	0.04-1.13	0.50
Right Palm (firing hand)	0.01-0.44	0.19	0.01-0.83	0.26
Left Back (non-firing) (hand)	0.01-0.12	0.03	0.01-0.07	0.02
Left Palm (non-firing) (hand)	0.01-0.15	0.04	0.01-0.13	0.03

---

* Micrograms

Table III

Frequency of Firearms Discharge Residue Detection

Sampling Area	Detection Frequency (%)	
(firing hand)	FAA	NAA
Right Back	85.0	82.0
Right Palm	56.0	50.0
(non-firing hand)		
Left Back	0.0	0.0
Left Palm	0.0	0.0

of the residue collection technique. A third is the criterion
used to define a "positive" result.

A "positive" firearms discharge residue result, as referred
to here, is based upon occupational hand blank studies reported
by several investigators (20,26,27,28). The 0.30 and 0.20
microgram quantities for barium and antimony are conservative
statistical estimates from average levels of these elements
found in hand blank determinations.

It should be noted that in no instance does the non-shooting
hand have a level of Sb which our lab would consider positive.
It should be further emphasized that the critical element in
firearms discharge residue determination is Sb, because of its
uncommon environmental occurrence. However, this common characteristic has led some investigators to consider using Sb alone
for the determination of GSR (26). The two methods are in good
agreement with regard to incidence of positives as indicated by
Table III.

Since both methods yield comparable results, which method
should a laboratory use for firearms discharge residue detection?
Three factors must be kept in mind: cost, turn-around-time and
personnel requirements.

The cost per sample of NAA analysis is high, involving
additional personnel and reactor, and detector and processing
systems. Additionally, with NAA, reactor accessibility, sample
workup and analysis do not lend themselves to rapid throughput,
especially where a heavy case load is involved. Reactor accessibility is limited, posing still further delays.

For the majority of laboratories, flameless atomic absorption is the more practical technique. It requires only a modest
investment and enables all work to be done in-house, thus
eliminating complex scheduling. These factors reduce the cost
per sample and speed up the analysis. Additionally, FAAS lends
itself to a wide variety of other analyses of interest to the
forensic laboratory.

In short, NAA is an excellent analytical tool, but for
firearms discharge residue, FAAS is the more practical technique.

Although only a limited number of test firings and a single
weapon were employed in this study, a much broader effort is
currently in progress. The latter study will involve as
varibles weapon caliber, barrel length, brand of ammunition,
firing and sample collection conditions. Results of this will be
reported subsequently.

Acknowledgment

The authors wish to acknowledge the assistance in this
investigation of Mr. Charles R. Midkiff and other staff members
of the Forensic Branch, Bureau of Alcohol, Tobacco and Firearms,
U. S. Treasury Department.

Literature Cited

1. "The Dermal Nitrate Test" FBI Law Enforcement Bulletin (1935)
    4, 5
2. "Further Observations on the Diphenylamine Test for Gunpowder
    Residue" FBI Law Enforcement Bulletin (1940) 9, 10
3. Harrison, H. C. and Gilroy, F. J. Forensic Science (1959)
    4, 184
4. Price, G. Forensic Science Soc. J. (1965) 5, 199
5. Guinn, V. P. Methods of Forensic Science Vol. 3 pp 41-68
    Interscience Publishers, New York (1964)
6. Kerr, M. F. RCMP Gazette (1959) 21, 9
7. Forschufvud, S., Smith, H. and Wassen, A. Nature (1961)
    192 103
8. Ruch, R. R., Guinn, V. P. and R. H. Picker Nucl. Sci. Eng.
    (1964) 20, 381
9. Guinn, V. P., Hackleman, R. P., Lukens, H. R. and Schlesinger
    H. L. "Applications of Neutron Activation Analysis in
    Scientific Crime Investigations" U.S.A.E.C. Report GA-9882,
    National Science and Technology Information Service, U. S.
    Department of Commerce, Springfield, Va., (1970).
10. Lukens, H. R. and Schlesinger, H. L. "Applications of
    Neutron Activation Analysis in Scientific Crime Detection"
    U.S.A.E.C. Report GA-10276, NSTIS, Department of Commerce
    Springfield, Va., (1970)
11. Guinn, V. P. "The Determination of Traces of Barium and
    Antimony in Gunshot Residue by Activation Analysis" Gulf
    General Atomic Report GA 8171 San Diego, (1967)
12. Scott, H. D., Coleman, R. F. and Cripps, F. H. "Investiga-
    tion of Firearm Discharge Residues" Atomic Weapons Research
    Establishment Report AWRE 0-5/66, England, (1968)
13. Kubotz, M., Tokunaga, O. and Nakamura, Y. Kagaka Keisatsu
    Kenkyusho Hokoku (1968) 19, 261
14. Krishnan, S. S., Gillespie and Anderson, D. J. J. Forensic
    Sci. (1971) 16, 144
15. Green, A. L. and Sauve, J. P. Atomic Absorption Newsletter
    (1972) 11, 93
16. Renshaw, G. C., Pounds, C. A. and Pearson, E. F. Atomic
    Absorption Newsletter (1973) 12, 55
17. Renshaw, G. D. Atomic Absorption Newsletter (1973) 12, 158
18. Cone, R. D. "Detection of Barium, Antimony and Lead in
    Gunshot Residue by Atomic Absorption Spectrophotometry"
    presented at the Spring Meeting of the Southern Association
    of Forensic Sciences, (1973)
19. Renshaw, G. D. "The Estimation of Lead, Antimony, and Barium
    in Gunshot Residues by Flameless Atomic Absorption Spectro-
    photometry" C. R. E. Report 103, Home Office Central
    Research Establishment, Aldermaston, England, (1974)

20. Goleb, J. A. and Midkiff, C. R., Jr. Applied Spectroscopy (in press)
21. Hoffman, C. M. Identification News (1968) 18 , 7
22. Goleb, J. A. and Midkiff, C. R., Jr. Applied Spectroscopy (1974) 29 , 382
23. Rudzitis, E., Kopina, M. and Wahlgren, M. J. Forensic Sci. (1973) 18 , 93.
24. McFarland, R. C. and McLain, M. E. J. Forensic Sci. (1973) 18 , 226
25. Hoffman, C. M. J. Assoc. Offic. Anal. Chem. (1973) 56 , 1388
26. Albu-Yaron and Amiel, J. Radionanal. Chem. (1972) 11. 123
27. Midkiff, C. R., Jr. Identification News (1973) 23 , 5
28. Guinn, V. P. et. al., Special Report on Gunshot Residue measured by Neutron Activation Analysis, Gulf-General Atomic Report GA 9829, August 10, 1970

12

Recovery and Identification of Residues of Flammable Liquids from Suspected Arson Debris

CECIL E. YATES, JR.

Chemical Science Research Unit, F.B.I. Laboratory, Washington, D. C. 20535

Estimates of the range of annual fire costs in the U. S. go as high as $5 billion. These estimates include physical damage, loss of use, fire suppression expenses and other factors (1). It is also estimated that as high as 40% of all fire damage is caused by arsonists. Therefore, the forensic chemist's examination in the laboratory and the subsequent court testimony to the identification of the flammable accelerant is extremely important to the success of the prosecution. Forensic chemists routinely receive debris associated with fires of incendiary origin and ordinarily attempt to establish whether or not a trace of a flammable liquid is present in the debris. The purpose of the forensic chemist's examination is that of establishing the "intent" of the arsonist, a requirement under most statutes (2). "Intent" eliminates suspicions of fires of natural and accidental origins.

This paper presents a current summary of methods and instrumentation utilized in the recovery and analysis of traces of flammable accelerants in arson debris.

Instrumentation

A Perkin-Elmer model 900 gas chromatograph with a hydrogen flame ionization detector is used in this work. The recorder is a Perkin-Elmer model 56 adjusted to produce a chart at 1 centimeter per minute for ease of interpretation and evaluation. Variations in attenuation are frequently necessary from specimen to specimen.

The column which gives the most effective separation of the mixtures of accelerants generally encountered is a Support-Coated, Open Tubular (SCOT) column commercially available from Perkin-Elmer Corporation. The stainless steel column is 0.020 inch inner diameter coated with DC 550 on an inert support and consists of two fifty-foot sections joined with a zero dead volume union.

The carrier utilized in analyzing accelerants is helium, set to produce a flow rate of approximately 5 milliliters per minute.

Procedure

Samples are introduced to the instrument with syringes of various types and sizes through a capillary injection system with a manifold temperature of 200°C. The type of syringe used depends upon the sample to be analyzed: headspace sample injections are made with 2ml disposable plastic syringes, and liquid samples are injected with 1µl microsyringes, usually using 0.1µl if the liquid is fairly pure.

A programmed run has been found to be highly effective in analyzing accelerants and is preferred over isothermal runs. The program determined to be best for most accelerant samples is:

Initial temperature (I.T.) - 70°C
I.T. held for 3 minutes at 70°C
Temperature Increase - 6°C per minute
Maximum Temperature - 145°C
Total Maximum Time - 45 minutes

It is not infrequent to obtain in this manner a chart with as many as 150 or more distinct peaks.

Methods of Recovery

Numerous methods are available in the recovery of trace quantities of flammable accelerants from arson debris. Of these, four basic methods are generally preferred and have been found to be adequate in most cases encountered by forensic chemists. Each of these methods possesses good and bad features and consideration must be given to those features in contemplating the recovery of accelerants from any particular piece of evidence.

Liquid. The most preferable of the methods available is the use of a liquid such as that found in an unconsumed, unbroken molotov cocktail or in a gasoline can containing the remains of the flammable liquid used in the initiation of a fire. This type of sample is transferred to an airtight container and subsequently subjected to examination with the gas chromatograph.

Pure liquid is the best source of material for the identification of flammable liquids and in the comparison of questioned material with known standards. A very small quantity of material is needed (0.1µl) and very little time is utilized since instrument programs can be pre-set, thereby eliminating the necessity for repeating runs with adjustments to the instrument.

Should the presumably pure liquid contain an unsuspected contaminant, it could cause damage to the instrument. Materials frequently encountered as contaminants in whole liquid are plasticizers, adhesives, and other materials soluble in accelerant mixtures. These substances can contaminate the detector and reduce or destroy the efficiency of the column.

Steam Distillation. Many types of materials received can be prepared for analysis by means of steam distillation. These items frequently possess readily detectable odors indicating that an adequate quantity of material is available in the specimens for recovery by distillation. These items include fragments of wood, soil, drapery and carpeting. Items to be examined must necessarily be suitable for "partial destruction," since fingerprints are lost, shrinkage frequently occurs, and other changes related to immersion in hot water are seen.

Generally, when the odor of an accelerant is strong, the success of recovery is assured. In addition, this method is ideal in the recovery of quantities of accelerant from substances such as plastics, rubber goods, resinous materials and others which either absorb or dissolve in flammable accelerants. However, this procedure is limited in recovering accelerants from mixtures of foaming agents such as soaps. These items are frequently encountered by the forensic chemist in sabotage cases and incendiary devices.

Although limited to a temperature maximum of 100°C, a good representation of the more volatile fractions can be recovered by steam distillation with a refrigerated condenser. While very simple and even clumsy in some aspects, this method is extremely effective with many types of evidence.

Solvent Wash. Hardwood, porcelain, glass, metal and similar hard-surfaced items lend themselves to the solvent wash technique of recovery. Usually, no odors can be detected and indications are that a very small quantity of only the high-boiling fractions of an accelerant remain for recovery.

After placing the specimen in a suitable container for washing, the item is given several washings of a solvent such as hexane. Virtually all of the fractions of an accelerant present can be recovered from arson debris in this manner, and the quantity can be concentrated by a careful evaporation of the solvent to a small quantity. Unfortunately, many contaminants are recovered along with the accelerant traces. Virtually any cleaning of the solvent wash will necessarily eliminate valuable quantities of the accelerant. Among the contaminants encountered by this recovery method are oils, adhesives, resins and plasticizers. These are frequently unobserved and may cause damage to the instrument.

Headspace. Recovering vapors from the atmosphere above a specimen in a sealed, heated container is often a satisfactory method of analyzing specimens which cannot be treated by the

other methods described. Such specimens include items of
clothing that cannot be altered or destroyed, leather goods,
canvas, items of fabric, specimens contaminated with foaming
agents such as soap, and absorbent plastics and rubber. A group
of items, such as pieces of clothing or several documents, can be
handled at one time and without destroying fingerprints, writing
or other aspects of forensic interest.

Although this method is the only one applicable in many
instances, several problems present themselves. Valuable time is
spent in attempting to further vaporize remaining traces of
accelerants. Additionally, since low boiling fractions are
usually already lost and the high boiling fractions are difficult
to vaporize, problems are frequently encountered in evaluating
the chromatograms obtained. Great variations are found to exist
from sample to sample due to the absorbancy of the materials
being examined and the environment existing where the specimen
was collected and sealed.

Other Methods. Other methods of recovery of traces of
flammable liquids used infrequently are vacuum distillation and
soaking in water. Most items of arson evidence are physically
more susceptible to analysis by other methods than by vacuum
distillation. Soaking in water will sometimes allow residues
from small pieces of wood to surface; they can then be collected
and analyzed. These methods are usually highly inefficient and
little success is experienced with them.

Comparison

The charts produced by the gas chromatograph quickly
indicate the success or failure of the techniques selected in
attempting to recover traces of accelerant. When compared with
charts of known standard accelerant specimens, the results range
from simple comparisons to charts extremely difficult to match.

Frequently, pure liquid samples produce charts that are
essentially a perfect match for each peak, both by retention and
quantity. This allows a quick and certain identification.
However, as individual samples of accelerants are "weathered" by
exposure to fire and air the more volatile, low-boiling fractions
are consumed or lost through evaporation. The compositions of
some accelerant mixtures such as gasoline are rapidly altered.
With passage of time, "weathered" accelerant mixtures become
more difficult to compare with charts of standard mixtures.

In addition, the mixing of two or more accelerants may
produce a sample that is virtually impossible to identify. The
chromatogram produced from such a sample is difficult to
associate with a single original accelerant or with a known
mixture of accelerants prepared by the forensic chemist since
he is estimating the ratios of accelerant mixtures he suspects
to be present in the questioned sample.

Frequently, the residual portion of the accelerant present in arson debris may be so small in quantity that the comparison of the resulting chromatogram with a known standard is inconclusive.

Recovery Problems

Numerous problems are encountered in the recovery of accelerant materials from submitted specimens. These problems limit the potential identification of accelerants and are often precipitated by the lack of care taken by the investigator in collecting and handling the specimens.

Many specimens obtained by the investigator are simply not appropriate. Rather than submitting a piece of drapery or carpeting, which are highly absorbent, pieces of glass, ceramics or similar small, hard-surfaced, non-absorbent materials are taken. Limited success is experienced with the non-absorbent materials.

Futhermore, difficulty is encountered with many specimens received for examination either because of the absence of accelerant or because of the type of material itself. Examples are (a) heavily charred wood, where all flammable accelerant has been lost, (b) a rag that was soaked in the water used by the fire department to extinguish the blaze, dried out, and forwarded to the forensic chemist for examination and (c) a sample of soap recovered near the site or origin. Analysis of the soap for an accelerant would exclude the solvent wash recovery method as well as any other method that might cause interference due to foaming.

Improper Handling

If a sample is prepared correctly, no vapors of accelerants will be lost once it is placed in an adequate container and properly sealed (3). Many good specimens are handled subsequent to recovery in such a way that the flammable accelerants present are lost. Upon reaching the forensic chemist, he either has very little accelerant to recover and examine, or he has none. Porous containers and wrappers such as paper bags, bundles of newspapers and cardboard boxes are frequently substituted for suitable airtight containers. In these instances, volatile materials are invariably lost through evaporation.

The quantity of debris received is frequently a great obstacle to the successful recovery of an identifiable amount of flammable liquid. Small amounts of dry, charred ashes, dry fragments of paper, and small fragments of glass could at the very best only contain extremely small quantities of accelerants and could easily preclude the possibility of effecting an identification of the material.

Conclusion

Through the use of the various methods of recovery discussed, it is often possible for the forensic chemist to obtain a satisfactory sample of accelerant residue for examination purposes. Through utilization of gas chromatography, the identification of the accelerant can often be effected and differences and similarities between recovered and known standard specimens can be shown. However, success in the recovery and identification of accelerant residues is highly dependent upon the type and quantity of material received for examination and the care that has been taken in the preservation of the items to be examined.

Obvious areas of potential research present themselves to the forensic chemist.

1. A need for additional and better methods of recovery of traces of accelerants. These methods must be inexpensive, practical and simple in order for lesser-equipped forensic laboratories to utilize them to the maximum.

2. A need for simple, inexpensive methods of removing contaminants from recovered traces of accelerants in order to allow a specific identification to be made of the accelerant without damage to the gas chromatograph.

3. A need for methods of specifically identifying two or more accelerants when found together in a recovered specimen.

4. A need for techniques to individualize accelerants by commercial brands or sources after recovery from fire debris.

Literature Cited

1. "A Study of Fire Problems," NAC-NRC publication 949, W.D.C., 1961.
2. O'Hara, C. E., "Fundamentals of Criminal Investigation," Charles C. Thomas, Springfield, Ill., 1973, pp. 219 - 230.
3. Hurteau, W. K., "Arson Investigation and The Collecting of Evidence," Security World, March, 1974, p. 18.

13

Forensic Applications of Differential Scanning Calorimetry

JESSE H. HALL and BRUCE CASSEL

Perkin-Elmer Corp., Norwalk, Conn. 06856

Over the last decade Thermal Analysis has made significant contributions to a surprising number of fields (1). In the multi-faceted field of polymer science, it has provided a universal tool for ascertaining and predicting the effect of preparation and thermal history on the physical properties of polymers. One reason for this is that a great deal of information about the over-all structural state of a complex macromolecular system is revealed in the heat capacity. Thus, while conventional analytical techniques give information about the total amount of various molecular substances and molecular subgroups present in the sample, thermal analysis gives quite different information about the system. It indicates changes in the morphology or molecular order as a function of changes in temperature.

Specifically, the physical phenomena studied by differential scanning calorimetry (DSC) and its other thermal cousins are these: first, the heat capacity, the power required to heat the sample at the designated rate; second, first-order phase changes such as melting; third, second-order phase changes such as the glass transition; fourth, thermally initiated heats of reaction such as cross-linking and oxidative or reductive degradation; and, finally, evaporation or sublimation. Thermomechanical analysis (TMA) and thermogravimetric analysis (TGA) monitor dimensional and weight changes in the sample as a function of temperature. The temperatures of occurrence of transitions and reactions are characteristic of the materials; and, if the associated y-coordinate (heat capacity, weight or dimension) is measured quantitatively, this can be used as a basis for analytical determination.

Despite the unique capabilities of the method, relatively few studies have been reported which specifically deal with the use of thermal analysis in the forensic sciences. Perhaps the most useful study thus far has been that of W. M. S. Philp (2), of the Toronto Centre of Forensic Science, who analyzed by DSC all of the common synthetic fibers in use today. He had outlined a procedure for analysis and tabulated the temperatures at which characteristic thermal events occur in some 50 commercial synthetic fibers. Philp's conclusion was that, using quantitative DSC, it is possible to identify from milligram quantities of fiber the class of polymer (nylon, polyester, triacetates, polyolefins, polyacrylonitriles, and modacrylics). In addition, he noted that certain differentiation can be made within each class, for example, in distinguishing the various types of nylons and orlons. Rather than duplicate Philp's work, it is the purpose of this present study to show how this approach can be extended through the use of second-generation instrumentation.

What are the particular demands or constraints inherent in forensic analysis? There are two basic functions of analytical instruments in forensic science. The first is to use them to obtain information about a material such as its chemical composition, for example, for the purpose of settling patent rights or for finding the origin of a material. The second function, which is the more applicable to thermal analysis, is as a comparitive technique to determine if two materials are from the same origin. In this case, the most common problem is to establish that an artifact linked to the crime--usually some item overlooked by the criminal--is of identical origin to a similar sample in the possession of the suspect. The samples collected in the field are frequently damaged, contaminated and diminutive, thus posing a considerable challenge for the forensic analyst. The particular virtues of thermal analysis of such samples are these: first, a great deal of information can be gleaned about a sample without destroying the sample for further analysis; second, the information is complementary rather than duplicative of spectroscopic and chromatographic evidence; third, nonpolymeric materials (e.g., dyes, soil, dried blood) are noninterfering; fourth, the method is rapid and does not require sample preparation.

While as a general means of material study the method is universal in its capabilities, it is primarily in the analysis of polymers that it is useful for forensic purposes. The area where it is perhaps most needed and which also demonstrates the methodological approach best is that of fiber analysis.

Experimental

The thermal analysis laboratory used in this study, as seen in figures 1-3, included the Perkin-Elmer Model DSC-2 scanning calorimeter, the Model TGS-1 thermogravimetric analyzer, the Model TMS-1 thermomechanical analyzer, and the Model AD-2 autobalance. These instruments, besides being among the most sensitive and quantitative on the market, have certain features which make them especially useful for forensic analysis. For instance, the scanning calorimeter was used with a freon-based cooler (The Intracooler II) which afforded the following capabilities: (1) Continuous operation from -70°C to 700°C without the need for hardware changes at high and low temperatures. (2) Reproducible program cooling rates of up to 80°C/min. over the transition range of the fibers. (3) Frost-free shock cooling of 100°C/sec. (over the same range) within the calorimeter dry box by placement of sample on the isothermal calorimeter block. (4) High resolution and fast response times for sharp peaks and short ($\langle$30 sec.) equilibration times. (5) TMA or TGA module programmable from the DSC as an accessory. The method of operation and the performance of these instruments have been amply described in the literature (3-5).

The materials used included dyed and undyed yarn and fiber samples obtained from the manufacturers and fabric and other polymeric materials from the marketplace. The samples were encapsulated without preparation and the experimental conditions are noted on each figure. Unless otherwise noted, the DSC samples were run in an atmosphere of dry nitrogen.

Procedure

A procedure has been outlined in figure 4 for the handling of small samples to obtain a maximum of information. The weighing of the sample before and after heating to 120°C gives a quantitative measure of the adsorbed water per weight of sample, an intrinsic polymer characteristic.

The use of thermomechanical analysis as the first step in the thermal analysis of the virgin sample has certain advantages. First, the processing of polymers with glass transitions above room temperature frequently have strains which result from processing history (drawing, extruding, etc.) which are relieved in a characteristic way at the glass transition. Second, the virgin glass transition temperature can usually be determined even in very small samples when it would be virtually impossible

Figure 1. The Perkin-Elmer laboratory for thermal analysis. From left to right: the DSC-1B differential scanning calorimeter with evolved gas analyzer, the TGS-1 thermobalance (top to bottom), the recorder chart control, model UU-1 temperature programmer control, and model TMS-1 control unit. At right is the model TMS-1 thermomechanical analyzer.

Figure 2. Model DSC-2 high performance calorimeter

Figure 3. Model AD-2 precision electronic microbalance (capacity 5g; sensitivity 0.1μg)

to see by DSC.

The next step in the analysis involves the use of DSC to observe the virgin melting profile. If a melt endotherm is not encountered, then the scan can be continued up to roughly 340°C to check for crosslinking exotherms.

Once the melt is completed, the sample is shock-cooled by removal from the calorimeter vessel and placement on the iso-thermal calorimeter block. This cools the sample sufficiently rapidly that most materials will be "trapped" in their metastable supercooled liquid state. A rescan of the sample over the same temperature span will show the cold recrystallization of the material followed by the melt. For maximum time efficiency and sensitivity, a fast scanning rate is recommended.

For additional confirmational information, the sample can be program-cooled from above the melt to below the recrystal-lization, then reheated at a slower rate. This melting profile is most likely to compare closely with other literature data on the material--both temperature and enthalpy data--since all proces-sing history has been erased and thermodynamic effects are predominant. The faster scanning and shock cooling of the earlier experiments tend to exaggerate kinetic differences between the materials in addition to the thermodynamic differ-ences.

Finally, the last stage of the thermal analysis involves observation of the calorimetry (DSC) or weight change (TGA) associated with the degradation of the sample as it is programmed to elevated temperatures. This can be performed in oxygen or nitrogen to obtain oxidative or reductive degradation, respectively. The advantage of using DSC is that exothermic and endothermic processes can be distinguished and processes involving no weight change can be observed. The advantage of TGS is that the inter-pretation is simpler and the results are more quantitative and reproducible.

This final degradative step in the thermal analysis can, of course, be replaced by some other analytical technique. Of course, water and possibly other volatile additives may have been lost. A novel approach which has been suggested involves trapping temperature fractions (e.g., 100-300°, 300-400°, etc.) from the heated effluent of a TGS-1 (or possibly of a modified DSC-2), on a substrate such as a charcoal or silica gel filter, removal by heat or solvent and running gas chromatography on the degradation products.

Results

The results are primarily an indication of the capabilities of the method using the specified instrumentation, rather than a source of reference data. In demonstrating the forensic use of TMA, the samples were not removed at 120°C and run on the DSC-2 as suggested in figure 4, but rather were scanned up through their melting points and fresh samples prepared for DSC.

Figure 4.   Sample size-limited test schedule

1. Weigh sample

2. TMA (0-120°C)   Obtain glass transition, stress relief and cold recrystallization temperatures

3. Reweigh   Obtain weight of dehydration

4. DSC (100 to 300°C,N_2) Obtain processing points, melting profile and/or crosslinking exotherm

5. Shock-cool   Then DSC (-20 to 300°C) Obtain glass transition, cold recrystallization and remelt profile

6. Program-cool   Obtain degree of supercooling, fusion profile

7. Slow heat   Obtain conditioned melting profile

8. TGS or DSC   Obtain degradation profile
    (200-700°C) or
    analyze by other means

Thermal Analysis of Fibers. One of the most common
forensic problems involving violent crimes is that of establishing that a fiber of clothing or hair left at the scene of the
crime belongs to the assailant or that found in the possession of
the suspect belongs to the victim. Since such samples may weigh
from a few micrograms to perhaps a hundred micrograms, there
are few techniques beyond microscopic analysis sufficiently
sensitive to give substantial information. Using TMA is possible
and is the most sensitive thermal analytical technique whenever
there is about 1/4" of fiber or more. The fiber is mounted with
one end on the recorder output. The weight of the probe is
counterbalanced by a completely submerged float. The amount
of tension (negative weight) applied to the fiber is independent of
probe displacement and is adjusted by adding or removing weights
from the probe-float system.

Cellulose triacetate. Figure 5 shows a typical TMA thermo-
gram, that of a single fiber of untextured cellulose triacetate
run on two different output sensitivities. From the high sensitivity curve, we see normal thermal expansion of the fiber at low
temperatures and contraction as water is lost above 100°C. At
roughly 180°the sudden expansion marks the onset of the glass
transition (6). On the lower curve, run at 1/25 the sensitivity
of the upper curve, the expansion and contraction are not apparent, but it can be seen that after a 5% expansion at the glass
transition there is another period of contraction before the final
melting or decomposition. This behavior is diagnostic of triacetate,and the transition temperatures differ between commercial types. The scanning calorimetry and thermogravimetry of
cellulose triacetate fibers have been described elsewhere and
were not pursued in this study (2).

Polyester. Various types of polyester fibers have been
run on thermal analysis instrumentation. In figure 6 the bottom
curve demonstrates the typical performance of an untextured
polyester such as that found in tightly woven fabric such as is
used in shirts. The fiber begins to contract shortly above room
temperature and does so at an increasing rate starting at about
the glass transition temperature. The derivative of this long
contraction often displays minima at around 140°and 220°C which
reflect processing conditions. The melt, of course, is a massive extension.

The upper curve of the textured polyester is typical for
crimped fibers of doubleknit fabric and sweaters. Here, the

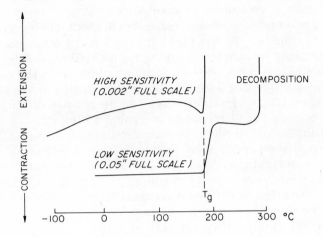

Figure 5.   *Flat cellulose triacetate extension analysis of single fiber*

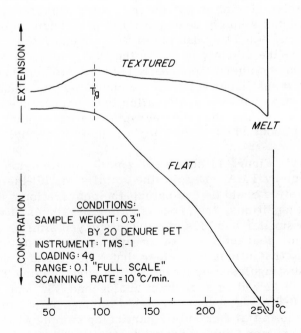

Figure 6.   *Extension analysis of polyester fibers*

crimp relaxation overcomes the normal thermal contraction.

In figure 7 we see on an insensitive range a sample of partially oriented polyester which has been shock-cooled and cold-drawn in spinning. At the glass transition the molecules sieze the opportunity to reorient causing a massive extension at the recrystallization point which continues right up to the melt. These three polyester samples show that while fiber samples may be chemically identical, they can be readily distinguished by TMA because of differences in process history.

Similarly, differences in manufacturing substantially affect the DSC melting profile (7). In figure 8 we see thermal curves of nearly identical polyester yarns. Sample one and two are identical in composition--both contain a dyability additive-- but were annealed at different temperatures as can readily be seen by the position of the annealing "scars" on the thermograms. The effect of the dyability additive apparently is that it lowers and broadens the melting peak destroying its characteristic first-run, double-peak behavior.

In figure 9 we see an 80 microgram sample of Burlington polyester fabric (textured fiber cut from a pick on a pair of double-knit slacks). Even in this small sample the processing temperature is apparent, and the double peak on the initial run indicates the material as polyester. The rerun after program cooling reveals a single peak and a flat pretransition baseline.

In figure 10 a 74 ug sample of flat polyester fiber obtained from a silk-like fabric was run in the DSC. In the first run appeared an endotherm apparently belonging to some sort of low molecular weight additive, then the characteristic double peak melt, this time with a much smaller low temperature peak. After shock cooling, the cold recrystallization exotherm was obtained at about 175°C, much higher than for the nylons.

Nylons. Figure 11 shows two small, single nylon fiber samples run by TMA. Despite the small size, all the major characteristics could be evaluated: the dehydration contraction, the glass transitions, the processing temperatures and the melt. These two similar samples of nylon displayed similar qualitative behavior characteristic of the nylons, and from the temperatures of the transitions it is clear that Nylon 6 and Nylon 6-6 can be easily distinguished by their melting curves using TMA.

Figures 12 and 14 show first and second DSC runs of Nylon 6 and Nylon 6-6 using seventy to eighty microgram quantities of fiber. In the initial run on this particular sample of Nylon 6, no thermal phenomena are discernable up to the melt, which is a

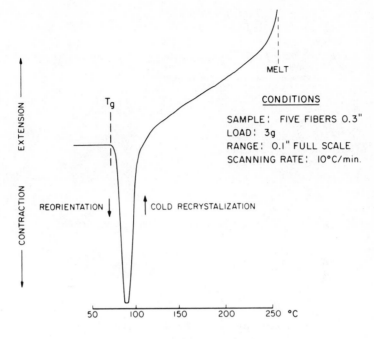

Figure 7.   Partially oriented polyester

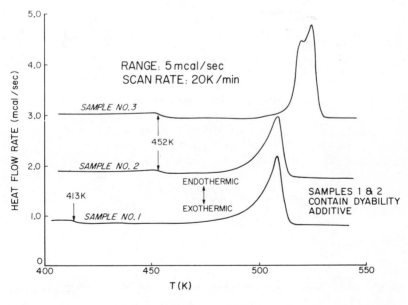

Figure 8.   Polyester finished paper showing differences between manufacturing lots

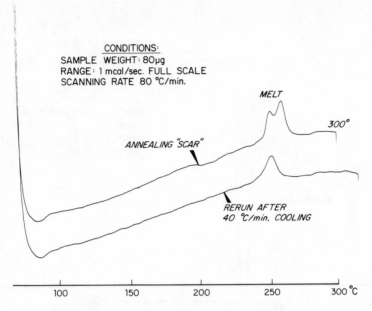

Figure 9.   Burlington double-knit polyester fabric

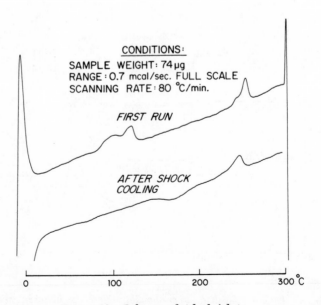

Figure 10.   Polyester finished fabric

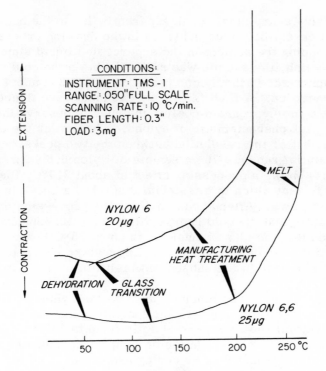

Figure 11.   Extension analysis of nylon single fibers

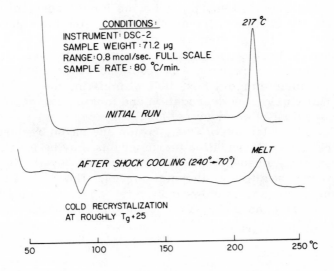

Figure 12.   Nylon 6 yarn

particularly sharp single peak apparently due to the highly
oriented crystalline state achieved in the drawing process (8).
After trapping the sample in the supercooled liquid state by
shock-cooling, the sample was rerun to obtain the cold recrystallization which in the nylons peaks out about 25° above the
glass transition. A final DSC scan was made (see figure 13)
after 20°C/min. program-cooling in order to observe the double
melting peak characteristic of nylons. The slower the cooling
rate, the better the resolution between the two peaks.

An initial run on a 76 ug sample of Nylon 6, 6 yarn (seen
in fig. 14) shows a processing effect at about 210°C, the same
temperature at which this material displayed a break in the TMA
extension curve. After shock cooling, the processing mark has
been erased; and the cold recrystallization peak appears--an
indication that the glass transition is about 25°C lower. Figure
15 shows the effect of program-cooling and the characteristic
nylon double peak in the subsequent melt (9).

Other fibers. The other major class of synthetic fibers,
the polyacrylonitriles (orlon, acrilon, etc.) like the cellulosics
(rayon, cotton) show no thermal activity up to 300°C. Above
these temperatures degradation of sample accompanies any
characteristic transitions or curing exotherms. To minimize
this effect, the samples are run in an inert environment such
as N_2, as seen in figure 16. Under these conditions reproducible
characteristic endotherms were obtained for identifying wool,
cotton and rayon. In roughly the same temperature region,
Philp has reported sharp exotherms for the acrylonitriles
which distinguish them from these and for the most part from
one another. His studies were run in air because of the incon-
veniences of hermetically encapsulating in nitrogen. Using the
DSC-2, the samples can be encapsulated within the nitrogen
purged calorimeter dry box, thus eliminating the uncertainties
of partially oxidizing degradation and making the identification
of the acrylonitriles more reliable.

The identification of wool, cotton and rayon by observing
their reductive degradation thermograms may be less reliable
because the presence of flame retardants, dyestuffs, etc.,
may somewhat alter the thermal curves. However, as a comparison technique, samples from a truly identical origin, encapsulated or run under the same conditions should give similar
results (10).

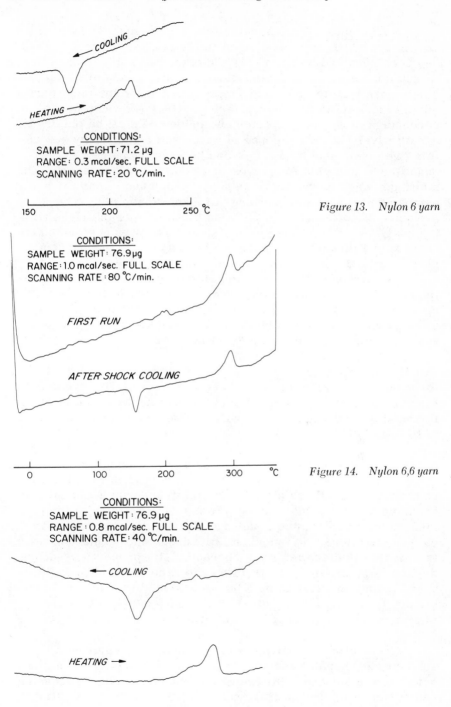

CONDITIONS:
SAMPLE WEIGHT: 71.2 µg
RANGE: 0.3 mcal/sec. FULL SCALE
SCANNING RATE: 20 °C/min.

150   200   250 °C

Figure 13.   Nylon 6 yarn

CONDITIONS:
SAMPLE WEIGHT: 76.9 µg
RANGE: 1.0 mcal/sec. FULL SCALE
SCANNING RATE: 80 °C/min.

FIRST RUN

AFTER SHOCK COOLING

0   100   200   300   °C

Figure 14.   Nylon 6,6 yarn

CONDITIONS:
SAMPLE WEIGHT: 76.9 µg
RANGE: 0.8 mcal/sec. FULL SCALE
SCANNING RATE: 40 °C/min.

← COOLING

HEATING →

0   100   200   300 °C

Figure 15.   Nylon 6,6 yarn

Fiber blends. The thermal analysis of unknown fabrics to obtain an identification and quantitative analysis of components has been reported by Gray (11) and others (2). Since the yarn or thread consists of a bundle of discrete fibers, each of which is a single polymer, the physical properties are for the most part additive and mutually noninterfering. Gray showed how the percentage of nylon, polyester and orlon could all be obtained quantitatively in the presence of rayon and a secondary acetate in a five component blend. As can be seen in figure 17, the quantitative analysis for polyester is obtained by measuring the melting energy in the previously weighed unknown sample and comparing to the melting energy of a known sample. The presence of cotton and rayon in the blend did not interfere with the analysis. While this particular analysis was performed on several milligrams of sample, an accuracy of a few percent should be possible at the hundred microgram level.

A second analytical technique for polymer blends involves the use of thermogravimetric analysis as seen in figure 18. Here again the percent polyester is determined in the presence of cellulosics. Such an analysis should have about the same accuracy for submicrogram samples as DSC (12).

Other Polymeric Materials. While the primary thrust of forensic research in thermal analysis has been with synthetic fibers, there are several other promising areas which require further investigation. These will now be evaluated on the basis of the available evidence.

Paints, lacquers, and other coatings. Thermal analysis is not usually necessary for the comparative analysis of pigmented coatings such as those obtained from hit-and-run accidents and breaking and entering because of the specific nature of the pigment blend which can be readily analyzed. However, should a case arise where this evidence is inadequate, thermal analysis is capable of determining the characteristic properties--dehydration, T_g, melting, contraction and decomposition--of the various coating substrates (13). Also, possibly a unique thermal history (fire, explosion, etc.) would leave a characteristic imprint on the heat capacity which could be of forensic use.

Wire coatings. Wiring from detonation devices could be subjected to thermal analysis to determine, by comparison, the origin of the sample. Differences in manufacturing processing can result in lot-to-lot differences in the degree of crosslinking,

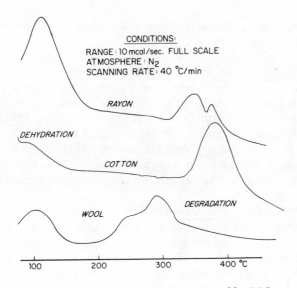

CONDITIONS:
RANGE: 10 mcal/sec. FULL SCALE
ATMOSPHERE: N₂
SCANNING RATE: 40 °C/min

RAYON

DEHYDRATION

COTTON

WOOL

DEGRADATION

100   200   300   400 °C

Figure 16.   Identification of fabric material by DSC

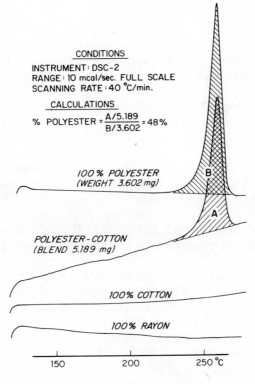

CONDITIONS

INSTRUMENT: DSC-2
RANGE: 10 mcal/sec. FULL SCALE
SCANNING RATE: 40 °C/min.

CALCULATIONS

$$\% \text{ POLYESTER} = \frac{A/5.189}{B/3.602} = 48\%$$

100 % POLYESTER
(WEIGHT 3.602 mg)

B

A

POLYESTER-COTTON
(BLEND 5.189 mg)

100% COTTON

100% RAYON

150   200   250 °C

Figure 17.   Blend analysis

T_g, residual cure, etc., which can be identified by thermal
analysis (14). See figure 19.

Tire rubber. Substantial differences can be seen in the
thermal curves of automotive tire rubbers from formulation to
formulation [and, one suspects, from lot to lot, since DSC is used
as a quality control monitor in tire manufacturing (15)]. If it can
be demonstrated that sufficient rubber can be obtained from a
skid mark to make such a determination, this could become a
valuable tool in hit-and-run forensic work. Because of its
sensitivity, perhaps TMA would hold particular promise.

Non-Polymeric Materials. Waxes, soaps, greases,
asphalts, oils. Complex mixtures of hydrocarbons of different
molecular weight when treated to a common thermal history
(such as slow program-cooling from above the melt) give
complex but highly repeatable characteristic DSC melting profiles (16, 17). In the absence of any other forensic evidence,
these thermal profiles should be sufficiently specific and repeatable to be definitive evidence.

Hair, Nail, Skin. Differences can be seen by thermal analysis between grossly different samples (e.g., bleached, unbleached
hair (18)), but this does not appear at present to be a promising
area for thermal analysis.

Drugs. The melting profile for a mixture of materials,
such as organic drugs, is a characteristic property of the mixture. In fact, in a mixture which is dominated by one component,
such as a semi-pure drug, the purity may be obtained directly
from the melting curve (19). This purity, which can usually be
determined to within a few hundredths percent, could be considered a characteristic property of the mixture. This technique
of drug identification would be most useful in the limit of very
pure drugs where a direct analysis of the impurities does not
provide sufficient comparitive evidence of the origin of the drug.

Packaging Materials. As in the case of fibers, thermal
analysis can easily distinguish between most polymeric films on
the basis of the glass transition and the thermal history dependence of the melt and recrystallization (20, 21). From the analysis of thin films--as, for example, used in plastic bags recovered with drugs--it should be possible to identify by comparison
the bag manufacturer and possibly the manufacturing lot.

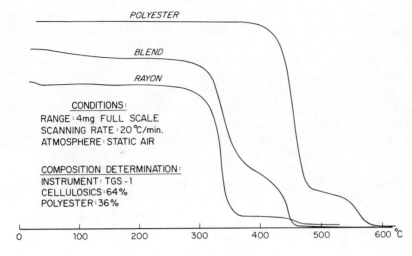

Figure 18.   Fiber analysis by TGA

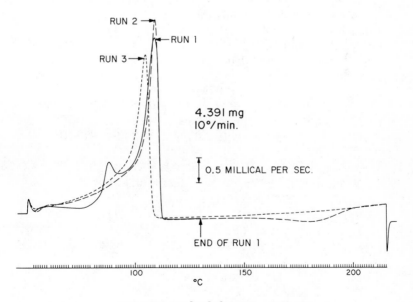

Figure 19.   Polyethylene wire coating

In conclusion, it can be seen that thermal analysis is able to make a considerable contribution to forensic science. Because of its capability to differentiate between manufacturing lots, it has for years been employed in quality control laboratories to monitor production of polymeric products. Its capability of differentiating between materials of identical chemical composition on the basis of differences in molecular weight distribution and thermal or mechanical history should be a capability quite unique and useful to forensic science. With the advent of second-generation instrumentation, this technique can be usefully extended to the realm of submilligram level analysis.

The greatest difficulty with the use of thermal analysis is that inherent to any new method--that of a shortage of prior experience on the part of most forensic scientists. However, since the method has been used in the polymer field for many years, it should be possible for the forensic laboratories to draw upon this reservoir of experience. In the interest of furthering this method, the Perkin-Elmer Microanalytical Laboratory would be prepared to help in demonstrating the capabilities of thermal analysis for forensic use.

Literature Cited

1. "Bibliography of DSC....," (600 references) (1973) Perkin-Elmer Order No. MA-23.
2. Philp, W.M.S., J. FOR. SCI. (1972), 17 (1), 132.
3. Gray, A.P.,in "Anal. Cal.,"Vol. I, Eds., Porter, R.S., and Johnson, J.F., Plenum Press, New York, NY (1968).
4. O'Neill, M.J., and Fyans, R.L., E. ANAL. SYMP., New York, NY, Nov. (1971).
5. Copies of the above references and technical descriptions are available from the authors.
6. Hall, J.H., and Goodwin, R.W., INSTR. NEWS, (1972), 21 (2), 1.
7. Brennan, W.P., THERM. ANAL. APPL. STDYS., (1973), 6, Perkin-Elmer Order No. TAAS-6.
8. Bell, J., TEXT. RES. J., (1972), 42, 292.
9. Abu-Isa, I., J. POLY. SCI., A-1, (1971), 9, 199.
10. Koktka, B.V., Valade, J. L., TAPPI, (1972), 55 (3), 375.
11. Gray, A.P., INSTR. NEWS, (1970), 16 (4),Order P-E MA-8.
12. Kokta, B.V., Lepoutre, P., and Valade, J.L., TAPPI, (1972), 55 (3), 370.
13. Sanders, C.I., J. PAINT TECH., (1970), 42, 405.

14. Brennan, W.P., (To be delivered at 1975 ANTEC Meeting, Atlanta, Georgia).

15. White, J.L., Lin, Y.M., J. APPL. POLY. SCI., (1973), 17, 3273.

16, Gray, A.P., INSTR. NEWS,(1970), 17(1), Order P-E MA-8.

17, Noel, F., J. INST. PETROLEUM, (1971), 57, 354. Noel, F., and Corbett, L.W., J. INST. PETROLEUM, (1970), Vol. 56, No. 551, 261.

18. Humphries, W.T., Miller, D.L., and Wildnauer, R.H., J. SOC. COSMET. CHEM., (1972), 23, 359.

19. Plato, C., and Glasgow, A.R., ANAL. CHEM., (1969), 41 (2), 330.

20. Spencer, L.R., FOOD PROD. DEV., (1973), 7 (1), 46.

21, Pals, D.T.F., et al., J. MACROMOL. SCI. PHYS., (1972), B6 (4), 739.

14

Ink Analysis—A Weapon Against Crime by Detection of Fraud

RICHARD L. BRUNELLE and A. A. CANTU

Bureau of Alcohol, Tobacco, and Firearms, U. S. Treasury Department, Washington, D. C. 20026

For decades, document examiners have searched for ways to detect fraudulent documents other than by traditional methods such as handwriting analysis, typewriting identification, obliterated and indented writing, deciphering and determination of the sequence of writings. New methods for detecting fraudulent documents developed slowly for several reasons: (a) analysis of ink and paper causes slight destruction to the document; (b) document examiners considered the preservation of the original condition of the documents very important; and (c) document examiners with few exceptions were trained in the areas of handwriting and typewriting analysis but lacked the scientific training to explore chemical and physical methods for use in detecting fraudulent documents.

The need for new and better methods to detect fraud has continuously been expressed by various agencies primarily within the Treasury Department and the Criminal Tax Division of the Justice Department. For example, agents of the Intelligence Division of the Internal Revenue Service need to know not only who signed a particular document, but when the document was prepared or signed. It is not uncommon for a dishonest taxpayer to backdate a receipt or series of records to substantiate a tax claim on his income tax return. Often documents are created or altered after an investigation begins in an attempt to account for taxable income, which in some cases involves sizable sums.

Firearms records are often created or altered after the start of an investigation of a suspected firearms dealer. Since certain types of weapons such as machine guns, grenades, sawed-off shotguns and others must be registered with the Bureau of Alcohol, Tobacco and Firearms (ATF), proof of their legal registration must be presented.

The Justice Department has an urgent need to detect fraud in many organized crime cases because it is often very difficult to associate a suspect with the particular offense except by the

detection of fraud through document analysis. The Securities
and Exchange Commission (SEC) is frequently concerned with fraud
in the illegal manipulation of the stock market. Many of their
cases involve the analysis of hundreds of documents which may
typically show the creation and dissolution of companies and the
sale of unregistered stock for the financial gain of a few
greedy people at the expense of the unknowing stockholders.

It is obvious that thousands of spurious documents are
passed daily to government and other agencies and, after traditional methods fail to detect fraud, only the application of
chemical and physical methods of analysis remain.

Both the ink and paper of a document possess potential
value in detecting possible fraud through the use of scientific
techniques. Within the Bureau of ATF, the Identification Branch
of the Laboratory met the challenge placed on its chemists by
the pressing needs of the many enforcement groups for this
scientific type of work. These chemists discovered that the
application of well established and proven scientific methods of
ink analysis (1) in conjunction with a well maintained up-to-
date standard ink library could lead to the identification and
dating of writing inks (2). This accomplishment has proven to
be extremely valuable whenever the date of preparation of a
document is questioned. Paper analysis, which can provide valuable information in these efforts (3), will not be dealt with in
this article.

The value of the systematic approach to ink identification
and dating used by the Bureau of ATF group is evidenced by the
many requests for the services of the Laboratory. Over the past
six years several hundred document cases have been processed and
the technique has been accepted by the courts. Furthermore,
this work has to the present detected several million dollars in
tax evasion.

Systematic Approach to Ink Identification

Prior to the research carried out by the Bureau of ATF
Identification Branch the specific identification and dating
of writing inks had not been accomplished. Ink dating was
limited to the determination of periods of time when gross
changes were made in their compositions. For example, the
change from oil base solvents to glycol bases provided a date
(circa 1952) prior to which glycol ballpoint inks did not exist.

In the new and rather unique approach to this problem, the
identification of inks on questioned documents depends on the
maintenance of an up-to-date standard ink library. The actual
identification is made by comparing the characteristics, or
points of identification, resulting from the analysis of the
questioned ink with the corresponding results obtained from
dried samples (on standard paper) of the known standard inks in
the library. Clearly, the larger the number of characteristics

that match, the higher the degree of reliability of the identification.

The methods of analysis used to compare the inks are well-
established laboratory techniques which have general acceptance
in the scientific community. The initial method for comparing
the questioned and known specimens is by performing non-destructive and somewhat simple but important tests to determine the
color, type (ballpoint, fiber tip, rolling marker, fountain pen,
etc.), and infrared luminescence properties. But most essential
are the chemical characteristics which require the removal of
micro-samples from the questioned ink writing. With such samples one can perform thin layer chromatography (TLC). This technique makes possible the separation of both non-volatile colored
and non-colored compounds used in the ink formulation. A paper
sample or control is usually examined simultaneously. The ink
chromatograms shown in Figures 1-5 show differences between similar colored inks of various types when analyzed by TLC. The differences are obvious from observation of the separated colored
components. Since the dyes and pigments in the writing inks are
colored and the separation of the dye components can be seen
visually, this phase of the identification process of a questioned ink can be utilized to rapidly scan through the standard
library to search for inks which may have similar TLC chromatograms. In actual practice, this procedure permits narrowing the
search to all but possibly a few inks. These inks with somewhat
similar chromatograms are further examined by observing fluorescent components on the TLC plate using ultraviolet light. If
this level of examination and comparison does not show uniqueness
and if sufficient questioned ink is available, other examinations
can be performed. These examinations include the use of different TLC media (plates) and different solvent systems. To obtain
further characterizing features with any of the TLC plates, relative amounts of the various dyes present in the formulation are
determined using spectrophotometry. These examinations usually
narrow the possibilities to only one standard ink in the library.

When we reach the point where these examinations cannot distinguish between the questioned and standard ink it is then possible to conclude with a high degree of scientific certainty that
the questioned ink matches in every respect a specific ink formulation in the library. To further conclude that two inks come
from the same formulation is based on the fact that, of about
3,000 writing inks in the standard ink library, all inks produced
by different manufacturers have been found to be distinguishable
when the difference is in the non-volatile components.

Once the questioned ink has been identified, i.e., matched
with a standard ink, the first production date of the standard
ink can be determined from information supplied by the manufacturer. Inquiries carried out by the Bureau of ATF Identification
Branch have shown that the various ink formulations change frequently, and every time a formula changes a date is provided

prior to which that ink was not in existence. As a result it is
possible on many occasions to determine that a questioned ink
used to prepare a document matched a standard ink which was not
in existence on the date the document was allegedly prepared.
Obviously, the effectiveness of the dating technique relies on
frequent formulation changes and on the degree of identification.

It should be mentioned that in some cases it may happen
that a questioned ink can be more positively identified through
presence of fluorescent or other unique components in the formulation. When sufficient questioned ink is available and the
proprietory formula composition has been furnished, further
analysis can lead to the identification of a component which may
provide additional proof of the identity of the ink. For
example, there are a variety of fatty acids, resins, and viscos-
ity adjusters added to inks which can be readily identified by
TLC or gas liquid chromatography (GLC), when sufficient ink is
available. As further examples, amorphous carbon and graphite,
which are common dispersion ingredients in ballpoint inks, can
be distinguished using electron diffraction methods.

The larger number of points of identification that are
determined, the more certain becomes the conclusion regarding
the identification of questioned inks. Such forensic scientific
philosophy is true not only of ink comparison but of other types
of physical evidence such as soil, paint, hair, bullets and fingerprints.

The Bureau of ATF Ink Library of standard ink samples is
essentially complete with respect to all domestic and most Euro-
pean-produced inks for the past few decades. However, the
library does not contain all of the inks produced in the world
nor will this ever be possible. This does not detract from the
practicability of the ink identification technique despite the
rare occurrence of a non-identification. However, since in actual
practice it is not possible to obtain all of the inks in the
world, the comparison is based on the probability or degree of
certainty that a questioned ink matches an existing standard ink.
The non-identification of questioned inks can occur when the
corresponding standard ink was not supplied, or when the questioned ink characteristics changed sufficiently due to deterior-
ating conditions such as photochemical degradation caused by
extreme exposure to light.

Application to Actual Cases

This systematic approach to ink identification and ink
dating as stated earlier has been applied to several hundred
cases over the past six years. In a large percentage of cases
examined, it was possible to show that documents were backdated
because the writing ink used was not in existence at the time
the document was allegedly written.

The courts have held that scientific methods of analysis are acceptable in the courts if the techniques used have general acceptance in the scientific community (Frye v. U.S.) (4). The ink identification technique satisfies these criteria because all of the methods used to analyze inks are well established and proven analytical tools and this point has been conceded by experts for the defense in several cases.

Usually the ink testimony is offered as corroborative evidence in a case and occasionally it has been used as primary evidence such as in Stoller v. U.S. (5) tried in Miami, Florida. In this case, testimony based on the ink dating technique was presented for the first time. Several inks were identified in travel and expense diaries for the years 1965, 1966, and 1967. The analysis revealed that a large number of the inks used in the diaries were not available commercially until after the years in question, indicating the entries were backdated. The testimony was used as a rebuttal to impeach the testimony of the defendant and placed considerable doubt on the authenticity of the diaries. Thousands of dollars of taxable income were involved and the defendant became liable for the tax assessed by the Internal Revenue Service.

In U.S. v. Wolfson (6), tried in the Southern District of New York, the defendant charged the government with using a spurious document to prosecute him for violation of SEC regulations involving the Capital Transit System. He claimed that one of a seven page document was altered and was not the original instrument.

Analysis revealed that ink prepared from the same formulation was used on each of the seven pages. This test, together with the findings from paper analysis and watermark examination conducted on the documents, helped to substantiate the authenticity of the questioned document. The ink testimony was accepted by the court as valid and persuasive and the examinations conducted by the Bureau of ATF Identification Branch were held in the balance by the court even though a large sum was spent on defense expert work and testimony.

In another case, an official of a large New York bank was accused of illegally awarding loans to small business concerns. In this case, U.S. v. Meyers (7), tried in the Southern District Court of New York, ink and handwriting analyses assisted in showing that many of the loan application forms were prepared by the bank official rather than the loan applicant. The scientific testimony presented for the government was accepted by the court and was not challenged by the defense.

In Memphis, Tennessee, the defendant was charged with perjury resulting from testimony given at the defendant's federal income tax evasion trial. In U.S. v. Sloan (8) a conviction was obtained and during the trial certain documents were offered as evidence. It was because of these instruments that perjury charges were made.

The defendant claimed he was investing money for an anonymous rich client through land purchases which were supposed to have been made from 1958 through 1966. Over a half a million dollars of taxable income was involved. The government claimed the defendant was investing his own money and was using the rich client scheme to avoid paying the tax.

To prove his case, Sloan introduced a four page agreement dated 1958, stating that the defendant was to invest sums of money for an anonymous client covering an indefinite period of time. Also introduced were a series of notes dating from 1958 to 1966 which presumably was the proof of these investments.

Ink analysis of the writing on each page of the agreement and the notes, showed that the same ink formulation was used on the documents. Figure 6 shows the similarity among these chromatograms. In addition, the findings revealed that the documents could not have been in existence in 1958, because a unique dye identified in the ink was first synthesized by Ciba Chemical Corp. in 1959 and the ink formulation was not produced until 1960.

The testimony involving the ink analysis was primary evidence and its use was sufficient to obtain a conviction of perjury even though three experts were employed by the defense to counter the ATF ink testimony.

The defendants in the case, U.S. v. Colasurdo (9), tried in the Southern District of New York, were allegedly connected with organized crime operations and were charged with the formation and dissolution of companies to achieve personal financial gain at the expense of the stockholders.

After almost two months of trial, testimony based on ink identification and ink dating was introduced by Bureau of ATF chemists. The findings, which were accepted by the court over objection of defense counsel, revealed that a document dated 1965 offered as evidence by the defense was backdated. The ballpoint ink used to prepare the signature on this instrument was not produced until 1968.

Although the defense secured the services of experts to counter the ATF ink testimony, the evidence was accepted by the courts.

The defense appealed the guilty verdict partly on the basis of the ink testimony, but the U.S. Court of Appeals for the Second Circuit affirmed the conviction. Later the U.S. Supreme Court denied certiorari.

Prior to the appeal of the Colasurdo decision, ink testimony was offered in the U.S. v. Bruno (10), tried in Philadelphia, Pennsylvania. The request for laboratory assistance was initiated by the Criminal Tax Division of the Justice Department. The charge involved the evasion of income tax from the sale of certain vending machines and the premises on which the equipment was located.

Analysis revealed that ink used to prepare a signature on a document dated 1965 was not available commercially until 1967. A combination of ingredients that was unique to one ink manufacturer in all of the U.S. and in Europe was identified.

In this case, the presiding judge after two weeks of trial, ruled that the evidence was not conclusive because the ATF Laboratory did not have access to all foreign inks. In addition, the ink testimony was the primary evidence and in the judge's opinion the state of the art of ink identification had not reached a reasonable degree of scientific certainty. This ruling was made despite five prior rulings by different courts in different jurisdictions upholding the ink identification technique as valid and persuasive.

The U.S. Court of Appeals for the 2nd Circuit affirmed the conviction of Colasurdo after considering an appeal based on reasoning that the ink identification technique was not yet proven. In their opinion, the Court considered the ruling made by the Judge in the Bruno Case, but were not particularly influenced by his failure to accept the ink identification technique.

The most recent decision regarding the acceptability of the ink method was the denial of the U.S. Supreme Court to review the Colasurdo Case. Since then ink analysis testimony has been accepted in at least eight cases.

In summary, it appears from the rulings made by the various courts that the ink identification and ink dating technique are generally acceptable for court purposes.

Future Developments in Ink Identification Work

Absolute identification of writing inks is difficult because all of the components which were originally put into the ink by the manufacturer cannot be determined on a sample taken from a questioned document. Positive identification is only possible when it can be established that a unique dye or combination of ingredients was used in the formulation.

The success of the present ink identification program depends largely on the cooperation of the various ink manufacturers who supply the known inks. Without their help, sufficient standard samples would not be available to compare with questioned inks for the approach to be practical. The Bureau of ATF Identification Branch has been very fortunate because ink companies have recognized the value of this type of program to the law-abiding citizens. They have been extremely cooperative in supplying us with ink specimens and with experts in ink technology to present testimony in court whenever necessary.

Since the effectiveness of the ink dating program depends on frequent formula changes, the Bureau of ATF Identification Branch is currently investigating the feasibility of a more absolute identification system that can be used by all ink manufacturers. It has been proposed that each producer add markers

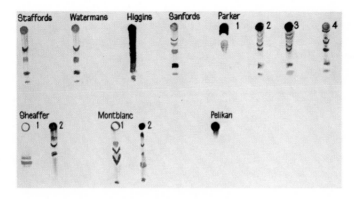

Figure 1. Chart demonstrating different TLC patterns of blue fountain pen inks

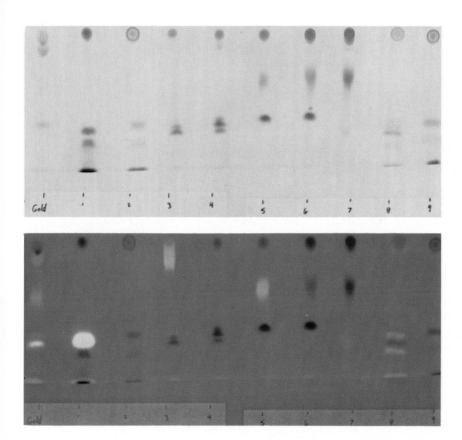

Figure 2. (top) TLC of blue ballpoint pen inks and one gold ballpoint pen ink. (bottom) Above, under UV light.

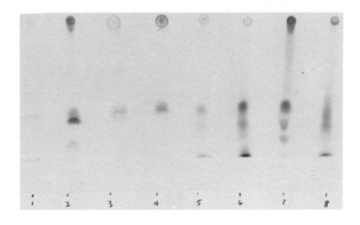

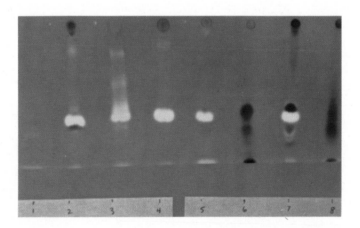

Figure 3.   (top) TLC of black ballpoint pen inks. (bottom)
Above, under UV light.

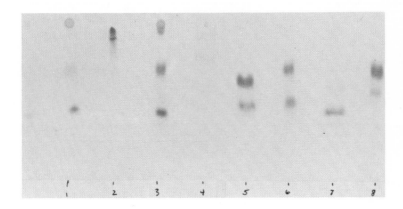

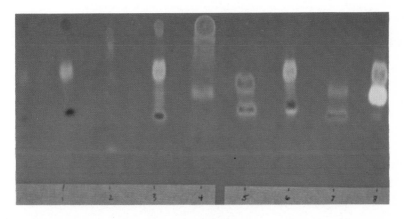

Figure 4. (top) TLC of blue fiber tip pen inks. (bottom)
Above, under UV light.

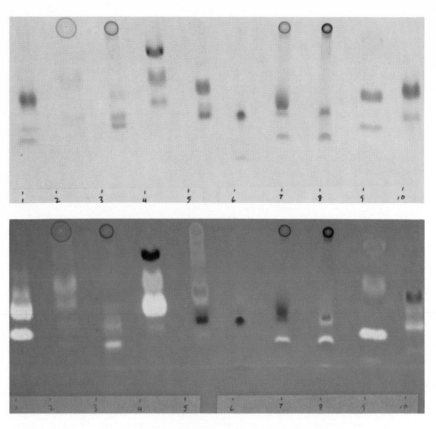

Figure 5. (top) TLC of black fiber tip pen inks. (bottom) Above, under UV light.

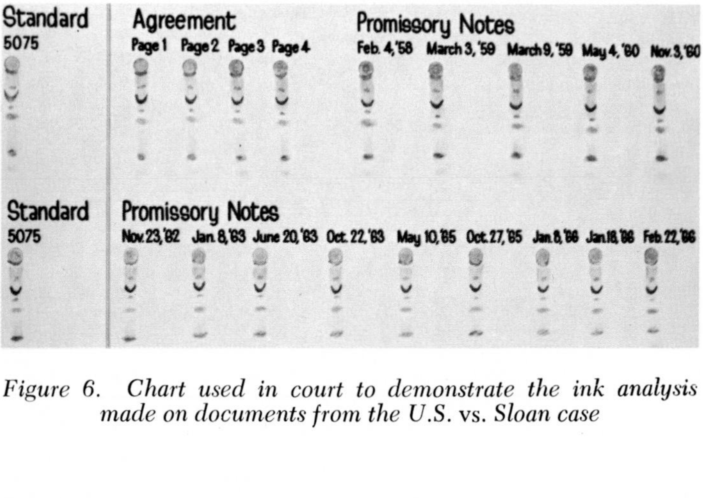

Figure 6. Chart used in court to demonstrate the ink analysis made on documents from the U.S. vs. Sloan case

or tags to make possible a positive identification of their product. This approach will allow the determination of the year
the ink was produced if the markers are changed yearly. This
will settle at least two current problems facing the effectiveness of the method: (a) Recently an increasing number of ink
manufacturers have not changed their formulations, particularly
their non-volatile components. (b) Non-identification sometimes
occurs due to severe aging conditions of a questioned ink. Ink
manufacturers can also benefit from ink tagging to settle custo-
mer disputes concerning the age of inks.

The value and applications of the Bureau of ATF Ink Identification and Dating Program to law enforcement problems is now
well recognized internationally. The International Association
of Identification, one of the world's largest professional organizations in forensic science, presented the highly coveted Don-
dero Award to a Bureau of ATF chemist for the outstanding contribution to the field of ink identification. This laboratory,
however, must continue to improve the effectiveness of its ink
identification and dating program through the development and
implementation of a suitable marking or tagging system.

Literature Cited

1. Tholl, J., POLICE (1960) pp7-15. See also references
    appearing on publication 2 below.
2. Brunelle, R. L. and Pro, M. J., J. ASSOC. OFFIC. ANAL. CHEM.
    (1972) 55, pp 823-826.
3. Brunelle, R. L., Washington, W. D., Hoffman, C. M. and Pro,
    M. J., J. ASSOC. OFFIC. ANAL. CHEM. (1971) 54, pp 920-924.
4. Frye v. U.S. 293 F. 1013 (D.C. Cir 1923).
5. Staller v. U.S., Miami, Fla. (1969).
6. U.S. v. Wolfson, N.Y., N.Y. (1970).
7. U.S. v. Meyer, N.Y., N.Y., (1970).
8. U.S. v. Sloan, Memphis, Tenn. (1970).
9. U.S. v. Colasurdo, New York City 1970 (Second Circuit of
    Appeals, Docket Nos. 71-1373-4-5-6, Dec. 6, 1971).
10. U.S. v. Bruno, Phil., Pa. (1971).

15

Forensic Bloodstains and Physiological Fluid Analysis

W. C. STUVER, ROBERT C. SHALER, and PETER M. MARONE
Pittsburgh and Allegheny County Crime Laboratory, Pittsburgh, Penn. 15219
RALPH PLANKENHORN
Pennsylvania State Police Crime Laboratory, Greensburg, Penn. 15601

The goal of forensic serology is to individualize blood stains by identifying genetic markers whose population frequencies have been established.

This goal may soon be within our reach. It appears, however, that this will not be a one step analytical procedure but a series of analyses utilizing several components of the blood from which a profile of genetic markers can be established. Since these markers in blood are inherited independent of one another and their frequencies within a given population are known, the profile obtained will permit a mathematical probability or uniqueness to be calculated. Thus, blood evidence will always remain in the realm of probability; however, as with fingerprints, the probability of two people having exactly the same profile may be so remote that a conclusion can be made as to its origin.

Blood is a multi-component system with formed elements of red and white blood cells as well as platelets, and a liquid fraction (plasma), each containing a vast array of biochemical constituents. The forensic serologist has chosen three classes of the blood constituents for their genetic information and use in individualization endeavors. These constituent classes are 1) the blood grouping and typing antigens, 2) the polymorphic enzymes and 3) the polymorphic proteins.

The fact that blood grouping and/or typing antigens exist has been known since Landsteiner discovered the ABO system around 1900 (1). Since then over 246 published antigens have been found; however, only three of these antigenic systems, the ABO, MN and Rh, have received crime laboratory acceptance (2). Until several years ago most crime laboratories did only ABO groupings; however, with the improvements of specific antisera and the increased sensitivity of detection techniques, the MN and Rh systems have also been adopted as reliable systems.

The ABO, MN and Rh systems, unlikely many of the other antigenic systems, have useful population frequencies. For instance, the four groups belonging to the ABO system occur in approximately the following percentage frequencies: O - 44%, A - 44%, B - 8% and AB - 3%. The MN system has three groups having the following frequencies: M - 30%, MN - 50% and N - 20%, and the Rh system basically has a five component antigen system giving rise to eight gene complexes or agglutinogens (3). Phenotyping using Rh antisera can be quite useful in obtaining individualizing information.

Recent advances have also been made in shortening the procedure for obtaining blood group antigen information. A quick, reliable procedure for the ABO grouping used in the Pittsburgh and Allegheny County Crime Laboratory involves a maximum of 45 minutes (4). This includes a 10 minute preparation and collection of threads, a 10 minute antibody incubation, a 3 minute wait, a 10 minute elution and a 10 minute rotation and examination period. Thus by shortening an otherwise lengthy technique, a serologist can efficiently process more samples in a given period of time with less material waste, thus permitting further analysis on the same sample. In addition, another advantage of this technique is that it uses only three bloodstained threads from the questioned source material to accomplish what normally would take significant quantities of blood.

The second main class of blood constituents used as genetic markers are the polymorphic enzymes. The enzymes of interest to the forensic serologist are primarily located within the red blood cell and are commonly referred to as isoenzymes. These can briefly be described as those enzymatically active proteins which catalyze the same biochemical reactions and occur in the same species but differ in certain of their physicochemical properties. (This description does not exclude the tissue isoenzymes that occur within the same organism; however, our consideration deals only with those of the red blood cell in particular.) The occurrence of multi-molecular forms of the same enzyme (isoenzymes) has been known for several decades; however, it was not until the Metropolitan Police Laboratory of Scotland Yard adapted electrophoretic techniques to dried blood analysis that these systems were catapulted to the prominence they presently receive (2). For many of the forensic serologists in the United States, the use of electrophoresis and isoenzyme determination is a recently-inherited capability shared by only a few laboratories.

Many isoenzymes have been identified from various human tissue sources; however, our consideration will deal with six erythrocytic systems that have received routine crime laboratory status. These are phosphoglucomutase (PGM), adenylate kinase (AK), adenosine deaminase (ADA), glucose-6-phosphate dehydrogenase (G-6-PD), 6-phosphogluconate dehydrogenase (6-PGD) and erythrocytic acid phosphatase (EAP).

The PGM system has received the greatest amount of attention for three reasons. First, it is a very stable enzyme and produces an easily interpreted zymogram; second, its population frequencies are very useful since the three phenotypes (commonly

found in the British population) have the following percentages:
PGM - I - 58%, PGM 2-I - 36% and PGM - 2 - 6%; and third,
phosphoglucomutase can be found in other forensically important
physiological fluids, namely, semen and vaginal secretions (5).
This last dimension has been extremely useful in further individualizing seminal stains found on garments and/or bed clothing
associated with sexual assault cases.

Adenylate kinase has also received quite a bit of attention
because it can be identified on the same electrophoretic zymogram
as PGM, thereby affording additional isoenzyme information from
the same blood sample, (Figure 1).

This ability to obtain multiple isoenzyme information from a
single electrophoretic zymogram is not new. Publications dealing
with human genetic studies have listed PGM, AK, ADA and 6-PGD
being determined on the same electrophoretic zymogram (6, 7).

Another isoenzyme with substantial interest is erythrocytic
acid phosphatase (EAP) (8, 9, 10). This system has three
autosomal allelic genes termed A, B and C. These can be homo-
zygous or heterozygous giving rise to BA, CA and CB phenotypes.
Each of these phenotypes is easily distinguished using starch gel
electrophoresis with very useful population frequencies of
approximately A - 13%, B - 35%, C - 0.2%, BA - 43%, CA - 3%,
CB - 6%. Erythrocytic acid phosphatase has been found to remain
viable for many months after drying and successful typing can be
performed on a minimum of several threads (9), (Figure 2).

A major disadvantage of many of the other isoenzymes, not
mentioned, and which could be identified in blood, is the frequency of variants (11). When utilizing these other systems in
screening blood samples to find differences between the victim
and suspect blood types, the odds are against the examiner. Many
have at least 98% of the population tested belonging to one of
the isoenzyme variants (i.e., phosphohexose isomerase). By
contrast, if the serologist should find that the victim's blood
does have a rare variant then the probabilities of the questioned
blood stain being from the victim are very high and of extreme
value as a form of associative evidence.

The third main class of constituents used as genetic markers
in the blood are polymorphic proteins (2, 11). Hemoglobin and
the haptoglobins constitute the most important members of
this classification. The haptoglobins are $Alpha_2$ globulins which
are responsible for binding free homoglobin released into the
plasma after destruction of red blood cells. Genetically, they
exist in three forms, $H_p I$, $H_p 2$ and $H_p 2$-I, with the following
population distribution: $H_p I$ - 14%, $H_p 2$-I - 53%, and $H_p 2$ - 32%.
Once again these frequencies are useful in screening blood for
differences, (Figure 3).

Hemoglobins can be useful to the forensic serologist, for
example, in differentiating fetal blood in cases of abortions,
since fetal hemoglobin is different from adult hemoglobin on a
molecular level, and also as an anthropological marker for

PHOSPHOGLUCOMUTASE

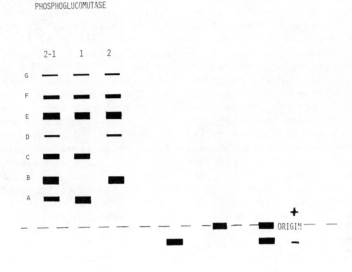

Figure 1. *Separation of PGM and AK electrophoresis was done for 22 hr at 6.5 V/cm at 4°C in a 1 mm, 14% starch gel prepared in .1M Tris, EDTA, maleic acid, $MgCl_2 = 7.4$ tank buffer diluted 1:10. The PGM side of the gel was stained at 1–2 hours before the AK using an agar overlay technique at 37°C. The visualized bands are precipitated with formazan.*

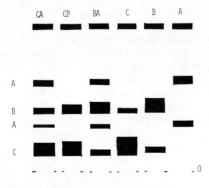

Figure 2. *Erythrocytic acid phosphatase schematic. A schematic drawing illustrating typical results of an EAP determination in a 13%, 1mm starch gel prepared in 0.24M NaH_2PO_4, 0.15M trisodium citrate tannic acid buffer diluted 1:100. The electrophoresis is carried out for 4½ hr at approximately 410 V. The gels are stained by the fluorescence produced after enzymatic hydrolysis by methylumbelliferyl phosphate at 37°C for 1½ hr.*

identifying negroid blood. Approximately 10% of the negroid
population retain a form of hemoglobin referred to as sickle cell
(11). Sickle cell hemoglobin (Hb-S) is caused by a replacement
of glutamic acid with valine at the sixth position on the beta
chain. Several electrophoretic techniques have proven useful for
differentiating the various hemoglobins A, F, S, D and E (12).

     Present research is being carried out to further the metho-
dology of the anthropological classification of bloodstains.
Two isoenzymes, peptidase A and glutathione reductase, have been
reported to have polymorphic forms in negro populations and
little or no variants in caucasians (13, 14, 15). Thus, should
the rare variant be demonstrated in a stain, there would be a
high probability concerning the ethnic origin of the blood. In
addition, research has been initiated into the use of Gm and Inv
typing to assist in the anthropological classification of bloodstains (2, 17). For example, the combination of Gm factors 1,
2, 17 and 4, 22 is found in caucasians, whereas Gm factors 1,
6 and 11 are found in negroes and Gm 1, 4 and 17 are found
strictly in mongoloids.

     Gm and Inv are amino acid sequences occurring in the light
and heavy chains of immunoglobulins (16, 18). Antibodies
specific to the Gm and Inv groups are found in some patients
suffering from rheumatoid arthritis and in some healthy people.
So far, 23 Gm types and 3 Inv types have been found. The success
of Gm and Inv typing will depend on the quantity of stain, and
the specificity, quality and availability of the antisera,
(Figure 4).

     Gm and Inv typing will not only be an asset in anthropo-
logical testing, but will also be valuable in individualizing
blood since only certain combinations of Gm and Inv types are
found in any one person's blood. For instance, the individual's
blood may type positive for Gm 1, 4, 17, 22, whereas another
person may type as 1, 5, 12 and 21.

     Current research involves the use of radioimmunoassay to
quantitate testosterone and estrogen in dried blood samples
(22, 24). The ultimate goal of this research will be to determine the sexual origin of the stains. In the past, researchers
have attempted this by identifying Barr bodies and Y chromosomes
using differential fluorescence staining with quinacine; however,
these tests required a substantial amount of blood deposited as a
thin film on a non-porous surface and are therefore limited in
their application (19, 20, 21). The sensitivity and basic
technique of radioimmunoassay will permit the analysis of bloodstains on virtually any surface and should also be applicable to
very small ones.

     Forensic serologists have had little success in identifying
menstrual blood. With the increase in the number of sexual
assaults (rape in particular) taking place each year, the analyst
confronts the problem of menstrual blood identification more
often. A recent publication reported the identification of

menstrual blood stains based on the electrophoretic separation and quantitation of lactate dehydrogenase (LDH) isoenzymes (25). They noticed a significant elevation in the LDH-4 and LDH-5 fractions or stained bands. The activity of these 4 and 5 bands is reported to remain for two weeks after the blood dries. Recent work in this laboratory has resulted in the development of LDH's and PGM's on the same plate. Through this technique, information can be obtained concerning the menstrual origin of the blood and also, possibly, information regarding the PGM type of the contributor. This can be also very meaningful when the menstrual blood is mixed with semen and the resultant mixture deposited on the suspect's clothing. In a recent case, such a mixture was tested. The woman was a PGM-I and the perpetrator a PGM 2-I. The PGM study of the stain revealed not only the "a" and "c" bands of the PGM-I type but also the "b" and "d" bands from a PGM-2 or PGM 2-I semen source.

Another interesting dimension to the LDH isoenzyme system resides in the fact that during the process of spermatoagenesis an LDH isoenzyme is formed that when separated by starch electrophoresis is found midway between the LDH_3 and LDH_4 bands. It is referred to as the LDH_x band (26). Efforts are being made to identify this band in semen. This could possibly be a solution to the dilemma of identifying seminal stains in cases where the perpetrator is azospermatic, aspermatic or has had a vasectomy (i.e., he is naturally or artificially incapable of producing spermatozoa), (Figure 5).

In the event that the LDH system does not solve the problem of seminal stain identification, research has been initiated to produce specific antisera to certain antigens only found in seminal fluid. Preliminary work indicates that at least five constituents of seminal fluid can be electrophoretically separated and antigenically introduced into rabbits (28, 29). (Commercial antisera now on the market have proven unsatisfactory (27).)

Electrophoresis has become a most vital technique for the separation and identification of the genetic markers in blood. In addition to blood, Adams and Wraxall (30), of the Metropolitan Polica Laboratory, have applied acrylamide electrophoresis to the identification of various sources of acid phosphatase (AP) activity found when vaginal swabs or washings are being tested for the presence of seminal fluid. This technique is capable of differentiating between vaginal and seminal (prostratic) acid phosphatase since prostrate AP moves faster in the gel. Differentiation between vaginal AP and prostratic AP has explained cases where it has been found that significant AP levels are present while no spermatozoa can be located microscopically. In one particular case, the high AP level was due to the vaginal enzyme and no bands of prostratic AP were detected. Thus the presence of high levels of AP does not necessarily confirm the presence of seminal fluid. This test is in agreement with the

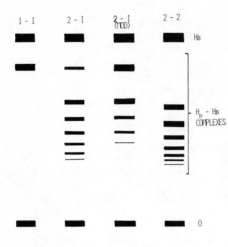

Figure 3. Haptoglobin separation schematic. A schematic illustrating typical results of a Hp determination run in 8 mm, 10% starch gel prepared with tris citric acid buffer at pH = 8.6. The tank buffer is boric acid, pH = 7.9. The electrophoresis is run at 100 V for 17 hr at 4°C. The Hp–Hb complexes are stained by virtue of the peroxidase reaction of hemoglobin which gives a color reaction with benzidine.

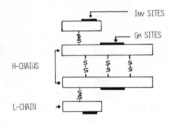

Figure 4. Schematic illustrating the positions of the Gm and Inv sites on the IgG molecule

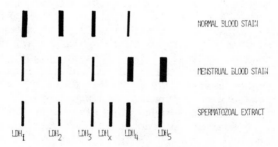

Figure 5. Lactic acid dehydrogenase schematic. This schematic illustrates the value of LDH isozyme patterns for the identification of menstrual blood and seminal material.

argument that many forensic serologists have made, namely that the chemical acid phosphatase test can only be regarded as a presumptive test until the specific source of the AP can be identified.

In conclusion, forensic serology has made great advances during the past 2-3 years and the next few years promise to be even more worthwhile. Since blood is so complex, it presents so many avenues for investigation that it will continue to be a fertile area for meaningful forensic research.

Literature Cited

1. Issett, P. D., "Applied Blood Group Serology", Spectra Biologicals, Oxnard, California (1970).
2. Culliford, B. J., "The Examination and Typing of Bloodstains in the Crime Laboratory", National Institute of Law Enforcement and Criminal Justice, Washington, D. C. (1971).
3. Issett, P. D., in ref. 1, p. 58.
4. Unpublished results from this laboratory.
5. Culliford, B. J., in ref. 2, p. 106.
6. Goedde, W. H. and Brinkmann, H. G., HUMANGENTIK (1972) 15(3), 277.
7. Hopkinson, D. A., Spencer, N. and Harris, H., NATURE 199, 969 (1969).
8. Wraxall, B. G. D., IV International Meeting of Forensic Sciences, Edinburgh, Scotland (1972).
9. Wraxall, B. G. D., personal communication.
10. Giblett, R., "Genetic Markers in Human Blood", Blackwell Scientific Publications, Oxford (1969).
11. Wraxall, B. G. D., J. FOR. SCI. SOC. (1972) 12(3), 452.
12. Lewis, W. H. P. and Harris, H., NATURE (1967) 215.
13. Kaplan, J. D. and Bentler, E., NATURE (1968) 217, 256.
14. Lewis, W. H. P., NATURE (1971) 230, 215.
15. Grubb, R. and Laurell, C. B., ACTA PATHOL. MICROBIOL., SCAND. (1956) 39, 390.
16. Blanc, M., Goity, R. and Ducos, J., J. FOR. SCI. (1971) 16(2), 176.
17. Popartz, C., Lenior, J. and Rovart, L., NATURE (1961) 189, 586.
18. Pearson, P. L. and Bobrow, M., NATURE (1970) 226, 78.
19. Renard, S., J. FOR. SCI. SOC. (1971) 11, 15.
20. Philips, A. P. and Gaten, E., LANCET (1971), Aug. 14, 371.
21. Furuyama, S., Mayes, D. M. and Nugent, C. A., STEROIDS (1970) 16(4), 415.
22. Hillier, S. G., Brounscy, B. G. and Cameron, E. H. D., STEROIDS (1973) 21(5), 735.
23. Boon, D. A., Keenan, R. E. and Slaunwhite, Jr., W. R., STEROIDS (1972) 20(3), 269.
24. Asaon, M., Oya, M. and Hayakawa, M., FORENSIC SCIENCES (1972) 1, 327.

25. Khalap, S., unpublished communication.
26. Baxter, S. J., MED. SCI. LAW (1973) 13(3), 155.
27. Beling, C. and Li, T., BERT. STERIL, (1973) 24(2), 132.
28. Hara, M., Kuyanag, Y., Inoue, I. and Fukuyama, T., NIPPON
     HORGUKU ZASSHI (1971) 25(4), 322.
29. Wraxall, B. G. D., personal communication.

Effect of Environmental Factors on Starch Gel Electrophoretic Patterns of Human Erythrocyte Acid Phosphatase

CORNELIUS G. McWRIGHT, JAMES J. KEARNEY, and JAMES L. MUDD

Biological Science Research Unit, FBI Laboratory, Washington, D.C. 20535

Human erythrocyte acid phosphatase (EAP) polymorphism was first described by Hopkinson, Spencer and Harris (1). EAP can be classified by electrophoresis into six different phenotypes, A, AB, B, CB, AC and C. From numerous distribution and family studies it has been determined that the six phenotypes are directed by three common alleles p^a, p^b, and p^c (2,3,4). Using crude hemolysates (5) and 1,000 fold pure homogeneous type AA and BB enzymes (6) some properties of EAP, such as thermostability, pH and substrate specificity and molecular size, have been examined. From the time EAP polymorphism was first described, the use of the enzyme as a means of typing human blood has been of interest to the forensic scientist. Investigators have described successes in typing dried bloodstains stored at 20 - 25°C for 5 - 8 weeks and stored whole blood kept at 5 C was typed for as long as 15 months (7). Difficulties in typing EAP types AB (1,3), B and C (8) have also been described.

Putrefactive bacteria, such as Clostridium welchii, which frequently invade human blood during the agonal period or immediately after death, produce the enzyme neuraminidase (9). Neuraminidase has been shown to effect the heterogeneity of electrophoretic banding patterns of the human prostate acid phosphatase (10). The effect of this enzyme on EAP is not known.

The purpose of this study was to compare two electrophoretic methods used to type EAP and to examine the stability of EAP phenotypes in red cell hemolysates, clotted blood and dried bloodstains stored at room temperature (25°C). A distribution study of the frequency of five EAP phenotypes among ABO, MN, Rh blood groups and among 137 metropolitan Washington D. C. area residents was made. The effect of neuraminidase on EAP was also studied.

Methods and Materials

Preparation of samples. Fresh and outdated blood samples
used in this study were obtained from blood banks of selected
medical institutions in the metropolitan Washington, D. C. area.

Red cell hemolysates were prepared by washing centrifuged
red cells twice with a 0.87% saline solution and then mixing one
volume of distilled water to one volume of packed red cells.
This mixture was then frozen and subsequently thawed just prior
to use.

Dried bloodstains were prepared by pipetting a mixed
suspension of red cells onto a clean piece of white cotton
sheeting which was then completely air dried. Accurately cut
10mm x 2mm cuttings were used for electrophoresis.

Samples to be taken from liquid hemolysates and pulverized
clotted blood were prepared by saturating 10mm x 2mm cuttings
with hemolysates or liquid from the pulverized clot and allowing
the cuttings to dry before application.

Starch-gel electrophoresis. Electrophoresis was carried
out for time intervals of 4 hours and 15 hours using the method
first described by Hopkinson and Harris ($\underline{11}$) with one slight
modification. The 0.245M NaH_2PO_4/0.15M $Na_3C_6H_5O_7$ bridge buffer
was prepared with 0.02M $MgCl_2$ and 0.01M EDTA at pH 5.5. Two
millimeter thick ($\underline{12}$) 10% starch-gels, pH 6.1, were prepared by
using a 1/100 dilution of the bridge buffer. Samples were
inserted into the gel approximately 40 minutes after the gel was
poured. Samples were overlayed with 0.1M Dithioerythritol
(Sigma) prepared in gel buffer and were allowed to incubate in
the presence of the thiol reagent for 10 minutes before
electrophoresis was started. Four hour electrophoresis runs
were carried out on cooling plates at 0 C at 20 ma/plate.
Fifteen hour runs were carried out in the refrigerator at 5°C at
8 ma/plate. For best results bridge buffers were only used once.

Measurement of EAP Activity. A 2 x 10^{-4}M 4-methyl-
umbelliferyl phosphate (Koch-Light Laboratories) solution
prepared in 0.05M citric acid/NaOH buffer, pH 5.0 ($\underline{13}$) was
used to saturate an appropriate sized piece of Whatman 1MM filter
paper. The saturated paper was placed on the gel surface
covering the area between the origin and anodic bridge. EAP
activity was developed by placing the gel in a 37 C incubator
for 30 minutes and then observing it under long wavelength UV
light. Less active samples required longer incubation times.

Photography and Densitometer Tracings. EAP activity was
photographed under UV light through a Tiffen Photar, #61, series
7 green glass filter using Polaroid type 55 film and a constant
focus Graphic camera box built by the Special Photo Unit of the
FBI Laboratory. Densitometer tracings were made directly from

the cleared negatives using a Joyce Loebl model 3CS densitometer.

Neuraminidase. Neuraminidase (Sigma) contained 500 units
of activity per ml.

Results

Comparison of 4 hour and 15 hour starch-gel electrophoresis.
The comparison of the banding patterns of five EAP phenotypes
obtained during electrophoresis with the same buffer but for
different time intervals is shown in figure 1. Banding patterns
obtained during 4 hour electrophoresis at 0°C were consistently
sharper and better defined than the more diffuse patterns
obtained during 15 hour electrophoresis at 5°C. The a' isozyme
band is clearly separated from the faster moving components
types AB and AC. In the 15 hour electrophoresis run the a'
isozyme band appears as a shoulder to the faster moving b
isozyme band in types AB and AC, making these types more
difficult to interpret. Patterns obtained from both systems are
consistent with those described by other investigators (1,3,4).

Densitometer tracings of the electrophoresis banding
patterns of five EAP phenotypes from a 4 hour electrophoresis
are shown in figure 2. All four isozyme bands making up the
five EAP phenotypes are clearly defined. The strong storage
band, s, is always associated with those phenotypes having
strong b isozyme bands such as types B, CB and AB. A weaker s'
storage band appears in phenotype A. The s' storage band is
associated with the strong a isozyme band of type A. The weaker
s' band also appears in types AC and AB but is so weak it is
difficult to observe. Strong s bands can be seen in figures 1
and 3, but the s' is too light to be seen or to be read with
the densitometer except in type A. The appearance and intensity
of the s and s' bands can be controlled somewhat by incubation
of samples in thiol reagents before electrophoresis. If the s
band becomes as strong as it appears in figure 3, in the absence
of a control showing the placement of the a isozyme band, a type
B may be falsely read as a type AB by an untrained examiner.

Stability of EAP during storage at 25°C. The loss of EAP
activity in dried bloodstains, fresh cell hemolysates, and
clotted blood during storage at 25°C is shown in figure 4.
Hemolysates and clotted blood lost nearly all EAP activity
after storage for 5 days at 25°C while EAP activity in dried
stains persisted for much longer periods of time. The loss of
activity of all five different EAP phenotypes was the same in
hemolysates and clotted blood stored at 25°C. In dried bloodstains, however, EAP phenotypes CB and AC lose activity at a
slower rate than do types AB, A and B. Type A is the least
stable of the phenotypes. Type AB was intermediate between
types B and A.

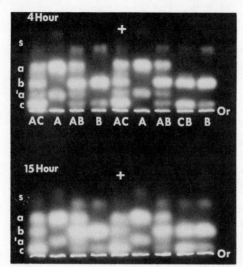

Figure 1. The comparison of the EAP phenotype electrophoretic patterns obtained during electrophoresis for 4 hr at 0°C and 15 hr at 5°C

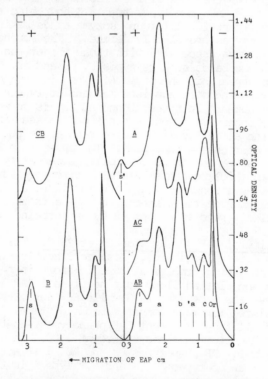

Figure 2. Densitometer tracings illustrating the isozyme migration patterns of five EAP phenotypes during electrophoresis for 4 hr at 0°C. The s and s' storage bands can also be seen.

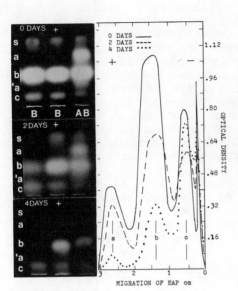

Figure 3.   Densitometer tracings and accompanying photographs of EAP phenotype B illustrating the loss of activity of the b isozyme and increase in activity of the c isozyme during storage at 25°C. Samples were taken from clotted blood. Electrophoresis was carried out for 15 hr at 5°C. The successive densitometer tracings shown were made from the EAP phenotype B pattern located on the left in the photograph.

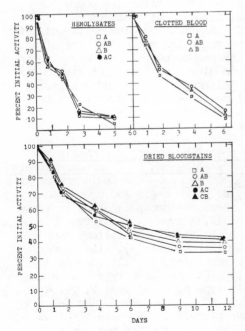

Figure 4.   Comparison of the loss of EAP activity present in red cell hemolysates, clotted blood, and dried bloodstains stored at 25°C. EAP phenotypes shown are types A, AB, B, CB, and AC.

As shown in table 1, dried bloodstains retain EAP activity for periods as long as 15 months. Dried bloodstains were typed blind up to 4 months without difficulty but beyond that period typing became very difficult. Dried bloodstains that could be typed after 4 months were saturated and required long incubation periods in the presence of freshly prepared thiol reagents.

During the course of storage studies, changes in the intensities of various components of the different EAP phenotypes were observed. The most striking changes are illustrated in figures 3 and 5. The faster moving components of types B and CB became weaker while the slower components became slightly stronger. As shown in figure 3, from the accompanying densitometer tracings, it is apparent that after 4 days a type B could be misinterpreted as a weak type C. Changes in the intensities of the different components of the EAP phenotypes did not occur often during the course of this study but did occur often enough to warrant discussion.

Whole blood containing citrate phosphate dextrose anti-coagulant and stored at 5°C was typed up to 10 months.

The effect of neuraminidase on EAP banding patterns during electrophoresis. The effect of neuraminidase on five EAP phenotype patterns is shown in figure 6. Selected fresh red cell hemolysates were treated with neuraminidase and stored at 25°C. Samples 1-4 contained no neuraminidase while samples 5-9 contained 10 units of neuraminidase/ml. After 114 hours, although all 9 samples had lost significant amounts of EAP activity, samples 1-4 remained typeable. Samples 5-9, containing neuraminidase had lost all observable EAP activity. The effect of neuraminidase on the five EAP phenotype patterns needs to be examined more closely but may involve the removal of sialic acid residues from the EAP enzyme. Although neuraminidase affects the heterogeneity of EAP phenotype patterns, it does not alter them in a manner which would lead to misinterpretation of pattern types.

Distribution of five EAP phenotypes among a randomly selected number of metropolitan Washington, D. C. area residents and among the ABO, MN and Rh blood groups. The incidence of five EAP phenotypes in 137 randomly selected negro and caucasian metropolitan Washington, D. C. area residents is shown in table 2. The computed frequencies of 10.2% type A, 44.5% type B, 38.0% type AB, 4.4% type CB and 2.9% type AC differs from those figures obtained by Giblett and Scott (3). They observed among 193 Seattle caucasians frequencies of 17.1% type A, 31.6% type B, 39.4% type AB, 6.73% type CB and 5.18% type AC. Among 164 negros frequencies of 7.32% type A, 60.4% type B, 29.3% type AB, 1.83% CB and 1.21% type AC were observed. No EAP type C's were observed in either study. If the data obtained by Giblett and Scott in the separate studies on negroes and

TABLE 1. EAP TYPING OF AGED-DRIED BLOODSTAINS
STORED AT 25°C

No. attempted	Age of stain	No. having EAP activity	No. typeable
	months		
6	1	6	6
6	2	6	6
8	4	8	8
6	5	6	4
5	7	5	4
6	10	6	3
8	12	7	2
8	15	3	0

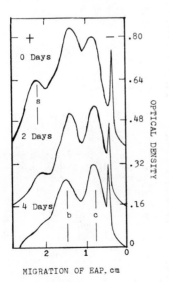

Figure 5. Densitometer tracings illustrating the loss in activity of the b isozyme of EAP phenotype CB in a dried bloodstain stored at 25°C

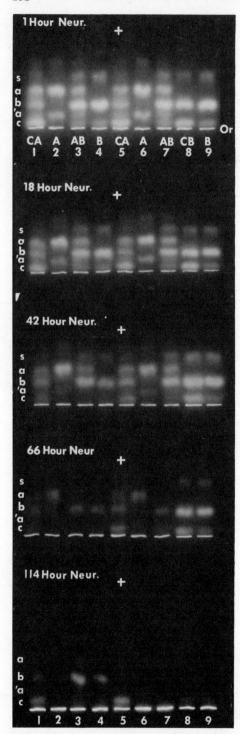

Figure 6. The effect of neuraminidase on the EAP phenotype patterns obtained during electrophoresis for 4 hr at 0°C. Samples 1–4 contained no neuraminidase. Samples 5–9 contained 10 units of neuraminidase activity per ml. All samples were incubated at 25°C. The photograph taken at 114 hr was exposed for 6 min to enhance EAP activity observed in samples 1–4. A 2-min exposure was used for photographs taken at the other times. The only EAP activity observed after incubation with neuraminidase for 114 hr was the c isozyme band of sample 5 (EAP phenotype AC). The c isozyme is the most stable of the four EAP isozymes (5).

caucasians are combined, it would then represent an approximate 60/40 mixture of caucasians to negroes. If new phenotype frequencies are then calculated, percentages of 12.2% type A, 44.8% type B, 34.4% type AB, 4.20% type CB and 3.36% type AC are obtained. The figures obtained by this combination are strikingly similar to the frequencies obtained in this study.

The distribution of five EAP phenotypes among blood groups ABO, MN and Rh is shown in table 3. Although the samples taken in some groups are small it is apparent that the incidence of EAP is not associated genetically with blood groups ABO, MN and Rh.

Discussion

EAP is a stable polymorphic enzyme which can, by electro-phoresis, be typed into six phenotypic patterns -- A, AB, B, CB, AC, and C (the rare type C was not observed in this study). Electrophoresis for 4 hours at $0^{\circ}C$ consistently gave sharper EAP banding patterns than electrophoresis for 15 hours at $5^{\circ}C$. The a' isozyme of types AB and AC was well defined during 4 hour electrophoresis and made the typing of EAP phenotype AB reliable and simple.

During electrophoresis runs, it is recommended that a fresh type AB or types A and B be used as controls to mark the migration and intensity of the various components of the six different EAP phenotypes. These controls will also aid in differentiating the true isozymes of the EAP types from storage bands s and s' which are associated respectively with the strong b and a isozymes. The rate of loss in activity of the five different EAP phenotypes during storage at $25^{\circ}C$ in hemolysates and clotted blood was determined to be the same. All five types lost essentially all typeable activity in 5-6 days under these conditions. In dried bloodstains, differences in the rates of loss in activity of the five EAP types was observed. Types CB, AC and B were observed to be the most stable, while type A was the least stable. Type AB is intermediate between types A and B. Dried bloodstains were typed blind up to 20 weeks but beyond that point caution should be exercised.

Occasional changes in activity of the b isozyme of types B and CB during storage at $25^{\circ}C$ in clotted and dried bloodstains were observed. This phenomenon is consistent with observations made by Luffman and Harris (5). During thermostability studies with five EAP phenotypes they found that the activity of the faster moving component (b isozyme) of type B became weaker as it was heated for 5 minutes at $52^{\circ}C$ while the activity of the slower component (c isozyme) became stronger. Both isozymes lost essentially all activity after 10 minutes.

Smith and Whitby (10) found that incubation of the human prostatic acid phosphatase in the presence of neuraminidase

TABLE 2. INCIDENCE OF EAP PHENOTYPES IN 137 RANDOMLY
SELECTED METROPOLITAN WASHINGTON D.C. RESIDENTS

EAP phenotypes	No. of individuals	Incidence %
A	14	10.2
AB	52	38.0
B	61	44.5
CB	6	4.4
AC	4	2.9
C	0	---
Total	137	

TABLE 3. DISTRIBUTION OF FIVE EAP PHENOTYPES AMONG
THE ABO, MN AND Rh BLOOD GROUPS

Phenotypes	ABO				MN			Rh	
	A*	B	AB	O	MN	M	N	+	-
A	3	2	0	1	2	1	2	4	1
AB	15	6	5	5	11	9	5	16	11
B	21	7	1	4	9	10	6	21	10
CB	4	0	0	0	2	0	2	3	1
AC	3	0	1	0	1	1	1	3	0
Totals	46	15	7	10	25	21	15	47	23

*Contains 2 A_2, each one having a different EAP
phenotype.

caused a redistribution of the faster moving electrophoretic components of this enzyme among its slower moving components. Although neuraminidase alters the heterogeneity of EAP electrophoretic patterns it does not alter them in a manner which would lead to misinterpretation of types.

The frequency of occurance of five EAP phenotypes was determined to be 10.2% A, 44.5% B, 38.0% AB, 4.4% CB and 2.9% CA among 137 randomly selected negro and caucasian metropolitan Washington, D. C. residents. These figures are in agreement with the results obtained by Giblett and Scott when the data obtained from separate studies among Seattle negro and caucasians were combined and new phenotype frequencies calculated. EAP is not genetically linked to the ABO, MN or Rh blood group systems.

Literature Cited

1. Hopkinson, D. A., Spencer, N., and Harris, H., Nature, (1963), 199, 969.
2. Hopkinson, D. A., Spencer, N., and Harris, H., Human Genetics, (1964), 16, 141.
3. Giblett, E. R., and Scott, N. M., Amer. J. Hum. Genet., (1965), 17, 425.
4. Sorensen, S. A., Human Heredity, (1973), 23, 470.
5. Luffman, J. E. and Harris, H., Ann. Hum. Genet., (1967), 30, 387.
6. Scott, E. M., J. Biol. Chem., (1966), 241, 3049.
7. Brinkmann, B., Gunnemann, M. and Koops, E., J. For. Med., (1972), 70, 68.
8. Fiedler, H., Arztl. Lab. (1967), 13, 507.
9. MacLennan, J. D., Bact. Rev., (1962), 26, 177.
10. Smith, J. K. and Whitby, L. G., Biochim. Biophys. Acta., (1968), 151, 607.
11. Hopkinson, D. A. and Harris, H., Biochemical Methods in Red Cell Genetics, 337, Editor J. J. Yunis, Academic Press, NY, 1969.
12. Wraxall, B. G. D. and Culliford, B. J., J. For. Sci. Soc., (1968), 8, 81.
13. Wraxall, B. G. D. and Adams, E. G., For. Sci., (1974), 3, 57.

17

Forensic Toxicology—The Current State of the Art and Relationship to Analytical Chemistry

BRYAN S. FINKLE

Center For Human Toxicology, University of Utah, Salt Lake City, Utah 84112

In general terms, toxicology is the study and understanding of the harmful effects of exogenous substances on living systems. Forensic toxicology is the practice of this biomedical science in a medico-legal context. In consequence, forensic toxicologists are to be found plying their professional expertise and technical skills in laboratories supporting the courts and the general criminal and civil justice system. Analyses of biological samples, and other materials thought to be poisoned, in order to produce factual data from which to interpret the condition of a poisoned victim or criminal suspect is the daily fare of the Forensic Toxicologist. Cases as various as drinking and/or drugged drivers, errant probationers and parolees with serious drug problems, drug involvement in homicide, grand larceny and other major crimes, assessing possible accident versus suicide and advising the coroner or medical examiner in fatal poisonings require high scientific acumen and professional maturity. Much of the necessary laboratory work can be realistically related to analytical chemistry, but the major professional aspect is a highly disciplined specialty of medical pharmacology.

There are some specific implications in the phrase, "State of the Art," which may shed some light and reason on the often mystified view other scientists hold of forensic toxicology and forensic science in general. It implies that there is more art than science in toxicology. This, of course, is simply not true, although the impression is consistent with a small, proud group of professionals (perhaps less than 300 in the U.S.A.), who until recent years were closed and communicative just between themselves and only showed their faces publicly via ridiculously dramatized and innaccurate accounts of their work in newspapers and T.V. series. The image is further fostered by the painful self-consciousness stemming from exposure in the charged atmosphere of the court room. Is there any other profession in which practitioners are routinely, aggressively cross-examined concerning the details of their work, qualifications, experience,

and even fitness for the job? Every effort is often made to
deprecate the science, and it is not surprising that the Forensic
Scientist has become perhaps too self-conscious of his awesome
responsibility in the life, liberty and death of others and
aware of his limitations to fulfill the role. Toxicologists are
not pseudo-scientists, much less warped chemists or clinical
biochemists, frustrated physicians, lawyers or police officers.
But their highly structured discipline is "people-science" and,
as such, cannot ignore the demands which go beyond cold objectivity. In this it is unique.

The quiet revolution in our justice system which has taken
place in the past decade has placed massive weight upon scientifically developed facts and "Expert Opinion". Forensic science
is no longer a luxury, jury-impressive, window dressing for the
trial attorney's case. It is a necessity. Today, no one can be
tried for drunken or drugged driving without evidence of blood
alcohol or drug concentration, and interpretation of those values
in terms of ability to safely operate a motor vehicle. Similarly,
prosecution for use or possession of narcotics or illegal drugs
requires scientific analysis and specific identification of the
suspect material. These are just two examples of many which
are bringing into focus the need for high caliber, trained and
experienced scientists in the forensic arena.

Efforts to bring forensic scientists together and to cor-
porately develop programs for professional progress and upgrading of standards have been successful through the American
Academy of Forensic Sciences and its Foundation. The formation
of the Federal Law Enforcement Assistance Administration, and
also the Drug Enforcement Administration, has greatly enhanced
recognition, and ultimately support, for needs in Forensic
Toxicology.

There is, however, a major gap which has barely been
addressed. The demand for trained forensic toxicologists is
increasing (similarly for clinical, environmental and industrial
toxicologists), but there is less than a handful of universities
in the United States offering appropriate education. It
should be stated that there are many with "toxicology" listed in
their catalogs, but what number of graduates are fitted when
they leave college to immediately enter the field and become
productive? Precious few indeed. Most current teaching is
solely academic and an adjunct to pharmacy, pharmacology or
biochemistry. Certainly the book knowledge is available, but
what is the purpose of all the knowledge if you don't know how
to use it? Forensic Science can only house people who know
how to apply their learning. Most forensic toxicologists
practicing today qualified in analytical chemistry or a life
science, then gravitated into the field via on-the-job training
and the slow accretion of practical skill and expertise in the
"school of hard-knocks". Ideally, a firm undergraduate
training in basic sciences, preferably chemistry and physics, is

required. This should be followed by graduate school education
with a major in pharmacology and a minor in biochemistry and
physiology. Concurrent training in laboratory techniques should
be emphasized, and, before graduation, a one-year internship
should be undertaken in an accredited forensic laboratory.
Forensic toxicologists are a very special breed, and they do require special training.

Although it is possible to discuss the practice of forensic
toxicology in broad, general references, it is important to
recognize that toxicology is local. It is local in terms of time
and place, and it is constantly changing. We live in a fast-
moving society, and forensic science mirrors the vogues, vanities
pleasures and abuses of society as no other profession does.
Drug abuse is illustrative of that fact: there are many drugs
popular on the West Coast that are rarely seen in the East, and
vice versa. Drugs which were a major problem perhaps five years
ago have now disappeared, to be supplanted by agents of greater
appeal, and usually of greater price. So it is with broader
toxicology. Accidental or deliberate misuse of pharmaceuticals
is the major cause of poisoning in the United States, but in less
developed countries it may be classic plant alkaloid poisons or
uncontrolled use of pesticides. In tropical countries it is perhaps snake and spider venoms. We are concerned with the forensic
toxicologist today--in the United States. What then are the types
of problems, how are they resolved, what techniques are used,
and what does the immediate future hold?

There are three major case-load areas in most forensic
toxicology laboratories. They are cases resulting directly from
the illegal use of drugs - "Drug Abuse", toxicology aspects of
broad, criminal investigations - "Police cases", and analytical
studies in support of the Medical Examiner to determine cause-of-
death - "Post-mortem cases". In addition, many forensic laboratories undertake to assist local hospitals and physicians with
clinical diagnoses and patient care in emergency poisoning
cases or those patients requiring complex drug therapy. Although
many hospital clinical laboratories are now developing the
specialized facilities and talent required for clinical toxicology, (currently there is also a mushroom growth of private
laboratories), in most areas the forensic laboratory is the only
available service. It fulfills a mutual need. The physician
requires rapid, specific identification of the agent involved,
and advice concerning the seriousness of the patient's condition.
The toxicologist requires, and is able to develop through
clinical experience, a broad analytical data and experience base
from which to assess drug involvement in police and post-mortem
investigations. It is desirable and necessary that collaboration
in the clinical and forensic areas continue if the tax-paying
community is to get the best possible service.

Court-issued Probation Orders regularly state that chemical
testing must be part of the rehabilitation program for any pro-

bationer with a drug abuse problem - juvenile or adult. Urine
samples, taken at the discretion of the Probation Officer at
irregular intervals, are analyzed to determine whether the
probationer is abstaining from drug use. A judge may command
that a blood or urine sample be obtained immediately from a
defendant appearing in court if he seems to be intoxicated.
This occurs surprisingly often! Analyses are frequently requested for inmates of county jails and minimum security prisons
where alcohol and drug problems are often rampant. Control and
treatment of heroin addicts through methadone clinics also
requires toxicological analyses in surveillance of their behavior and response to treatment. It is not unusual for a
thousand cases of this type to be submitted each month to a
laboratory serving an urban community of one million
people.

In the category of "Police cases", the toxicologist's
greatest load comes from drinking and drugged driver cases.
This is an enormous social problem with difficult and demanding
analytical toxicology implications. These cannot be fully
discussed in this paper. Suffice it to say that 10,000-15,000
cases annually from a million population is not unusual.
Certainly, most involve only alcohol and can be efficiently
processed by excellent mechanized or semi-automated methods,
but those involving other drugs pose extremely difficult
problems. The number and variety of drugs and active metabolites
to be detected and quantitated in perhaps five milliliters of
blood is legion, and toxicologically effective concentrations
are infinitesimal - nanograms/milliliter. To further complicate
matters, definitive interpretation is demanded: a metabolite
of an antidepressant drug; having sworn to tell the whole truth,
state unequivocally whether this substance did in fact impair
the defendant's ability to drive. That is when the forensic
toxicologist is put on his mettle. Adequate analytical procedures and techniques are only now being developed to satisfy
this type of case, and yet strong laws are already in the
statute books of most states. The resulting dilemma for the
toxicologist results from the not uncommon human propensity to
put the cart before the horse: to promulgate laws to regulate
a subjectively apparent social problem without thorough study
of needs and priorities and before the means for effective
enforcement have been developed.

It has been determined that,in some areas, ninety percent
of all crime is drug-related, whether it be burglary to raise
cash to buy drugs, or violent crimes perpetrated under the
influence of drugs. All these police investigations now
involve the toxicologist. The increase in these types of cases
and the accompanying demand by investigators and courts for
prompt service has forced the analyst into the forefront of
sophisticated methodology development which now includes
mechanized immunoassays and mass spectrometry. Additionally,

there is a myriad of criminal cases brought to the laboratory.
They range from adulterated candy given to children at Halloween,
dead dogs perhaps poisoned in a neighborhood dispute, to child
abuse and revenge and spiteful episodes en famille or between
once-loving friends. There is no wrath to match that of the
scorned lover! They all demand care and analytical ingenuity.
     The Coroner or Medical Examiner is responsible for deter-
mining cause-of-death in the sudden or unexplained demise of
all persons in his jurisdiction. The terms of his work are
legally defined whether he operates on a state or local, county
basis. To assist him he relies heavily upon trained investigators, forensic pathologists and of course the toxicologist.
At least one thousand autopsies per year (many more in major
cities) are routine in most Medical Examiner Offices. The
bulk of the cases for the toxicologist are suspected suicides,
accidental overdose cases or deaths in which it is important
to establish whether the victim was taking prescribed medication,
for example, a known epileptic who was on chronic anticonvulsant
therapy, a middle aged business executive on drugs to control
hypertension or a heart ailment, the controlled diabetic and
the thousands for whom tranquilizers have become a daily necessity. For any of these individuals, dying in an automobile
accident, in their sleep, or following sudden collapse at
work, it is obviously important to ascertain the extent to which
their drug use (or lack of it) may have contributed to the total
circumstance surrounding their death. There are a remarkable
number of people who manage to poison themselves by self-medi-
cation with multiple, apparently harmless over-the-counter drugs
or left-over prescription tablets in the medicine cabinet.
Despite spectacular advances in pharmacology and pharmacy
and Federal control, there are too many people poisoned as a
result of medical mismanagement, pharmaceutical company
propaganda, and public advertising of the latest cure-all
wonder drug. This fact alone is likely to keep the forensic
toxicologist in business with indefinite job security.
     Samples of blood and organ tissues taken at autopsy are
rarely in a physiological state when received for analysis, and
therefore present a particular challenge to accomplish clean
extraction of the toxicological agent. Accurate quantitative
data are often extremely difficult to obtain in these cases,
and, in consequence, interpretation of results as to lethality or
toxicological significance within a set circumstance surrounding
the death generally requires the deft, cautious touch of experience. Collaborative efforts to pool and discuss case experiences
by members of the International Association of Forensic Toxicologists and local groups such as the California Association of
Toxicologists and their counterparts in Great Britain and
Europe have enormously improved the real basis upon which such
opinion is founded.
     Alcohol in combination with other central nervous system

depressants, tranquilizers and narcotics are the major offenders. Carbon monoxide is still a popular means of suicide; and aspirin and antihistamines are particularly common in children. Although these agents generally present uncomplicated problems, the analysis of multiple drugs and their metabolites in degraded or frankly putrified tissue require specialized methods. Unfortunately, the latter is the usual situation. Methods sensitive in the picogram range are necessary for many CNS, highly lipid soluble, or highly polar drugs including cocaine, tricyclic antidepressants and pesticides, together with their active metabolites. Resolution of a major pharmacological problem, e.g., toxic drug interaction or another thalidomide, a public health crisis, e.g., thallium or pollutants in drinking water, proper disposition of a will or insurance benefit, or pinpointing a new drug of abuse may well depend upon the skills of the forensic toxicologist.

Any toxicological analysis involves two broad steps; the first is extraction of the toxic agent from the biological matrix and the second is identification and quantitation of the isolated material. There are very few useful tests which can be applied directly to body fluids. Exceptions are urine screening tests for salicylate, ethclorvynol, and phenothiazine drugs. Most notably, enzyme, radio, and spin-label immunoassay techniques have been developed to determine some narcotics and sedative hypnotics in urine and this has been of immense assistance in analyzing the very large numbers of urine samples related to drug abuse control programs. These methods are rapid, extremely sensitive and require very little sample. Unfortunately they are plagued by cross reactions which severely limit their specificity. If this technique could be extended to plasma for a broad range of drugs it would be a major breakthrough to rapid screening of samples from intoxicated drivers. It is also possible to very quickly screen gastric lavage samples from overdosed victims in the hospital emergency room by chemical ionization mass spectrometry but this is not yet common practice.

Almost all commonly encountered toxic agents are organic and therefore the extraction and identification methods have much in common with classic organic chemical analysis. The exceptions are obviously the heavy metals, for example, arsenic, lead, mercury, thallium,etc.. These inorganics are usually identified by atomic absorption spectroscopy, although energy dispersive x-ray is finding increasing application. The latter is rapid, requires minimal sample preparation, is non-destructive and combines the ability to screen a large number of elements and simultaneously quantitate those detected. For the organic drugs and poisons however, liquid-liquid extraction has remained the method of choice. Use of various organic solvents and solvent mixtures to directly extract homogenized biological samples at appropriate pH, is the basis of most schemes. Extraction at strong alkaline, weak alkaline (pH 8.5) and acid pH

into chloroform will efficiently isolate basic drugs, amphoteric
drugs such as morphine, and weak acids such as barbiturates. Of
course, many drugs are neutral and extract at any pH value.
n-Butyl chloride is a favored solvent for many basic drugs,
and chloroform : isopropanol 4:1 is best for morphine and its
analogues. Prior protein precipitation may be necessary in
particularly intractable samples and ion-exchange or charcoal
absorption have some applications.

The extracted drugs in the solvent fractions are concentrated before further separation and identification. Gas chromatography (GC) and thin-layer chromatography are the staple
techniques, and GC also permits quantitation using suitable
internal standards. Ultraviolet spectrophotometry continues
to be important as a quantitative method and the massive files
of available reference data ensure its future in toxicology.
These and other procedures are well reviewed by Jackson (1)
Sunshine (2) and Finkle (3), and are recommended to those
interested in the routine methods.

The necessity to specifically identify sub-microgram
amounts of extracted drugs and metabolites has been revolution-
ized by the advent of gas chromatography-mass spectrometry(GC-MS),
The demand for analyses with a high degree of accuracy, precision and qualitative specificity has become acute in the face
of wide-spread drug abuse and the medical need to monitor
patients undergoing complex drug therapy. Chromatographic methods
are empirical and do not of themselves provide a solution.
They generally lack sensitivity and a direct relation to molecular
structure. GC-MS is fast, direct, and very sensitive, and the
spectrum provides a result which puts identification beyond
dispute. Computer-assisted systems are now available which embody
extensive drug reference libraries and can be automatically
searched to identify unknown spectra. The further development
of chemical ionization and mass fragmentography methods using
stable isotopes now permits very accurate quantitative work.
Only the current cost of the equipment prevents this instrumentation from becoming the toxicologist's prime tool. High pressure
liquid chromatography is also destined for a long future in
toxicology. The ability to separate polar metabolites is an
outstanding problem that could be overcome by this technique.
It too may soon be married to the mass spectrometer. The
need and tendency, then, is away from crude macro methods towards semi-automated rapid and sensitive instrumental procedures,
with an emphasis on specificity.

The interpretation of the data in relation to case circumstance is a perennial problem requiring much further work.
Efforts are underway, and must continue, to compile reliable
reference data on plasma and tissue concentrations of drugs
following therapeutic dosage; similarly in post-mortem cases.
The ability to analyze this data so that its essence can be
used to predict or evaluate future cases has barely begun to

grow and this remains a major task of tomorrow.

Meanwhile, the forensic toxicologist has come far in our fast-moving society from the days of hemlock and arsenic to pesticides and narcotics. There is much work to be done, but with good science and a sense of personal involvement much will be accomplished. This light, broad-brush picture of the forensic toxicologist at work is a glimpse at best, but perhaps the curtain has been raised and the interest of his fellow scientists stimulated to inquire further into the analytic arts.

Literature Cited

1. Jackson, J.V., The Pharmaceutical Press, (1969) Ed. E.G.C. Clarke, Extraction Methods in Toxicology in Isolation and Identification of Drugs.
2. Sunshine, I., Manual of Analytical Toxicology, Chemical Rubber Company, (1971).
3. Finkle, B.S., Anal. Chem. Special Report $\underline{44}$(9), (1972) Forensic Toxicology of Drug Abuse.

18

A Comparison of Heroin Samples

S. P. SOBOL and A. R. SPERLING

U. S. Department of Justice, Drug Enforcement Administration,
Special Testing and Research Laboratory, McLean, Va. 22101

The comparison of evidence is a well-established function of the forensic laboratory. Fields of expertise such as document examination, fingerprint analysis, firearms examination, as well as a myriad of other types of examination, all rely on the comparison of an exhibit with either a reference collection or another specific exhibit.

Little attention, however, has been given to the comparison of drug exhibits. The potential value of such types of analyses is equally as great as in other fields. If correlations among drug exhibits can be made, then distribution systems may be identified and conspiracy cases developed. Also, comparisons of exhibits can provide more specific information to the investigator or intelligence analyst.

One means of comparing drug exhibits is to identify the impurities which are present in the material and to determine their relative concentrations. Although some previous work has been reported regarding impurities associated with clandestinely produced methamphetamine (1,2) most of the comparison analyses have dealt with heroin.

As a result of the clandestine processes used in the production of heroin, the final product may contain not only heroin but also monoacetylmorphine, acetylcodeine, opium alkaloids, and other trace impurities. At the street level, heroin exhibits also contain adulterants such as quinine, procaine, methapyrilene, and various sugars. The determination of all these substances provides a good basis on which to compare heroin exhibits.

Schlesinger et al (3) reported that non-destructive neutron activation analysis (NAA) can be employed to compare drugs sold in illicit channels through the determination of their elemental compositions. This early work was amplified by Pro and Brunelle (4), combining atomic absorption analysis with NAA. Although the determination of elemental composition can be useful, this approach suffers from the fact that it may not be used when heroin has been packaged differently or adulterated with another material.

Lerner and Mills (5) reported the presence of O^6-monoacetyl-morphine as a common constituent in heroin and suggested that the ratio of heroin to monoacetylmorphine would not change during adulteration. Others have dealt primarily with the identification of the adulterants present, either other drug substances or sugars (6,7). Grooms (8) and Miller (9) have attempted to include the analysis of adulterants with the presence of monoacetylmorphine. In each of these cases, the resolution of the various components was insufficient to provide good quantitative data.

We have developed method for the quantitative determination of heroin, O^6-monoacetylmorphine, acetylcodeine, morphine, and codeine which is applicable to a wide variety of heroin samples. Since the relative proportion of these substances should remain unchanged during any additional handling of the material, this method enables one to compare seemingly unlike heroin samples. This information, coupled with other analytical information such as the physical appearance of the exhibit and the presence or absence of adulterants, provides a good basis on which to compare exhibits.

Two procedures are presented for the analysis of these heroin impurities, one involving derivatization of the material followed by gas chromatographic analysis, and the other a direct gas chromatographic analysis. The derivatization method is the preferred procedure in that all components are well resolved on the chromatogram whereas O^6-monoacetylmorphine and acetylcodeine are not totally separated in the direct method. Also, the reproducibility of the former has been found to be superior.

Although the derivatization method is preferred, it is not applicable to many heroin exhibits, due to the adulterants present. Sugars, in particular, will react with silylating reagents, thus causing incomplete reaction of the reagent with the impurities of interest or interfering with the peaks of interest in the chromatogram. Therefore, preliminary screening consisting of microscopic examination, color and crystal tests, and thin-layer chromatography must be performed to tentatively identify the adulterants present, if any.

Derivatization Procedure.

Transfer a portion of the exhibit equivalent to approximately 25 mg of heroin to a 1 ml glass-stoppered test tube. Add 0.2 ml of chloroform and 0.3 ml of N,O-Bis-(trimethylsilyl)-trifluoroacetamide (BSTFA). Mix and heat at 75°C for ninety minutes giving the tube an occasional shake. Use 2-5 microliters of the solution for gas chromatographic analysis.

Due to the wide differences in concentrations of these substances usually found in heroin exhibits, the peak areas must

be determined on an electronic integrator. To obtain a
relative concentration of these components, the area normalization technique is utilized. The peak area of each component of
interest is divided by the sum total peak area obtained in the
chromatogram and multiplied by 100.

For example, the percentage of morphine would be determined
by the following formula:

$$\frac{\text{Area of morphine-TMS peak}}{\text{Total peak area in chromatogram}} \times 100 = \%$$

Equipment:
    Gas Chromatograph: Perkin-Elmer Model 900
    Electronic Integrator: Infotronics CRS-101

Gas Chromatographic Conditions:
              Detector: flame ionization
         Carrier gas: nitrogen
          Flow rate: 60 ml/min.
             Column: glass column, 6 ft. x 1/4 in. packed
                     with 3% OV-25 on Gas Chrom Q*,
                     100/120 mesh

Injector
Temperature: 265°C

Column
Temperature: approximately 240°C

Detector Temperature: 265°C

The column temperature should be adjusted to give the
following retention times:

COMPOUND	APPROXIMATE RETENTION TIME IN MINUTES
Morphine-TMS	5.6
Codeine-TMS	6.7
O^6-monoacetylmorphine-TMS	9.8
Acetylcodeine	12.4
Heroin	19.0

A typical chromatogram is shown in Figure 1.
Morphine and codeine usually occur in the samples at very
low concentrations. Under the conditions used the practical
lower limit of detection is approximately 15 to 25 nanograms.
Linearity studies were run and the compounds were found to
be linear in at least the ranges indicated.

---

*Applied Science Laboratories, Inc., State College, Pa.

COMPOUND	RANGE
Codeine-TMS	25 nanograms to 2 micrograms
Morphine-TMS	25 nanograms to 4 micrograms
O^6-monoacetylmorphine-TMS	1 microgram to 7 micrograms
Acetylcodeine	1 microgram to 9 micrograms

To check on the reproducibility of injections, four samples were studied. They were injected ten times each at a concentration of 60 mg/ml and ten times each at a concentration of 10 mg/ml. The range and coefficients of variation were calculated and are given in Table I.

Direct Gas Chromatographic Analysis.

As mentioned above, complete separation of components using this procedure cannot be achieved, (Figure 2). Acetylcodeine is not completely resolved from O^6-monoacetylmorphine and thus the peak areas represent only a good estimate of the ratios. Also, because of the additional substances present in adulterated samples, the peak area normalization method is applied only to those peaks due to heroin processing, including opium alkaloids, if present.
To approximately 30 mg of sample, add 0.5 ml of methanol. Use 2-5 microliters for gas chromatographic analysis.
Equipment:
    Chromatograph: Perkin-Elmer Model 900
    Electronic Integrator: Infotronics CRS-101

Gas Chromatographic Conditions:
        Detector: flame ionization
    Carrier Gas: nitrogen
    Flow rate: approximately 60 ml/min.
      Column: glass column 6 ft. x 1/4 in. packed with 3% OV-25 on Gas Chrom Q*, 100/120 mesh

Injector
Temperature: 275°C

Column Temperature: 265°C

Detector Temperature: 275°C

---

* Applied Science Laboratories, Inc., State College, Pa.

Using these conditions, the retention times are as follows.

TABLE I

	60 mg/ml Range Percent	Coef-Variation	10 mg/ml Range Percent	Coef-Variation
Sample 1				
Morphine	.031 – .040	8.0%	--	--
Codeine	.006 – .008	9.6%	--	--
O^6-monoacetyl-morphine	1.31 – 1.65	6.9%	1.20 – 1.31	3.8%
Acetylcodeine	5.06 – 5.72	4.7%	4.92 – 5.22	2.9%
Heroin	92.7 – 94.0	0.4%		
Sample 2				
Morphine	.022 – .033	12.5%	--	--
Codeine	.007 – .009	9.9%	--	--
O^6-monoacetyl-morphine	1.54 – 1.75	4.3%	1.35 – 1.52	5.5%
Acetylcodeine	7.07 – 7.95	4.1%	6.79 – 7.13	6.9%
Heroin	90.5 – 91.4	0.3%		
Sample 3				
Morphine	.684 – .722	1.5%	.610 – .787	7.5%
Codeine	.114 – .122	3.1%	.101 – .170	17.1%
O^6-monoacetyl-morphine	7.64 – 7.99	1.7%	6.59 – 7.50	4.5%
Acetylcodeine	10.68 – 11.32	1.9%	10.54 – 11.37	2.5%
Heroin	80.68 – 81.44	0.2%		

TABLE I (Continued)

	60 mg/ml Range Percent	Coef-Variation	10 mg/ml Range Percent	Coef-Variation
Sample 4A				
Morphine	.143 — .160	3.7%	.135 — .166	6.2%
Codeine	.029 — .037	7.9%	.020 — .028	2.9%
O^6-monoacetyl-morphine	2.50 — 2.81	3.3%	2.26 — 2.40	4.2%
Acetylcodeine	5.41 — 6.18	6.2%	5.16 — 5.68	3.3%
Heroin	91.7 — 91.9	0.1%		
Sample 4B				
Morphine	.151 — .158	1.4%		
Codeine	.034 — .036	2.6%		
O^6-monoacetyl-morphine	2.45 — 2.52	0.7%		
Acetylcodeine	5.46 — 5.59	0.1%		
Heroin	91.7 — 91.9			

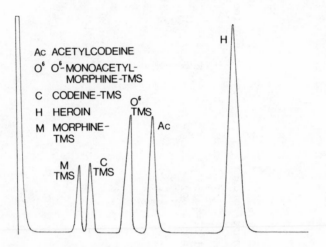

Figure 1.   *Derivatized heroin*

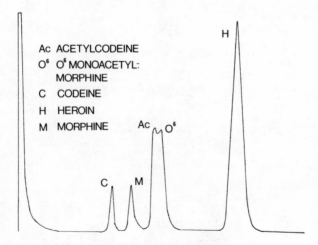

Figure 2.   *Underivatized heroin*

COMPOUND	APPROXIMATE RETENTION TIME IN MINUTES
Methapyrilene	1.0
Procaine	1.1
Acetylprocaine	2.5
Codeine	3.4
Morphine	3.9
Acetylcodeine	4.5
0^6-monoacetylmorphine	4.7
Thebaine	5.7
Heroin	6.6
Papaverine	13.5
Noscapine*	32.2

* Noscapine has been found to occur in such low concentrations that it is not usually detected under the above conditions.

The above techniques have been used in this laboratory on over 100 different heroin exhibits in the past two years. For the most part, the analyses have been limited to specific exhibits where intelligence had indicated a probable connection between two or more cases. The laboratory examination was requested to prove or disprove this connection. The following studies demonstrate how the analytical information can be used.

Table II shows the percent of heroin-HCl in eight exhibits. The first six exhibits are associated with a case originating in Texas; the last two exhibits are associated with a case originating in Michigan. The microscopic appearance of the three uncut heroin exhibits was identical (T 1775, T 1776, M 1832). The microscopic appearance of the five samples cut with lactose revealed the presence of poorly crystallized lactose monohydrate. The X-ray diffraction patterns of all the cut samples were similar. Table III shows the ratios of the impurities present in each of the exhibits. Even though many of the exhibits had been cut, a constant relationship of the relative concentrations of the by-products was found, except with the last sample (M 1833). From these results, we concluded that the heroin in one of the exhibits (M 1832) in the Michigan case did correspond with those found in Texas. We also concluded that all exhibits of the Texas case came from a common source, and, finally, that two sources of heroin existed in the Michigan case.

The comparison of heroin exhibits has also been used successfully in court in helping to establish a conspiracy. Comparative analyses were conducted on five exhibits from two different cases. The preliminary examination revealed that the excipients and diluents in each case were: sucrose, quinine hydrochloride, mannitol, corn starch, and lactose monohydrate.

TABLE II

Heroin Comparison

Lab. No.	Percent Heroin-HCl	Lactose
T 1771	30.2	+
T 1772	32.6	+
T 1774	31.4	+
T 1775	94.9	-
T 1776	93.0	-
T 1777	36.0	+
M 1832	95.1	-
M 1833	19.3	+

TABLE III

Ratio of By-Products

Lab. No.	Morphine	O^6-Monoacetyl-Morphine	Codeine	Acetyl-Codeine	Heroin-HCl
T 1771	–	1.70	0.13	2.69	95.5
T 1772	–	1.81	0.09	2.85	95.2
T 1774	–	1.89	–	2.88	94.7
T 1775	0.03	1.90	0.06	2.97	95.0
T 1776	–	1.95	0.12	3.25	94.7
T 1777	–	1.80	–	3.01	95.2
M 1832	0.03	1.92	0.10	3.13	94.8
M 1833	0.03	2.40	0.30	3.35	93.2

TABLE IV

Packet #	Assay, % Heroin·HCl	Quinine·HCl	O^6 Monoacetyl-morphine	Profile, %[1] Acetylcodeine	Heroin
Exh. 1					
1	17.1	4.62	1.76	0.82	97.4
2	16.5	5.43	2.09	0.80	97.1
3	16.5	4.64	3.98	0.69	95.3
			3.27	0.80	95.9
5	19.2	4.49	3.27	0.80	95.9
Exh. 2					
1	14.0	4.49	4.19	0.82	95.0
2	18.7	4.88	3.98	1.18	94.8
3	17.0	3.24	2.53	0.73	96.7
4	18.1	3.93	4.05	0.71	95.2
5	17.7	4.18	3.59	0.68	95.7
6	17.8	4.39	2.14	1.02	96.8
7	17.3	4.33	2.66	1.14	96.2
8	17.7	3.90	2.66	1.14	96.2
9	18.5	3.94	4.00	0.79	95.2
10	17.1	3.69	2.86	0.85	96.3
11	17.1	4.32			
Exh. 1					
1	17.9	4.32	2.57	0.90	96.5
2			3.77	0.85	95.4

TABLE IV (Continued)

Packet #	Assay,% Heroin·HCl	Quinine·HCl	Profile,%[1] O⁶ Monoacetyl-morphine	Acetylcodeine	Heroin
Exh. 2					
1	17.7	4.24	6.07	0.77	93.2
2	18.4	3.97	1.78	0.80	97.5
3	18.1	4.35	5.57		94.4
4	18.2	4.02	3.50	0.86	95.6
5	17.7	3.76	2.73	1.11	96.2
6	17.2	4.57	6.64	0.68	92.7
7	18.1	4.09	3.43	0.79	95.8
8	17.0	4.26	4.76	0.76	94.5
9	15.9	5.37	2.50	0.85	96.7
10			1.86	0.92	97.2
Exh 3					
1			2.05	0.93	97.0
2	16.6	4.56	1.72	0.90	97.4

(1) These percentages are determined by dividing the area obtained for each alkaloid by the total area for all three alkaloids.

Quantitative analysis showed that the concentrations of heroin
and quinine in all exhibits were approximately equal. The
determination of the relative concentrations of heroin impurities are given in Table IV, and were all similar. Expert
testimony was given that all five exhibits originated from a
common source and this testimony was an integral part of the
prosecution's case establishing a conspiracy.

Work is continuing on the analysis of heroin exhibits
to develop a larger data base. Work is also continuing on
more quantitative methods for adulterated heroin samples.

In conclusion, methods have been presented for the
comparison of heroin samples. These analytical procedures have
been successfully used for both intelligence purposes and court
testimony.

Literature Cited

1. LeBelle, M., Sileika, M., and Romack, M., (1973)
J. PHARM. SCI., 62, 862.

2. Barron, R., Kruegel, A., Moore, J. and Kram, T.,
J. ASSOC. OFFICIAL ANAL. CHEM. (in press).

3. Schlesinger, H., Pro, M., Hoffman, D., and Cohan, M.,
(1965), J. ASSOC. OFFICIAL ANAL. CHEM., 48, 1139-1147.

4. Pro, M. and Brunelle, R., (1970), J. ASSOC. OFFICIAL ANAL.
CHEM., 53, 1137-1139.

5. Lerner, M. and Mills, A., (1963), U.N. BULL. NARCOTICS,
15, 37.

6. Fulton, C., (1965), INTERN. MICROFILM J. LEGAL MED., 1,
Card 2, G-1.

7. Broich, J., DeMayo, M., and Dal Cortivo, L., (1968)
J. CHROM., 33, 526-529.

8. Grooms, J., (1968), J. ASSOC. OFFICIAL ANAL. CHEM., 51,
1010-1013.

9. Miller, M., (1972), J. FORENSIC SCIENCES 16, 150-163.

New Applications of Photoluminescence Techniques for Forensic Science

PETER F. JONES

The Aerospace Corp., El Segundo, Calif. 90245

I shall describe the useful properties of photoluminescence and the current application of these properties in forensic science. New applications of photoluminescence developed or being investigated in our laboratory are also described. We have used photoluminescence techniques to: (a) locate and identify seminal stains, (b) detect lead and antimony gunshot residue at the nanogram level, and (c) discriminate between different glass and human (head) hair samples. All of these techniques can be carried out rapidly in the crime laboratory.

Luminescence is a general term and has different meanings depending on the field of application. I am concerned here with photoluminescence, which can be defined as the light emitted by a chemical species in the ultraviolet-visible wavelength region of the electromagnetic spectrum (300 to 700 nm) when excited with ultraviolet radiation (190 to 380 nm). Absorption of ultraviolet radiation by a luminescent molecule causes it to undergo an electronic transition from the ground state, i.e., the state of lowest energy, to a higher energy or excited state. When a molecule in the excited state returns to its ground energy state, a portion of its excess energy is released through the emission of light. Luminescent properties of use are (a) the excitation and emission spectra, i.e., intensity versus wavelength (the excitation spectrum is a plot of the variation in the luminescence intensity as the wavelength of the exciting radiation is varied), (b) the decay time of the luminescence once the excitation source is extinguished, and (c) the quantum yield of emission, i.e., the ratio of the number of molecules that emit light to the number of molecules that absorb excitation. The luminescence can consist of both fluorescence and phosphorescence. The fluorescence of most molecules appears at shorter wavelengths and has a fast decay time (10^{-9} to 10^{-6} sec), whereas the phosphorescence appears at longer wavelengths and has a longer decay time (10^{-6} to 10 sec).

Photoluminescence analysis has the advantages that (a) it can be highly selective because the absorption, emission, and lifetime parameters must match; (b) it is highly sensitive; (c) it is often nondestructive; (d) it is inexpensive to perform; and (e) it often does not require the separation of complex mixtures.

Current Uses of Photoluminescence in Forensic Science

The most beneficial advantage of photoluminescence analysis is its high sensitivity, which is less than a nanogram for efficient emitters. Because of this sensitivity, it has been used extensively in forensic science for a variety of applications involving inspection with ultraviolet light. Typically, a hand-held low-pressure mercury lamp is used with filters as an ultraviolet excitation source, and the materials of interest are visually inspected (sometimes making use of another filter to discriminate luminescence colors). Applications include the examination of documents, e.g., for forgeries; the location of body fluid stains; the comparison of oils, greases, paint chips, and glass fragments; and, most frequently used, the visualization of spots in paper or thin-layer chromatography. Occasionally, emission spectra have been obtained with a recording spectrophotofluorometer to compare paint, ink, glass, minerals, paper fillers, and plastics. More recently, it has been shown to be useful for drug analyses such as screening for morphine in body fluids (1) and for the comparison of motor oils (2). Udenfriend (3), Guilbault (4), Konstantinova-Shlezinger (5), and Kirk (6) have summarized many of these applications.

New Applications of Photoluminescence Techniques

The high sensitivity and specificity of photoluminescence analysis should make it possible to individualize clue materials, e.g., hair and glass, by the characteristic luminescence properties of trace constituents or impurities. Of particular significance are the newer techniques of analyzing the luminescence decay curves. For example, even when the absorption and luminescence spectra of the impurities are similar, it is possible to determine their concentrations if their luminescence lifetimes differ. The usefulness of this technique is illustrated in Figs. 1 and 2, where it is shown that the fluorescence spectra of naphthalene (N) and 1,6-dimethyl napthalene (DMN) are too similar for fluorescence spectral analysis of their mixtures (Fig. 1); yet their relative concentrations can be readily determined from the fluorescence decay curve (Fig. 2). As indicated by the dashed curve in Fig. 2, the observed decay is the sum of exponential decays from a shorter lived component, i.e., DMN (lifetime ~ 50 nsec) and a longer lived component, i.e., N (lifetime ~ 100 nsec). St. John and Winefordner (7) have discussed this technique in general and Hoerman and co-workers (8,9) have been

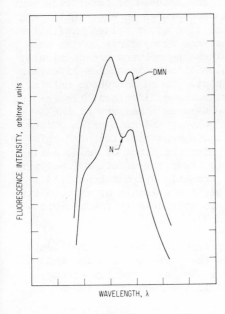

Figure 1. Representation of the fluorescence spectra of naphthalene (N) and 1,6-dimethylnaphthalene (DMN)

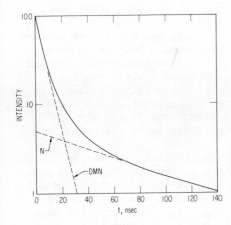

Figure 2. Fluorescence decay curve for pulsed excitation of a mixture of naphthalene (N) and 1,6-dimethylnaphthalene (DMN) with a concentration ratio of 5:95. The fluorescence intensity (arbitrary units) is plotted on a logarithmic scale.

investigating the possibility of using it for differential
identification of micro-organisms and body connective tissue.

Luminescence decay curves are also often used to verify that
samples do not contain impurities. The absence of impurities can
be established if the luminescence decay curve is exponential and
if the spectrum does not change with time after pulsed excitation.
However, in some cases, the luminescence decay curve can be nonexponential even if all of the luminescing solutes are chemically
identical. This occurs for molecules with luminescence lifetimes
that depend upon the local environment. In an amorphous matrix,
there is a variation in solute luminescence lifetimes. Therefore,
the luminescence decay curve can be used as a measure of the
interaction of the solute with the solvent and as a probe of the
micro-environment. Nag-Chaudhuri and Augenstein (10) used this
technique in their studies of the phosphorescence of amino acids
and proteins, and we have used it to study the effects of polymer
matrices on the phosphorescence of aromatic hydrocarbons (11).
This sensitivity of the luminescence of a molecule or atom to its
micro-environment is a very important attribute in the individualization of clue material.

Seminal Stains. As previously reported, we have used luminescence decay properties to detect the presence of semen on
strong fluorescent backgrounds (12). We have recently extended
the use of this technique as an aid in the identification of
semen (13).

In the crime laboratory, absolute proof that a stain is of
seminal origin is only afforded by the microscopic observation of
intact spermatozoa. However, one laboratory reported that spermatozoa were observed in only approximately 50% of the cases where a
stain was suspected to be of seminal origin. In cases where no
spermatozoa are found, alternate methods have been developed for
seminal stain "identification."

Two methods commonly used to test for seminal stains are the
acid phosphatase test and the Florence test. Both tests were
developed on the basis of the reaction of an introduced compound
with substances that are present in seminal fluid. Positive
results for these tests are either the formation of a characteristic color or the formation of specific crystals. Since the substances tested are also present in other body fluids and in
vegetable juices, the specificity of these tests has been
questioned (14).

It has been well-established that certain amino acids, i.e.,
phenylalanine, tyrosine, and tryptophan, both fluoresce and phosphoresce (15). We believe that a combination of these amino acids
is responsible for the observed luminescence of seminal fluid.
Furthermore, it seems reasonable that either this combination of
amino acids would not be present or would not occur in the same
proportions in other body fluids or substances of biological
origin. Therefore, differentiation between seminal fluid and

other substances on the basis of phosphorescence behavior appears
to be an attractive technique.

The approach in our study was to use the phosphorescence
examination as an adjunct to the acid phosphatase test. Stains of
the different materials were prepared, and their luminescence
properties were visually noted using hand-held, short- and long-
wavelength excitation lamps. The results of this simple test are
given in Table 1. Only four of the materials tested, i.e., vaginal fluid, almonds, rice and rattlesnake venom, gave phosphorescence results that were difficult to separate from those of
seminal fluid. However, all but the vaginal fluid were easily
distinguished by other luminescent characteristics. Thus, when
the phosphorescence and acid phosphatase tests are combined with
the recently introduced electrophoresis procedures for the separation of vaginal and seminal acid phosphatase (16,17,18), a
positive identification of semen is possible, even in the absence
of spermatozoa.

Detection of Gunshot Residue. When a suspect has been appre-
hended following a shooting, detection of gunshot residue on his
hands may provide significant evidence in the investigation.
Previous methods of gunshot residue detection, which are of ques-
tionable reliability because of their lack of sensitivity or
specificity, include the color test for nitrates (19) and the
color tests of Harrison and Gilroy (20) for antimony (Sb), barium
(Ba), and lead (Pb), the three most characteristic metallic elements found in gunshot residue. Until recently, the method in
general use for detecting residue on hands, although the use of
this method is not nearly as widespread as need would dictate, was
the application of neutron activation analysis to detect antimony
and barium (21). This method has serious drawbacks, e.g., the
time and inconvenience of sending samples out for analysis and the
inability to detect lead.

I describe here the results of our preliminary study (22) of
the application of photoluminescence techniques to gunshot residue
detection. The key objective in this study was to develop a
rapid, reliable, and convenient method of detection for use in the
crime laboratory on the basis of the detection of lead, antimony,
and barium. We did not attempt to repeat the extensive work
already carried out with neutron activation analysis concerning
the importance of the detection of these elements and the interpretation of findings. The literature concerning photoluminescence was surveyed for methods of analysis for antimony, barium,
and lead that would be (a) reliable, sensitive, and quantitative;
(b) that would not involve a great deal of wet chemistry; and
(c) that would be capable of simultaneous determination of more
than one of the three elements. No satisfactory procedure for
detection of barium was found. Low-temperature chloride ion com-
plexing with lead (II) and antimony (III) provides the most sensitive, convenient, and rapid method of luminescence analysis known

Table 1. Low-temperature phosphorescence properties of fresh stains on cloth

Material	Phosphorescence Properties		Comments
	Short-Wave Excitation	Long-Wave Excitation	
Semen	Blue	None	
Vaginal Fluid	Blue	None	
Human Milk	Very weak blue	Weak yellow ring	
Expressed Almonds	Blue	None	Cloth fluorescence quenched
Human Urine	Weak blue	Weak green	
Bind Weed (Morning Glory)	None	None	
Rice, Whole Grain	Blue	None	Cloth fluorescence quenched
Lucerne (Alfalfa)	None	Weak yellow	
Cow's Milk	Blue	Blue	
Clover	None	None	
Rattlesnake Venom	Blue	None	Yellow fluorescence
Cauliflower	None	None	
Brussel Sprouts	None	None	
Apple Mold	None	None	
Bread Mold	None	None	
Sweet Potato	None	None	

for these two ions; it also provides the capability of simultaneously analyzing for both ions (23,24). As shown in Figs. 3 and 4, the emission spectrum for lead (II) peaks at 390 nm, and for antimony (III) the emission peaks at 620 nm. The band peaking at 425 nm (Fig. 3) is a combination of scattered light and hydrogen chloride impurity emission. The excitation spectra (Figs. 3 and 4) peak at 276 nm for lead (II) and at 250 nm and 300 nm for antimony (III). These emission spectra have been corrected for the variation with wavelength of the response of our photomultiplier and grating. The excitation spectra have not been corrected for the variation in the lamp intensity versus wavelength. Thus, the excitation maxima can differ for different lamps. For lead, however, the band is so sharp that no dependence upon the lamp is expected (if we assume that the spectral output of the source does not vary rapidly with wavelength).

Rapid, convenient detection of gunshot residue on the hands of a suspect, following a shooting, can thus be accomplished by the photoluminescence determination of the presence of lead and antimony. Following the firing of a gun, the backs of both hands are washed in a stream of distilled water. Each handwashing is filtered, and the residue, collected on a membrane filter, is dissolved in hydrochloric acid. Upon excitation of the solution, cooled to 77 K, the lead and antimony complexes emit light with maxima at wavelengths characteristic for the two metallic elements. By the use of this procedure, it is possible to detect as little as 1.0 ng of lead and 10 ng of antimony on the hand. The total time for sample collection and analysis is less than 30 min.

Glass. Glass frequently provides evidence in criminal cases involving burglaries, hit-and-run driving, and auto accidents. Criminalists currently use physical properties such as density, refractive index, and dispersion for comparison purposes to determine if glass particles found on a suspect may have originated from glass broken at the scene of a crime. Unfortunately, because of the close correlation, measurement of more than one of these physical properties provides little additional information. One method that offers potentially more promise in establishing common origin of glass samples is the comparison of the trace elemental composition, but it is time consuming and expensive.

Currently, we are studying the luminescence of glass as a means of comparison. Luminescence in glass arises from the presence of ionic impurities or additives such as aluminum and copper. There is evidence that this luminescence is also sensitive to the heat treatment of glass. Our preliminary experiments suggested that the luminescent properties of glass could provide a rapid, reliable, improved method for determining the origin of glass. We therefore collected approximately 400 glass samples from crime laboratories in California and Canada. We measured the refractive index of the 143 California samples that had parallel

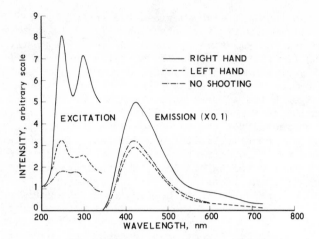

Figure 3. Analysis of three handwashing samples, re-ceived as unknowns, for antimony (Sb). The solid line and broken line spectra refer to the right and left handwash-ings, respectively, of a person who had fired two rounds from a .380 Browning automatic pistol with his right hand. The dashed-dotted line spectrum is from the right hand of a second person at the scene of the shooting, who did not fire a weapon. The solid, broken, and dashed-dotted line spectra indicate 0.18 μg, 0.03 μg, and no detectable anti-mony, respectively. See text for a definition of excitation spectra.

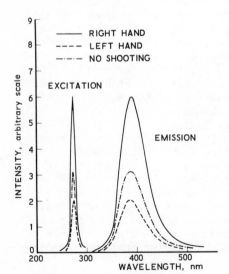

Figure 4. Analysis of three handwashings for lead. The three samples are the same unknowns analyzed for antimony in Figure 3. Analysis of the right hand (shooting hand) of the person who fired the gun yielded 0.60 μg lead. See text for a defini-tion of excitation spectra.

surfaces. Seventeen percent of the samples were indistinguishable with the experimental precision of ±0.0002. Fifty percent of the samples had a refractive index between 1.5160 and 1.5180. These data demonstrate the need for improved methods of comparison.

We are currently investigating the luminescence properties of the same glass samples, and, to date, we have studied 13 samples that were indistinguishable by measurements of their refractive index. All samples exhibit phosphorescence with two broad bands that peak in the green (540 nm) and the red (730 nm). The ratio of the green to the red band is dependent upon the wavelength of excitation, but for a given wavelength of excitation, the ratio of the phosphorescence bands varied among the samples. Indeed, twelve of the thirteen samples (previously indistinguishable) were distinguishable by this measurement. This is a tremendous improvement in the individualization of glass by a simple procedure.

Hair. Until recently, the application of luminescence specifically to the analysis of human hair has not been attempted in any systematic manner. It has been shown that three of the amino acids, i.e., phenylalanine, tyrosine, and tryptophan, found in hair protein both fluoresce and phosphoresce (15). It has been established that for other proteins that contain all three of the amino acids, the luminescence (both fluorescence and phosphorescence) is predominately the result of the tryptophan chromophores, with possibly some contribution from the tyrosine (15). More directly related to the luminescence of hair are the studies of Konev (25) involving the luminescence of wool keratin. He observed both fluorescence and phosphorescence from wool fibers that were characteristic of tryptophan.

Some researchers state that the energy initially absorbed by the tyrosine chromophores in protein is transferred to the tryptophan chromophores before the former have a chance to luminesce. This energy transfer process would explain the predominant emission from the tryptophan. However, it is known that the tyrosine and tryptophan fluorescence is readily quenched by interactions with the environment, i.e., by proton transfer, hydrogen bonding, or charge transfer; and it has been suggested that these interactions favor the tryptophan emission. Konev (26) has argued that because of the high sensitivity of tryptophan fluorescence to the micro-environment of a cell, the fluorescence acts as an indicator of perturbations in the molecular organization of the cell. There is evidence that disulfide bonds, such as those present in hair keratin, can affect the protein emission (26). This sensitivity of the tryptophan and tyrosine emission to the microscopic environment suggests that it should be possible to distinguish hair samples from different individuals by the use of individual luminescence properties. Studies of the differences in the keratins forming hair clearly indicate that no constant chemical composition of keratins can be expected. Indeed, the process of keratinization probably depends upon such physiological and environmental variations as nutritional supply, temperature, and solar radiation (27). Our preliminary work indicated that hairs phosphoresce when excited by ultraviolet light, at 77 K, as a result of the presence of amino acids in the protein of the hair.

Differences in excitation and emission spectra as well as phosphorescence decay times exist for hairs from different individuals. Examples of the luminescence results are given in Fig. 5. The typical phosphorescence spectra for the hair of two different individuals and for three different wavelengths of excitation with ultraviolet radiation are shown. In addition to the slight differences in the spectra for different individuals, a significant variation in the relative intensities is evident. Of particular interest is the variation in the ratio of phosphorescence intensities for 250 versus 350 nm excitation. The variation in the spectra for different wavelengths of excitation indicates that more than one species is phosphorescing. This is also evidenced by the rate of decay of the luminescence upon extinguishing the excitation. If the molecules emitting were the same type and if all of these had the same environment, the emission would decay exponentially with time. The decay curves as shown in Fig 6 are, in fact, nonexponential.

Analysis of the phosphorescence decay curves in Fig. 6 indicates a variation in the decay curves for different individuals and suggests the possible use of the decay curves for individualization of hair samples. We therefore undertook a more extensive investigation of the phosphorescence decay curves. Because frequently only a limited number of hair samples are available in a criminal case, we refined our techniques so that we could observe the phosphorescence spectra and decay curves for single strands of hair.

The emphasis of our studies to date has been to investigate the use of the phosphorescence technique as an adjunct to microscopic examination (28). Hairs from light-haired individuals, all approximately the same color, were examined microscopically. Hair from eight individuals that could not be differentiated on the basis of color, diameter, morphology of the hair root, presence or lack of medulla, and cuticular scale pattern was selected.

We measured the phosphorescence decay times at 77 K for ten single strands of hair from each of the eight individuals. The decay time (t) is defined here as the time required for the phosphorescence intensity to drop from the initial steady-state value (I_0) to $I_0/5$. In Fig. 7, average values of t for 250 nm excitation for each individual's hair are given as vertical bars. The bars incorporate a ±1 standard deviation in the mean value of t for the ten hairs of each donor. The amount of overlap in decay time did not make it feasible to make positive identification of an individual from his hair on the basis of t alone. However, in several cases, hairs with approximately the same t can be distinguished by their structured phosphorescence spectra. Thus, for this group of eight individuals, whose hair was indistinguishable by microscopic

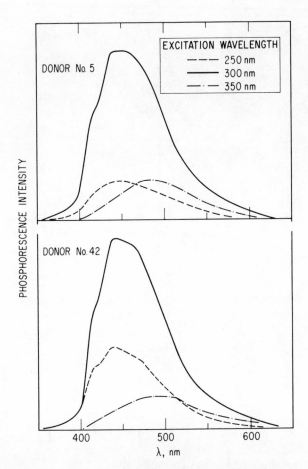

*Figure 5. Phosphorescence spectra at 77 K of the human
(head) hair from two different individuals for different
excitation wavelengths*

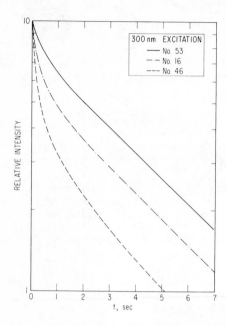

Figure 6. Representative phosphorescence decay curves at 77 K for hair samples

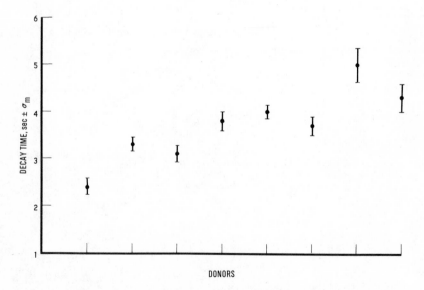

Figure 7. Phosphorescence decay times (t) for hair samples from eight blond-haired donors. The error bars represent ±1 standard deviation from the mean value of t for 10 hair samples from each donor.

examination, differentiation through phosphorescence properties
was possible. For very large populations, luminescent properties
alone are not expected to be sufficient to individualize a hair
sample. However, with a proper statistical analysis, the certainty to which phosphorescent examination of hair can be used for
its individualization can be properly evaluated.

Conclusion

Considerably more work is required before these techniques
can be introduced in court, but our studies and the work of others
show that photoluminescence techniques have potential for wide
application in forensic science. Indeed, because of the significant advances demonstrated in recent years, one can expect to see
spectrophotofluorometers become as commonplace as infrared spec-
trometers in a crime laboratory. Although luminescence spectrometry is not, in general, as specific as infrared spectrometry, it
is considerably more sensitive and convenient.

Acknowledgments

The effort of the entire staff of the Forensic Science
Laboratory at The Aerospace Corporation is acknowledged. Particular thanks are extended to A. R. Calloway, D. J. Carre, Q. Kwan,
and R. Nesbitt. The author also benefited from numerous discussions with Dr. S. Siegel.

Literature Cited

1. Mule, S. J., and Hushin, P. L., ANAL. CHEM. (1971), 43, 708.
2. Lloyd, J. B. F., J. FORENSIC SCI. SOC. (1971),11,83,153,235.
3. Udenfriend, S., "Fluorescence Assay in Biology and Medicine,"
    Vol. II, pp. 585-91, Academic Press, New York, 1969.
4. Guilbault, G. G., "Practical Fluorescence," pp. 609-12,
    Marcel Dekker, Inc., New York, 1973.
5. Konstantinova-Shlezinger, M. A., ed., "Fluorimetric
    Analysis," pp. 304-10, Israel Program for Scientific Trans-
    lations, Jerusalem, 1965.
6. Kirk, P. L., "Crime Investigation," Interscience, New York,
    1953.
7. St. John, P. A., and Winefordner, J. D., ANAL. CHEM. (1967),
    39, 500.
8. Adelman, S. L., Brewer, A. K., Hoerman, K. C., and
    Sanborn, W., NATURE (1967), 213, 718.
9. Hoerman, K. C., Balekjian, A. Y., and Boyne, P. J., J. DENTAL
    RES. (1969) 48, 661.
10. Nag-Chaudhuri, J. and Augenstein, L., "Quantum Aspects of
    Polypeptides and Polynucleotides," ed. M. Weissbluth,
    pp. 441-52, Wiley, New York, 1964.

11. Jones, P. F., and Calloway, A. R., J. CHEM. PHYS. (1969), 51, 1661.

12. Calloway, A. R., Jones, P. F., Siegel, S., and Stupian, G.W., J. FORENSIC SCI. SOC. (1973) 13, 223.

13. Jones, P. F., Calloway, A. R., Carre, D. J., and Siegel, S., "Low Temperature Phosphorescence As An Adjunct to the Acid Phosphatase Test for the Identification of Seminal Fluid," submitted to J. FORENSIC SCI. SOC.

14. Kind, S. S., "Methods of Forensic Science," Vol. III, pp. 267-88, Interscience, New York, 1964.

15. Udenfriend, S., "Fluorescence Assay in Biology and Medicine," Vol. II, Chap. 5, Academic Press, New York, 1969.

16. Walther, G., J. FORENSIC MED. (1971) 18, 15.

17. Anzai, S., REP. NAT. RES. INST. POLICE SCI. (1964) 17, 163.

18. Adams, E. G., and Wraxall, B. G., FORENSIC SCI. (1974), 3, 57.

19. Cowan, M. E., and Purdon, P. L., J. FORENSIC SCI. (1967), 12, 19.

20. Harrison, H. C., and Gilroy, R., J. FORENSIC SCI. (1959), 4, 185.

21. Schlesinger, H. L., Lukens, H. R., Guinn, V. P., Hackleman, R. P., and Korts, R. F., "Special Report on Gunshot Residues Measured by Neutron Activation Analysis, Gulf General Atomic, Inc., San Diego, 1970.

22. Jones, P. F., and Nesbitt, R. S., "A Photoluminescence Technique for Detection of Gunshot Residue," to be published, J. FORENSIC SCI.

23. Solov'ev, E. A., and Bozhevol'nov, E. A., ZHURNAL ANALITICHESKOY KHIMIT, (1972) 27, 1817.

24. Kirkbright, G. F., Saw, C. G., and West, T. S., TALANTA, (1969) 16, 65.

25. Konev, S. V., "Fluorescence and Phosphorescence of Proteins and Nucleic Acids," pp. 132-8, Plenum Press, New York, 1967.

26. Konev, S. V., "Fluorescence and Phosphorescence of Proteins and Nucleic Acids," pp. 147-72, Plenum Press, New York, 1967.

27. Rothman, S., "Physiology and Biochemistry of the Skin," pp. 343-65, Univ. of Chicago Press, Chicago, 1955.

28. Jones, P. F., Calloway, A. R., and Siegel, S., "Luminescence Properties of Hair," paper presented at 3rd Semiannual Meeting of Mid-Atlantic Association of Forensic Scientists, April, 1974.

INDEX

INDEX

A

ABO antigenic system 142
ABO blood group 156, 160
Accelerant residues 108
Acetylcodeine 171
Acid phosphatase test 186
Adenosine deaminase (ADA) 143
Adenylate kinase (AK) 143, 145
Alcohol abuse cases 165
Alloys, ferromagnetic 67
Aluminum 66
Anthropological classification of
bloodstains 146
Antigenic systems 142
Antimony 88, 92, 99, 103, 190
Antisera 48
Arson debris 108, 109, 110, 112
Asphalt 130
Atomic absorption
spectroscopy 97, 100, 167, 170
Auto paint color chips 50

B

Bacteria, putrefactive 151
Ballistics file searching system,
automated 84
Ballistics identification system,
computer-based 85
Barbiturates 32, 34
Barium 88, 91, 99, 102
Biological matrix, extraction of toxic
agent from 167
Biological samples, analysis of barbiturates from 32
Biological samples, extraction of
homogenized 167
Blend analysis 129
Blood
analysis 48
antigens 142
dried 53
EAP phenotypes in clotted 151, 155
frequency distribution data 48
genetic markers in 147
groups ABO, MN and Rh 156, 160
identification 49, 146
polymorphic proteins in 142
samples for drug or alcohol abuse
cases 165
Bloodstain
analysis 48, 142
anthropological classification of 146

Bloodstain (continued)
EAP activity loss in dried 155, 157
EAP typing of aged 157
Gm and Inv typing of 146
identification through genetic
markers 53
radioimmunoassay 146
stability of EAP phenotypes,
dried 151, 157
Bullet 83, 85, 86, 88

C

Calibration data 90
Cavitation, ultrasonic 66
Cellulose triacetate 120
extension analysis, flat 121
Central-Limit Theorem 94
Chemical ionization 168
Chemical potential 64
Chromatography 32, 34, 108
Cloth 188
Coatings 128, 131
Codeine 171
Cold-worked crystals 62
Cold working 66
Comparison microscope 83
Composite products characterization,
organic–inorganic 61
Compositional analysis (EDA),
energy dispersive 75, 76
Computer-based ballistics identifica-
tion system 85
Computerized crime laboratory infor-
mation system, nationwide 50
Copper 99
Corroborative evidence 138
Cost of the forensic science degree
program 18
Cotton swab technique 88, 99
Coupled analyses 78
Court acceptance of scientific tech-
niques 56
Court cases, ink analysis in 138
Crime scene examinations 28
Criminal
Investigation, role of physical evi-
dence in 24
justice education consortium,
national 29
justice system, crime laboratory in .. 23
Criminalistic laboratory
case-load areas in 164

Criminalistic laboratory *(continued)*
in the criminal justice system,
role of 23
effectiveness of 47, 55
exercises 25
information system 50
investigations 28
management and evaluation of 45
proficiency testing 54
techniques 48
for thermal analysis 117
Criminalistics (*see* Forensic science)
Crystals 62, 63, 80

D

Death, determining cause of 166
Decay
curves 185, 194
properties 186
time 183
Deformation of metal, plastic 62
Densitometer tracings, photography .. 152
Derivatized heroin 171, 176
Differential scanning calorimetry
(DSC) 114, 117, 128
Diffraction analysis, x-ray 70
1,6-Dimethylnaphthalene 185
Direct extraction of homogenized
biological samples 167
Discharge residue detection,
firearms 104, 105
Dislocation motion through a crys-
talline array 63
Distillation recovery of arson debris,
steam 110
Double knit polyester fiber 124
Drugs 33, 130, 164, 165
Dyes, ink 32, 33

E

Eaton's corrasable bond paper 34
Education consortium, national crimi-
nal justice 29
Education, forensic science 1, 4
at Northeastern University,
graduate 28
programs 13, 35
Educators in forensic science 10
Electrical resistivity 67
Electrochemical serial number
recovery 64, 66
Electroetching 66
Electron diffraction methods 137
Electronic microbalance 117
Electrophoresis
of EAP phenotypes 154, 156, 158
for genetic marker identification
in blood 147
PGM and AK 145
starch-gel 152

Electrophoretic patterns, EAP
phenotype 131, 154
Elemental constitution 75
Emission spectra 183
Encoding system 68
Energy dispersive compositional
analysis (EDA) 75, 79, 80
Energy dispersive x-ray 167
Environmental factors on starch gel
electrophoretic patterns 151
Enzyme 167
Enzymes, polymorphic 142
Erythrocytic acid phosphatase
(EAP) 143
activity 152, 155, 157
among blood groups, distribution of 156, 160
electrophoretic patterns 151, 154, 156, 158
phenotypes 151
schematic 145
stability of 151, 153
typing of aged bloodstains 157
Erythrocytic systems 143
Etching, visualization of metal
defects by 64
Ethyl acetate liver extract of barbiturates 34
Evidence
applications, forensic 75
corroborative 138
physical 14, 24, 28
Examinations, crime scene 28
Excitation, spectra 183
Expert witness 17
Extension analysis of fibers 121, 125

F

Fabric 124, 128
Ferromagnetic alloys 67
Fiber(s)
analysis by TGA 131
blends, TMA of 128
double knit polyester 121, 124
flat cellulose triacetate extension
analysis of 121, 125
nylon single 121, 125
thermal analysis of 120, 126
Filler metal 77
Financial support of student tuition ... 40
Firearm residue 88, 97, 104, 105, 187
Firing
and non-firing hands, antimony
from 103
and non-firing hands, barium from 102
pin impressions 77
test data 92
Flameless atomic absorption
spectroscopy 100
Flammable accelerant residues 108

Flat cellulose triacetate extension
  analysis 121
Florence test 186
Fluids, physiological 53, 142
Fluorescence 72, 185
Forensic
  applications of differential scanning
    calorimetry 114
  bloodstains and physiological fluid
    analysis 142
  chemistry at Northeastern Uni-
    versity 28
  curriculum of M.S. in 38
  disciplines, personnel in the 44
  evidence applications 75
  materials 49
    science 58
  science 46
    curriculum 16, 37
  degree program, staffing problem
    in 19
  education 1, 4
  educators in 10
  laboratory (see Criminalistic
    laboratory)
  law enforcement course 22
  materials science approach to 33
  milestones in 2
  origins of 3
  personnel policies in 8
  photoluminescence techniques
    for 183
  program symbol, FTU 15
  research 31, 43
  scientist 23
  serology 142
  toxicology 162, 163, 164
Fry's reagent 65
FTU forensic science program symbol   15

G

n-Gamma reactions 98
Gas chromatography (GC) 168, 171
  for flammable accelerant residue
    detection 108
  for heroin sample analysis 173
  –mass spectrometry 168
Gas–liquid chromatography (GLC) .. 137
Genetic markers in blood 48, 53, 142, 147
Glass 50, 189
Glucose-6-phosphate dehydrogenase
  (G-6-PD) 143
Gm sites on the IgG molecule 148
Gm typing of bloodstains 146
Graduate education in forensic chem-
  istry at Northeastern University .. 28
Greases 130
Grinding swarf 77
Gunshot residue 88, 97, 104, 105, 187

H

Hair 130, 191, 193, 194
Hallucinogenic drugs 33
Handblank values 90, 91, 92
Handwashing samples for antimony
  and lead analysis 102, 103, 190
Haptoglobins 144, 148
Headspace recovery of arson debris .. 110
Hemoglobin 144, 146
Hemolysates, red cell 151, 155
Heroin 170, 171, 173, 176
High pressure liquid chromatography 168
Holographic recording techniques 86

I

IgG molecule 148
Immunoassay, mechanized 165
Immunoassay techniques 167
Information system, nationwide computerized crime laboratory 50
Infrared luminescence properties 136
Ink(s)
  analysis 134, 138
  chromatography of 32, 136, 137
  color, type, and infrared lumi-
    nescence properties of 136
  dyes, spectrophotometry of 136
  electron diffraction of 137
  formulations 136
  identification and dating 135
  library, standard 135
  testimony 138
Inorganic components, identification
  of paper by 33
Inorganic composite products characterization, organic– 61
Inorganic solids characterization, nonmetallic 60
Institute of chemical analysis, applica-
  tions and forensic science 30
Instrumentation 28
Insulation, safe 79
Internship 17, 39
Inv sites on the IgG molecule 148
Inv typing of bloodstains 146
Isoenzyme(s) 143
  EAP phenotype 154, 155, 157
  lactate dehydrogenase (LDH) 147

J

Job placement 40
Justice, philosophy of 7
Justice system, criminal 23

K

Knit polyester fiber, double 124

L

Laboratory, forensic science (see
  Criminalistic laboratory)

Lacquer 80, 128
Lactate dehydrogenase (LDH)
  isoenzymes 147
Lactic acid dehydrogenase schematic 148
Laser holes, encoding system using ... 68, 69
Law enforcement program, forensic 22
LEAA's forensic science research
  program 43
Lead 99, 190
Lectures 24
Liquid
  chromatography 32, 34, 168
  —liquid extraction 167
  recovery of arson debris 109
Liver extract of barbiturates, ethyl
  acetate 34
Luminescence 183
  decay properties 183, 186
  excitation and emission spectra of .. 183
  glass identification by 189
  properties of inks, infrared 136

M

Magnetic methods on serial number
  recovery 67
Management of forensic science
  laboratories 45
Management training 6
Marijuana 80
Marking system, serial number 67, 68
Mass fragmentography methods 168
Mass spectrometry 165, 168
Materials characterization 58
Materials science approach to forensic
  science 33, 58
Menstrual blood identification 146
Mercury radiation 72
Metabolites, drug 33
Metal(s) 59
  cold worked 66
  defects 64
  filler 77
  hardness differences 66
  number stamped on 63
  plastic deformation of 62
Metallic samples, characterization of 60
Microbalance, electronic 117
Microscope, comparison 83
Migration pattern, isoenzyme 154
Mineral components of paper, inor-
  ganic 33
MN, antigenic system 142
MN blood group 156, 160
Monoacetylmorphone 171
Morphine 171
M.S. programs in forensic chem-
  istry 36, 37, 38

N

Nails 130
Naphthalene 185

National criminal justice education
  consortium 29
National Institute of Law Enforce-
  ment and Criminal Justice 43
Neuraminidase 153, 156, 158
Neutron activation analysis ... 88, 97, 100, 170
Nonmetallic inorganic solids charac-
  terization 60
Non-polymeric materials 130
Northeastern University 28, 31
Nylon fibers 122, 121, 127
Null hypothesis 93
Number stamped on metal 63

O

O^6-monoacetylmorphine 171
Oils 130
Organic
  —inorganic composite products
    characterization 61
  solids characterization 61
  toxic agents 167

P

Packaging materials 130
Paints 50, 79, 128
Paper
  ashed 34, 71
  EDA spectra of 80
  identification 33, 58, 70, 72
  polyester finished 123
  SEM x-ray energy spectrum of 34
  separations 72
  untreated 71
Personnel in the forensic disci-
  plines 8, 9, 44, 59
PGM electrophoresis 145
Ph.D. program 41
Phenotype EAP (see EAP phenotype)
Philosophy of justice 7
Phosphoglucomutase (PGM) 143
6-Phosphogluconate dehydrogenase
  (6-PGD) 143
Phosphorescence 188, 193, 194
Photography tracings 152
Photoluminescence techniques ... 183, 184
Photomicrographs, SEM 77, 80
Physical evidence analysis 14, 24, 28
Physiological fluid analysis, forensic 53, 142
Plastic deformation of metal 62
Police cases 164, 165
Polyester 120, 121, 123, 124
Polyethylene wire coating 131
Polymeric materials 128
Polymorphism 142, 151
Polypeptides 51
Population frequencies 142, 143, 144
Post-mortem cases 164, 166
Potential, chemical 64
Primer, barium from 88

Proficiency testing, criminalistics
    laboratory 54
Proof, problem of 6
Proteins in blood, polymorphic 142
Putrefactive bacteria 151

Q

Quantum yield of luminescence emis-
    sion 183

R

Radiation, mercury 72
Radioimmunoassay 146, 167
Red cell hemolysates 151, 155
Reference collections of forensic mate-
    rials, standard 49
Refractive index glass 50
Replica-producing techniques 86
Research, forensic science 28, 31, 43
Residue, firearm 88, 97, 104, 105, 187
Residues, flammable accelerant 108
Resistivity, electrical 67
Restoration methods 66
Rh antigenic system 142
Rh blood group 156, 160
Rubber tire 130

S

Safe insulation 79
Sample collection 99
Sample-size-limited test schedule 119
Scanning calorimeter 117
Scanning electron microscopy
    (SEM) 72, 86
    comparison of wood samples 81
    in forensic evidence applications 75
    for paper identification 72
    photomicrographs 77, 80
    x-ray energy spectrum 34
Scientific techniques, court accept-
    ance of 56
Scientist in criminal justice system,
    role of 23
Search systems, bullet 83
Searching system, automated
    ballistics file 84
Semen 52
Seminal stains 147, 186
Serial number marking system, im-
    proved 67
Serial number recovery 58, 61, 63, 64, 66, 67
Serology, forensic 142
Sickle cell hemoglobin 146
Significance level 93
Single fibers 125
Skin 88, 130
Soaps 130
Sodium chloride crystals 80
Solids characterization 60, 61
Solvent systems, TLC of 136

Solvent wash recovery of arson debris 110
Spectrophotometry 26, 136
Spin-label immunoassay techniques .. 167
Staffing problems in forensic science
    degree program 19
Stains on cloth 188
Standard reference collections of
    forensic materials 49
Starch-gel electrophoresis 151, 152
Steam distillation recovery of arson
    debris 110
Steel 64, 69
Surface-analyzing methods, bullet 85
Surface characterization 75, 85
Swab technique, cotton 89, 99
Swarf, grinding 77

T

t-distributions 91, 92, 94
t-test 95
Technique(s)
    court acceptance of scientific 56
    evaluation of 56
    limitations of 5
Test schedule, sample-size-limited 119
Testimony, witness 28
Textbooks 26
Thermal analysis 117, 120, 126
Thermogravimetric analysis
    (TGA) 114, 131
Thermomechanical analysis (TMA) .. 114
    cellulose triacetate 120
    of drugs 130
    of fibers 120, 122, 128
    of hair, nail and skin 130
    non-polymeric materials 130
    of packaging materials 130
    of paints, lacquers, and other
        coatings 128
    of polymeric materials 128
    of tire rubber 130
Thin layer chromatography (TLC) 136, 168
Tire rubber 130
Topographical analyses 76
Toxic agents 167
Toxicological analysis 167
Toxicologogist, forensic 162, 163
Toxicology, forensic 162, 164
Training, management 6
Tuition, financial support of 40

U

Ultrasonic cavitation 66
Ultraviolet spectrophotometry 168
Underivatized heroin 176
Universities, response of 11
University, Northeastern 28, 31
Urine sample for drug or alcohol
    abuse cases 165

V

Variant polypeptides 51
Vehicle information number 77
Vehicles, auto paint color chips for 50

W

Wash recovery, solvent 110
Waxes 130
Wire coatings 128, 131

Witness testimony 17, 28
Wood samples 81

X

X-ray diffraction analysis 70
X-ray energy spectrum 34

Y

Yarn 125, 127

Z

Zymogram 143